Pilgrimage in Islam

Traditional and Modern Practices

SOPHIA ROSE ARJANA

ONEWORLD
ACADEMIC

Oneworld Academic

An imprint of Oneworld Publications

Published by Oneworld Academic, 2017

ISBN 978-1-78607-116-3
eISBN 978-1-78607-117-0

Typeset by Silicon Chips
Printed and bound in Great Britain by Clays Ltd, St Ives plc

Oneworld Publications
10 Bloomsbury Street
London WC1B 3SR
England

CONTENTS

LIST OF ILLUSTRATIONS

FOREWORD

There are places, objects, and people where the veils between this world and the other worlds become quite thin. For a few breaths, it seems as if lightning flashes, and a darkened sky lights up. The boundary between this world and others is revealed as what it was all along: porous. These people, places, and objects are said to contain *barakah*, a Divine force that is palpable to all those who have hearts. The God of the infinite cosmoses shows up nearby.

This is one purpose of pilgrimage. We journey to find what has been with us all along. We find the presence that has been with us, inside us, around us, all around. But we have to go on the journey to find the treasure we have been sitting on. When we return, we are transformed, no longer who and what we had been before. Ultimately, pilgrimage is not to a place, but to a different state of being.

All religious traditions involve some notion of pilgrimage. In Islam the major pilgrimage, the *hajj*, is well-known, as we retrace the footsteps of a slave woman, Hajar, and reconnect to the Abrahamic foundations of faith. The pilgrimage to Mecca is even listed as the fifth pillar of faith. We come from the periphery of existence to the center, to the center of the center – which is to say the heart. Standing at the marrow of the universe, we are one, and connected to the One.

Every year, millions of Muslims gather in Mecca for what is, for most of them, a once in a lifetime pilgrimage. The *hajj* is intimately private and unavoidably communal at the same time. They, we, have come from every background, every race, every class. The *hajj* has become something of a Rorschach test for Muslims and for the world: we see in it whatever we imagine about Islam and Muslims. To so many, it is the ultimate symbol of Muslim unity, where white and black, yellow and brown skins stand shoulder to shoulder, united before the One. To others, it is a symbol of how the consumerist capitalist culture, symbolized by the high-rise luxury hotels over Mecca, have thwarted and distorted the radical egalitarianism of Islam. Some see a fabulous exchange of the richness of Muslim cultures, food, learning, and stories. Others see a chance to express geopolitical tensions.

Every one of those pilgrims walks in the footsteps of a black woman, a maiden or a slave (depending on the story you prefer), a woman left in God's care, or abandoned by a husband, a co-wife, or the victim of Sarah's jealousy. Every pilgrim walks in the footsteps of our mother Hajar/Hagar, a noble, tired, exhausted woman living as a single mother in the desert, without family, without support, without money, without water...

> Death was close.
> God was closer.
> She clutched her son so close that he breathed the air she
>   breathed.
> Her faith in God, and love for her baby, saved them both.

Hajar/Hagar figures differently in the Bible than she does in the Qur'an, partially because of how differently Isaac and Ishmael fare in the two scriptures. The Bible was written by the descendants of Isaac. So Ishmael and his mother Hagar, "the stranger", are cast out. In the Qur'an, Isaac and Ishmael are both God's prophets, and both Sarah and Hajar/Hagar are treated as wives of Abraham. Yet this much is agreed upon: Abraham left Hagar and Ishmael in the desert.

Here is how the story of Hagar is told in the biography of Muhammad:

> It was not long before both mother and son were overcome by thirst, to the point that Hagar feared Ishmael was dying. According to the traditions of their descendants, he cried out to God from where he lay in the sand, and his mother stood on a rock at the foot of a nearby eminence to see if any help was in sight. Seeing no one, she hastened to another point of vantage, but from there likewise not a soul was to be seen.[*]

During pilgrimage, all the pilgrims engage in a ritual called *Sa'y*, where they rush between the hills of Safa and Marwa, quite literally tracing the footsteps of Hajar. On the *hajj* we are reminded that we don't merely have faith, we do religion. Religion is ritual, ethics, history, myth and mysticism all mingled.

Countless pilgrims to Mecca have detailed their experiences on this journey, few more famously than Malcolm X. The telling and re-telling of these pilgrimage stories themselves stand at the very formation of communal identity.

Yet, as significant as the pilgrimage to Mecca is, it is not the only place that the boundary between this world and the other world is thin. Over the centuries, millions of Muslims have been unable to travel to Mecca and Medina to experience God there. For many, it was simply too expensive, too far. Is it not the case that so many of the most tender and lovely poems in praise of the Prophet's Medina have been written by far-away lovers who had to bring Medina to the heart, because they knew their feet would never walk on its soil? So they went, and they continue to go, to local vicinities where God is nearby. They come to places that are nearer, more intimate, more familiar, where the sacred speaks in a vernacular.

---

[*] Martin Lings, *Muhammad: His Life Based on the Earliest Sources*, p. 2

Some of these places attract millions of visitors, whether it is Mawlana Jalal al-Din Rumi's shrine in Konya, Imam Hossein's in Karbala, or that of Mu'in al-Din Chishti in Ajmer Sharif. This is part of the brilliance of Sophia Arjana's wonderful new book before you: it broadens the discussion of pilgrimage to what actual Muslims do on the ground, with all of the complexity, particularity, and ambiguity involved.

Allow me to end with one measure of these ambiguities. Years ago I found myself in the tomb of Mawlana Jalal al-Din Rumi. They were all there, pilgrims and tourists from near and far. Some came and took selfies, and then put their phones away to raise their hands in prayer. The Japanese Buddhist monks were there too, as were the hippie Americans with their much beloved meditational books of prayers. But mostly, the shrine was packed with Turkish village grandmothers. They came with their scarves wrapped tightly around their round faces, with their earnest faces and thick bodies, moving en masse to the front of the area where Rumi's grave was, and they squatted down. They would not be moved. They had waited too long, had too much love in their hearts, had come too far to say a quick prayer. I was reminded again and again of a saying attributed to the Prophet: "May you have the faith of old women."

There were state-sponsored security guards in the shrine. They seemed to have one job, and only one job. The guards kept pleading with the grandmothers: "Mother, please keep moving… Mother, wrap up your prayer, there are others behind you." In those days of uber-secularism in Turkey, everything was allowed inside the shrine, except… prayer. There was a wholesale museumification of the Shrine: one had to purchase a ticket – a ticket! – to access the place of this "offspring of the soul of the Prophet", as Rumi was called even in his own life. One could get headphones, and move from station to station to listen to the official state-sponsored narrative: this was the shrine of a humanist who taught humanity how to improve himself by preaching a rational, scientific, moderate version of Turkish Islam. You could go to the gift shop, and buy one of hundreds of miniature dolls of Rumi. You could buy a small doll, a medium doll, or a large doll. You could do all of that, but you were not allowed to pray. You could not pray the formal Muslim prayer (*namaz* or *salat*), and even the more informal supplication from the heart to God could be done only if it did not slow down the steady stream of visitors, tourists and ticket-purchasing pilgrims.

This was the audible sound that reverberated through the shrine: "Mother, please keep moving… Mother, wrap up your prayer, there are others behind you."

I stood there for hours, observing the faces of the pilgrims. Some with tears rolling down their faces. Some asking for brides and grooms for their children. Some standing silent, overwhelmed. Some weeping with joy, grateful to be in the vicinity of the "Friend of God" (*wali*) whose poems and teachings had so shaped their heart. Some came with a lover, holding hands. There was the unmistakable fragrance of *barakah* everywhere.

I shared in joyous conversation with some of the pilgrims. One woman's words have stayed with me. I asked her if she was praying *to* the friend of God. She looked at me with puzzlement, and said: "No! I pray to God. But I pray *near* this friend, because he is dear to God. My prayers are more likely to be answered by God, when I am in the vicinity of this friend of God." That distinction is at the very heart of these vernacular pilgrimages that often are devoted to friends of God or descendants of the Prophet.

The museum kept official 9–5 hours. At five o'clock the guards began to lead all the people outside. The guards told the last remaining Turkish grandmothers to wrap up their prayer, and leave. Finally, they politely but firmly escorted the last of the grandmothers out of the shrine. I was seated discreetly on the ground, in the back, mostly hidden behind a pillar. They did not see me, and I did not volunteer to move.

Then it happened. The very same guards who for eight hours had been telling faithful grandmothers not to pray too much and to keep moving... They themselves stood before the presence of God in the vicinity of God's friend. Their own hands went up in prayer, slowly, as slowly as the dance of any whirling dervish. And they stood there, in prayer, in front of the same tomb as the Turkish grandmothers, with the same hands raised up to heaven. There they stood, wearing the uniform of the secular state.

Pilgrimage is deliciously complicated. It is as beautifully subtle and complicated as we human beings are. This complexity, ambiguity, and even tension is fascinating to me. It reveals us as most human, not less so.

Sophia Arjana's primer on Muslim pilgrimages, in the universal and the vernacular, is a lovely way to explore these important rituals. What a vivid reminder that religion is not simply about what we believe, but how we embody faith with and through our bodies. We are indebted to Dr. Arjana for such a wide-ranging and enchanting book on this key Muslim practice. May the veils between this world and the other worlds become thin for you.

Omid Safi
Series Editor for Foundations of Islam

INTRODUCTION: BEYOND *HAJJ*

The annual journey to Islam's holy city includes men, women, and children of all ages and nationalities. Thousands of tents mark the path, offering everything from food and water to phone stations and resting places. The pilgrims wear veils, turbans, and modest clothing – *abayas*, *jallabiyas*, *niqabs*, and *caftans* – offering protection from the desert heat. It is important that they approach their destination in a pious state; while some walk, others may crawl. Once they reach their destination, the pilgrims say prayers, read the Qur'an, weep, and ask for forgiveness of their sins. The holy pilgrimage is a major life event, strongly encouraged by religious clerics. It is the largest pilgrimage in the world. This is not *hajj*. It is *arbaeen*, the annual pilgrimage to Karbala in Iraq. Over twenty million pilgrims a year travel to the shrine in Iraq where Husayn, the grandson of Prophet Muhammad, is buried. For some, the journey to Karbala is secondary to *hajj*, but for others it supersedes the pilgrimage to Mecca.[1] As one popular Shi'i tradition says, "A single tear shed for Husayn washes away a hundred sins."[2]

Husayn's tomb is rarely mentioned alongside *hajj* in introductory textbooks on Islam and world religions. Nor is the shrine of Sayyida Ruqayya, or Rumi's tomb, or the graves found in Damascus where some of the Prophet's closest companions are interred. Such oversights misrepresent the huge variety of pilgrimage traditions in Islam. This book remedies this problem, providing an expansive study of

Islamic pilgrimage that is inclusive, geographically diverse, and attentive to the rich traditions that characterize Muslim religious life.

The roots of *arbaeen* and many of the other journeys examined in this book are often, but not always, situated in early Islamic history. For Shi'i Muslims, the Battle of Karbala is the seminal event that inspires numerous pilgrimages in Iraq, Iran, Syria, Lebanon, Palestine, and elsewhere. In 680, Prophet Muhammad's grandson Husayn went to battle against the entire 'Umayyad army at Karbala. The story of this battle is told in great detail on the anniversary of Husayn's death, the tenth day of the month of Muharram, also known as 'Ashura'. When pilgrims visit the tombs of Husayn and other members of Prophet Muhammad's family, they commemorate the past, mourning the death of a pious and just Islam, and pray for the return of the Mahdi, the messiah who announces the End

Figure I.0 Sayyida Ruqayya's Shrine, Damascus, Syria (photo courtesy of author).

of Days. Husayn's statement, "I see death as salvation, and life with the oppressors as misfortune," is apropos here, for Shi'i pilgrimage is not just about the past but also about the present conditions of life.[3]

In addition to Husayn and the other martyrs of this battle, survivors of Karbala became the focus of other pilgrimages. Among these was a little girl named Ruqayya – Husayn's young daughter. Stories of her death include one version I was told when visiting the shrine in 2010. In this telling, Yazid, the 'Umayyad caliph, showed little Ruqayya her father's decapitated head and she immediately dropped dead. Another version of the story claims that she died at the age of four while imprisoned by Yazid, as a result of her ill treatment at the hands of her captors. The shrine of Sayyida Ruqayya is newer than many Shi'i sites and probably dates from the fifteenth century. The iconography of the site includes numerous inscriptions that reflect Shi'i beliefs about the Prophet's family, although non-Shi'i Muslims also visit the shrine.[4] Visitors are often struck by the intense display of emotion for the child buried within the tomb. As is the case for most Shi'i shrines, men and women have their own sections, allowing for public performances of grief that are unconcerned with expectations and boundaries surrounding gendered behavior.

Millions of Muslim pilgrims have visited Ruqayya's tomb. Within the walls of this shrine, pilgrims have said prayers, mourned the death of the Prophet's relatives, wept tears of sadness and grief, and asked for healing, relief, and forgiveness. Shi'i are not the only Muslims who have extensive networks of pilgrimage sites, however. Located near Ruqayya's shrine is the 'Umayyad mosque in Damascus, which houses the heads of Husayn, John the Baptist, and other martyrs. This is one of the thousands of pilgrimage sites worldwide that are focused on the dead. Muslim pilgrims often visit these places to receive a blessing (*barakah*; pl. *barakat*) from the saint or holy person, a tradition that dates from the Prophet's lifetime.

The association of *barakat* with pilgrimage traditions was an established practice by the ninth century. When Sayyida Nafisa (the daughter of al-Hasan b. Zayd b. al-Hasan b. Ali b. Ali Talib) died in Cairo in 824, the people asked that her body be kept in Fustat so that her blessing/*barakah* would be present for them.[5]

Pilgrimage in Islam goes far beyond the great pilgrimage to Mecca, although the rituals performed by Muslim pilgrims at other sites often mirror what happens at *hajj*, some of which are often rooted in pre-Islamic practices. "Many of the rites associated with the pilgrimage to Mecca and visitation of other shrines parallel funerary and mourning practices attested in other contexts, such as circumambulation of the tomb, the wearing of certain sorts of clothing, and restrictions on certain types of behavior."[6] Muslim pilgrimages also involve religious and cultural traditions adopted from Christianity, Hinduism, and local practices in their rituals, reflecting the myriad ways that Muslims adapt to and borrow from the communities they have conquered, or who have conquered them, or, in some cases, communities among whom Muslims live. As one example, in Java, Brawijaya V's life story employs both Hindu and Islamic beliefs: "the last episode of Brawijaya's life is depicted both in terms of Javano-Islamic mystical anthropology of *sangkan paran* as well as in the Hindu understanding of *moksa*."[7] Indonesia is by no means the only place where there is such a mixture of cultures, practices, and religions. This book includes practices that inform pilgrimages more identifiable with Islam, as well as those more closely aligned with traditions that are associated with non-Muslim figures and historical sites.

Muslim pilgrims travel to a wide variety of places. Countless holy sites (*mazarat*) – graves, tomb complexes, mosques, shrines, mountaintops, springs, and gardens – can be found across the world, in large cities like Mashhad, small villages in Turkey, trade outposts in the deserts of

Samarkand, African metropolises like Fes, and the forests of Bosnia. All of these places are located within an Islamic universe that is present with the spirit of Allah and holds the promise of *barakat* – the blessings that pilgrims seek. Although monumental sites exist, such as the great shrines at Mashhad, Karbala, and Konya, Islamic pilgrimage sites are more often established according to religious qualities, such as the popularity of a saint, the amount of *barakah*, and the numbers of miracles witnessed, rather than the magnitude of the site's architecture. "Muslim writers frequently mention other sacred qualities manifesting themselves at sacred places which were not perceived visually, but spiritually, in particular pilgrimage places possessing a friendly atmosphere (*uns*), awe (*mahāba*), reverence (*ijlāl*), dignity (*waqār*), and blessing (*baraka*)."[8]

This book makes a sincere attempt to be inclusive of the great varieties of Islamic pilgrimage, journeys that cross sectarian boundaries, incorporate non-Muslim rituals, and involve numerous communities, languages, and traditions. In the interest of providing accessibility to a variety of readers, I incorporate the reified categories of "Sunni," "Shi'i," and "Sufi," while simultaneously observing how scholars attach these identities to Muslim ritual and community in over-simplified ways. This tension is crystallized when we look at the complexities of Muslim religious experience – a Sunni site visited by Shi'i, the cohabitation of Shi'ism and Sufism, and the problems inherent in defining who is and is not a Sufi. For example, the concept of sainthood is involved in many Islamic movements including those within the Sunni and Shi'i traditions. "This blurring of lines with regard to defining *walāyah* [sainthood] has engendered a Sufi tradition that celebrates many such figures whose teachings, upon closer inspection, are actually found to be copied word-for-word from the Imams but without any credit or reference given."[9] Shi'i and Sufi pilgrimages – including those popular with Sunni Muslims – have numerous commonalities, from the belief in the power of the dead to the importance of visiting those close to Prophet Muhammad. These commonalities point to larger questions about the ways in which Muslim communities and their traditions are constructed in Western scholarship. My work interrogates these constructions through an examination of pilgrimage.

Islam encompasses a huge variety of sects, rituals, traditions, languages, and communities. The vast majority of the world's Muslims go on pilgrimage to places other than Mecca. This has been true from the very beginning, when visiting Jerusalem was viewed as an alternative to Mecca, equal in religious merit.[10] Annemarie Schimmel is one of many scholars who point to these replacement *hajj*s.[11] The performance of pilgrimage outside of *hajj* is not typically an arbitrary choice in which one tradition eliminates the other. For example, Maqbaratu al-Baqi and Masjid an-Nabawi, the cemetery and mosque in Medina that are often part of the great pilgrimage, are also part of a larger collection of sites held sacred by Muslims.[12] *Hajj* is often one of several pilgrimages that Muslims undertake over the course of their lives. Most Muslims never see Mecca during their lifetime, due to finances, geographical distance, or poor health. Many communities have vast networks of pilgrimage sites that function as the central practice in their lives. One example is found in the Ughyur context, where pilgrims frequent shrines ranging from "low mud lumps decorated with rags to monumental mausoleums with green-tiled domes."[13] The large number of these places and traditions means that they cannot all be covered in one volume; however, every effort has been made to include pilgrimages from every region of the world.

Scholarship on Islamic pilgrimage is mostly focused on *hajj* and *'umrah* (the lesser *hajj*) and occasionally on Shi'i Twelver traditions, especially in introductory texts on Islam and world religions. I include scholarship from religious studies, anthropology, and other fields to provide an opening up to these different scholarly voices, as well as to the great variety of experiences that fall under Islam. Scholars often adopt a myopic focus on their subject, as J.Z. Smith points out when he writes, "We may have to be initiated by the other whom we study and undergo the ordeal of incongruity. For we have often missed what is humane in the other by the very seriousness of our quest."[14] This book is an effort to respond to this critique.

Academic studies often classify religious practices into different categories depending on community, but Islamic pilgrimage is often a nonsectarian activity. It is true that Shi'ism has a distinct set of pilgrimage traditions that surround the tombs of the Prophet's relatives, but these sites are not as restricted as some would think. Sunnis visit the shrine of Sayyida Zaynab in a suburb of Damascus, although not in the numbers that Shi'i Muslims do.[15] This is far from the only case of mixed intra-religious sites. Sunnis and Shi'i visit the shrine of Husayn in Cairo and Sunnis visit numerous "Shi'i" tombs in Syria, Iraq, and Iran. When 'Abd al-Ghani al-Nabulusi did a series of *ziyarat* (pilgrimage; see p. 103) journeys between 1688 and 1701, he did not limit the places he visited by sect (he was a Sunni) nor by *tariqah* (he was a member of both the Qadariyya and Naqshbandiyya orders), in part because Sufis do not perform pilgrimage in these ways.[16] This is a problem when considering the ways Islamic pilgrimages are typically represented – the presentations do not accord with history or agree with the realities of Muslim religious life.

The vast majority of Islamic pilgrimage traditions are commemorative, focused on the dead and the power of the bodies being visited. This is one reason why the material aspect of pilgrimage is so important. As Elizabeth Hallam and Jenny Hockey have written, material objects have a great capacity to "bind the living and the dead, to hold a fragile connection across temporal distance and preserve a material presence in the face of embodied absence."[17] Holy people, including

Prophet Muhammad and his relatives, Sufi *shaykhs*, and others, remain important after their death because they are believed to have the power to offer blessings to their followers. Pilgrims visit the graves of the dead for a number of reasons. In the case of Chor Bandi and Shahi Zinda in Uzbekistan, sick people (*dardmand*) go to the graves in search of good health, childless people (*bifarzand*) ask for fertility, and others go to ask for a successful marriage or business.[18] In Islam, bodies and associated relics function as religious and political symbols: "Objects that confer legitimacy may do so merely because they belong, or once belonged, to a person whose sanctity inheres in his possessions as well as in himself."[19] Other sacred places visited by Muslims include those associated with births, miracles, and other wondrous events, such as the dreams associated with Khidr/Hizir in Turkey, in which pilgrims go on dream-quests (*istikharah*) in the hopes of encountering the mysterious figure of Khidr.[20] Pilgrimages may also involve shared sites, including Mary's house near Ephesus and John the Baptist's tomb in Damascus, also visited by Christians. Furthermore, pilgrimages may be more seriously focused on ecology and the natural world. In Bangladesh, several shrines are associated with wildlife, resulting in pilgrimages that involve not just the memory of the saint but the preservation of animals and entire ecosystems, and the Muslims, Christians, and others visit these sites and feed and observe the wildlife – ranging from monkeys to birds – all in the hope of gaining a blessing from God.[21]

In addition to physical pilgrimages like *hajj* and the visitation of tombs, graveyards, shrines, and nature reserves, this book includes traditions that imitate these journeys, often described as symbolic substitutions or *virtual* pilgrimages. These cases are not to be confused with cyber-pilgrimages, journeys involving technology like computers, the Internet, and mobile devices, which are also part of this study. Virtual pilgrimages and cyber-pilgrimages are distinct categories of experience. Virtual pilgrimages are physical activities that reenact or imitate the pilgrimage to which they correspond. One example is the *Hussainiya* that Shi'i sometimes construct in their homes or communities that serve as miniature replicas of Karbala. Cyber-pilgrimages use the worldwide web to journey to a pilgrimage site, often through a live camera feed or virtual landscape. All of these journeys – physical, virtual, and cyber – represent some of the different ways that people perform Islam, conduct ritual, and perform pilgrimage.

Islamic pilgrimages number in the thousands. In the Kotan prefecture in China alone, there are more than two thousand *mazars* and of these, only a small number, perhaps twenty, are known to Muslims outside the region.[22] Due to the fact that this book covers such a large corpus of material, I have made an effort to organize the subject in a way that gives equal weight to the experiences of different Muslim communities. I admit this is not perfect, but I have made considerable effort to include a geographical and cultural diversity of sites and traditions. In this spirit, I begin with a discussion of Islamic pilgrimage and its examination in the field of religious studies. This includes a discussion of some of the challenges faced by scholars who study Islam or pilgrimage, issues that are revisited in the afterword. Chapter 2 examines the holy cities of Jerusalem, Mecca, and Medina and includes a lengthy discussion of the importance placed by Muslims on Jerusalem in Islam, *hajj*, *'umrah*, and related traditions in Medina. Chapter 3 examines the pilgrimage traditions surrounding Shi'i Muslims, including Zaydis, Isma'ilis, Twelvers, and two groups that are associated with Shi'ism – the 'Alawis and Alevis. The following chapter focuses on Sufi pilgrimages, traditions that exist in many corners of the world and are undertaken by Sunnis, Shi'i, and other Muslim sects. This chapter addresses the problems in studying Sufism, a field of enquiry influenced by Orientalist notions of "mysticism." This chapter also looks at some of the pilgrimages that are shared among Muslims and other groups, such as Christians, Hindus, and Jews. Chapter 5 focuses on the topics of materiality and modernity – commodification, tourism, pilgrimage mementos, and virtual pilgrimages. It also examines the topics of technology and cyber-pilgrimage, offering a reflection on the ways in which modernity is changing Islamic pilgrimage and offering new ways of experiencing sacred sites. A careful reflection on the entire project, including some of the theoretical issues it presents, is contained in the afterword. These chapters are designed to be used independently or collectively in academic courses. As a whole they present a comprehensive study of the topic, one that I hope engenders more discussion both in the classroom and in academia on the subject of Islamic pilgrimage.

1

RECONSIDERING ISLAMIC PILGRIMAGE: THEORETICAL AND SECTARIAN DEBATES

Discussions of Islam and sacred space often point to the ways in which people living in the West define space differently than Muslims do, arguing that secularism is a value held solely by those who do not hold Islam as their guiding principle. This position neglects those Muslims who live in Europe, North America, and elsewhere, while insisting on a simplified view of how religious people negotiate the modern world. In fact, religion is more complicated than this binary suggests, involving movement, production, and circulation. In the case of pilgrimage, movement is a key component, making a division between secular and religious space impossible. Engseng Ho argues that this is especially true of pilgrimage, which is "a movement of persons" that entails "a movement of texts" that travel through prayers, poems, stories, countries, and other media.[1]

Despite the tendency in religious studies to categorize "other" people's religion as static and traditional, many contemporary scholars consider mobility, action, and movement as important parts of the religious experience. As Annelies Moors argues, "Things do not have either a religious or secular, non-religious, status; rather the ways in which forms become or cease to be religious may well shift in the course of their production, circulations, and consumption, and depends on the intentions of those engaging with them."[2] In recent years, scholars of pilgrimage have agreed with this analysis, often defining space as an ongoing, fluid, and active construction, a product of human agency rather than one created solely by modern secular institutions or by religious motivations. According to the French philosopher Henri Lefebvre, space is constructed through the interaction of physical, mental, and social fields; as a product of this interaction, space is not fixed.[3] Islamic pilgrimage helps to demonstrate this vision. For example, a pilgrim visiting the tomb of Rumi negotiates a number of elements during his or her journey, such as place of origin, social class, gender, religiosity, imagination, and embodiment. These all contribute to the experience of the individual and result in a particular construction of space. Edward Soja frames this idea with his tripartite notion of Firstspace (physical space), Secondspace (imagined space), and Thirdspace, which is where the physical, political, imaginary, and social all come together. He describes Thirdspace as a site where numerous activities and movements congregate, "the real and imagined, the knowable and the unimaginable, the repetitive and the differential, structure and agency, mind and body, consciousness and the unconscious, the disciplined and the transdisciplinary, everyday life and unending history."[4] Following this logic, shrines, tombs, graveyards, and other sites associated with Islamic pilgrimage are in constant movement, a consequence of the fact that human beings are "active participants in the social construction of our embracing spatialities."[5]

Muslims have a vast set of traditions that suggest the dead are able to hear the living, a belief that helps to explain the active quality to which Soja points. The practice of saying *talqin*, "reminding (or instructing) the deceased of the basics of religion, so that he will know how to answer when the angels of destruction interrogate him," suggests just how pervasive this belief is.[6] Pilgrimage sites are not simply ritual sites – they are places involved with history, memory, and imagination. Often, a pilgrimage involves a site at which memory and the imagination come together, serving as "representations of cultural artefacts associated with sacred places and conceptual narratives that become a commemoration of history as well as an imagination of it."[7]

New pilgrimage sites demonstrate the active and complex nature of the construction of sacred space. An interesting case is the tomb of Ahmad Shah Masoud, the military leader of the Northern Alliance in Afghanistan. Masoud was killed shortly before September 11, 2001, by two Al Qaeda suicide attackers and buried in northern Afghanistan. He was a mythic figure. Nicknamed the Lion of Panjshir, Masoud was admired even by his enemies – first the Soviets, then various competing warlords, and the Taliban. Tales of heroism were accompanied by claims of Masoud's deep religiosity. According to his widow, she would often wake in the middle of the night to find him praying. On one occasion, she found him weeping while kneeling on his prayer mat. Afghans believe that only the *awliya* (friends of God or saints, also known as Sufis) can wake themselves to pray in the middle of the night.[8] Like many other saintly figures in Islam, Masoud reportedly experienced miraculous events and had premonitions.

Masoud injured his leg in a battle against Communist soldiers. He sent his troops to a small valley inside Panjshir called Shaaba. Masoud could not walk very fast, however, and both he and his bodyguard Kaka Tajuddin were in danger of being caught by the enemy. Suddenly a horse appeared in front of them, which they mounted. As they traveled through the villages, they asked about the horse but no one had ever seen it before. After a week they arrived in Dasht-e Rawat, a safe place, and spent the night. When they awoke the horse

Figure 1.0 Tomb of Ahmad Shah Masoud, Afghanistan (photo courtesy of Wakil Kohsar).

was dead. In another tale, before starting his fight against the Communists, Masoud dreamt that he saw a holy man with long white hair and a beard. This man tied a green belt around Masoud's waist.[9] The tradition of tying a belt around a man's waist is an important one in Afghanistan, symbolizing the assignment of an important job. Many years later, shortly before his death, he had another dream. In it the same holy man untied the green belt. While Masoud's friends thought this meant the Taliban would be defeated and peace would come to Afghanistan, Masoud knew that his job was done, that his soul would soon leave his body and return to God. Shortly thereafter, he was assassinated.[10]

After his death, Masoud's tomb quickly became a pilgrimage site visited by those who fought alongside him in battles against the Russians, opposition forces, the Taliban, and Al Qaeda, by his countrymen who remember him from the Soviet–Afghan War and the conflagration that followed, and by young Afghans who were born in the last days of his life.

Although Masoud is a modern figure and the pilgrimage to his tomb is new, pilgrims to this site follow in the footsteps of their ancestors, for numerous graves, mosques, tombs, and other sites exist in Afghanistan and like other religious and political figures, Masoud fits into a larger cultural milieu. Most students of religion may have never heard of Masoud's tomb, or the cloak of the Prophet that lies in a shrine in Qandahar, but Afghans have a long history of shrine visitation that extends into north India. The fact that Afghans had "ties to numerous Sufis, living and dead," and the history of "Afghan notables as keen patrons of non-Afghan Sufis and their shrines," is absent from most of the scholarship on Islamic pilgrimage.[11] In addition, Shi'i shrines have had a presence in Afghanistan for a millennium, and of course there are *ziyarat* traditions that are historical, political, and local, defined in many ways by many communities. This concept of *ziyarat*, then, is where we must begin.

Figure 1.1 *Mazar* with flags, Xinjiang, China (photo courtesy of Brian Spivey).

ZIYARAT

Islamic pilgrimages are commonly referred to as *ziyarat* (sing. *ziyarah*). The Arabic word *zara* is the source of many words connected to pilgrimage, including *ziyara*, which means "visitation" and the Persianized *ziyaratgah*, or "place of pilgrimage," as well as *ziyarat gah mogaddas*, a phrase that refers to "places to visit." The vocabulary used to refer to pilgrimage sites is large, due to the wide geographical distribution of Muslims around the world. In medieval pilgrimage manuals, pilgrimage sites were often referred to as *mazarat*, but sometimes *qubbah* (pl. *qibab*) if a domed structure, *mazar* (a shrine), *qabr* (pl. *qubur*) if a tomb, *darih* (a tomb or cenotaph), *mashhad* (a place of martyrdom or witnessing), *masjid* (pl. *masajid*) in the case of a mosque that might contain a body or something else of religious significance, or *maqam* (a place a holy person had visited, such as a footprint or small structure, or a place associated with a vision), or *turbah* (pl. *turab*; mausoleum).[12] These descriptors denote the Arabic words used for pilgrimage sites, representing only a small sample of the philological communities associated with pilgrimage traditions in Islam. In addition to pilgrimages connected to architectural structures like shrines and mosques, others involve hidden places that have disappeared through the ravages of time and the environment, such as the *mazar*s buried beneath the dunes in Xinjiang, and the temporary shrines that are also found in this part of Asia, "fragile and ephemeral" constructions that are rebuilt time and again.[13]

Ziyarah has multiple meanings beyond the Arabic "visitations" connected to pilgrimage. It is also the word used for visiting a Sufi *shaykh*, literally meaning "visitation."[14] The plural *ziyarat* is also referenced in these cases, signifying the offerings or gifts brought to the *shaykh*, which in the Nilotic Sudan might include things like "livestock, cloth, slaves, honey, flour, butter, silver, rings, money (*māl*)."[15] In these cases, the visitation or pilgrimage is to a living person rather than a tomb, relic, or holy site, illustrating one of the many ways in which pilgrimage in Islam is an expansive category. The late scholar Shahab Ahmed defined *ziyarah* as "visitation of saint-tombs to benefit from the cosmic economy of the Sufi's *barakah* or spiritual power."[16] However, pilgrims visit sacred sites and bodies for a variety of reasons, as we shall see, and they do not always involve Sufi saints.

The use of "saint" in this book acknowledges that a large number of words are used to describe or identify holy people in Islam. In Christianity, the word "saint," which comes from the Latin *sanctus*, denotes "a charismatic individual who attains the Christian ideal of perfection in his or her lifetime and who is posthumously recognized."[17] Obviously, this book is not about Christian pilgrimage (although at times it is involved in the production of Islamic practices); however, the idea of saint is used in this project to discuss holy individuals who, while having a more fluid and broader definition, are viewed as spiritually admirable, or even perfect, in their character.

Ziyarah has a wide number of meanings that involve pilgrimage practices. In Shi'ism, *ziyarah* refers to the practice of visiting shrines and holy sites but it is also the name of the prayers recited at holy places. "By recollecting the events of Karbala, the *ziyara* at the holy places helps the pilgrim internalize the martyrdom and sufferings of al-Husayn and revives a spirit of revolt within him."[18] In some South Asian Sufi orders, the display of relics belonging to Prophet Muhammad is part of a ceremony called *ziyarat*.[19] *Ziyaratnama* is the genre of literature focused on pilgrimage.[20] It includes manuals that help pilgrims negotiate cities like Jerusalem, Damascus, and Qom, providing locations of sites as well as the prayers that should be recited there. As Schubel points out, for Shi'i *ziyarat* has three meanings – the visitation of sacred objects at *imambargahs* (where Shi'i gather in community), the Arabic salutations made at the end of a *majlis/majalis*, or prayer gathering, and the ritual performed on the twelfth day of Muharram.[21] In Java, *ziyarah* refers to the "public visitation of a saint," in a more specific usage of the term.[22] These connotations are in addition to the general usage of the word to refer to pilgrimage to, or visitation of, a holy place or person.

As these examples show, Islamic pilgrimage is a diverse phenomenon. Ibn 'Uthman (d. 1218) has a section in his Egyptian pilgrimage guide that reflects the important role played by ritual in these journeys and includes twenty rules (*wazaif*) for conducting pilgrimage, including that one should be sincere, perform the pilgrimage on a Friday, avoid sitting on and walking among graves (yet another indication that the dead knew when visitors came), greet the dead like the living, and read the Qur'an.[23] Prohibitions against kissing the grave and seeking a blessing from the grave are also part of the history of Muslim pilgrimages; however, these traditions, as well as many others, are still in vogue today.

In academic discourse, non-*hajj* pilgrimages to the tombs of Imam 'Ali, Sayyida Ruqayya, and others are frequently referred to as *ziyarat*. Scholars often characterize these traditions as deviations from "normative" Islam and describe them as small, local pilgrimages. Such a description does not fit *arbaeen*, the summer festival of Sufi music and prayer at Hacibektas, the *'urs* (death anniversary; literally "to marry") at Ajmer, or the countless other sites that feature large and transnational pilgrimages. Some of these pilgrimages may involve tens of thousands or even millions of pilgrims. The large numbers of Muslims at these gatherings is not something new. In the nineteenth century, over 100,000 pilgrims from India and Iran visited sites in Iraq, a number that is exponentially greater now.[24] Pilgrimages may also be daily activities, common in communities with rich cemetery cultures, such as the Kyrgyz, whose cities of the dead often incorporate "un-Islamic" elements that are part of local Muslim practice.[25] These examples point to some of the problems in classifying Islamic pilgrimages outside of *hajj* as local, small, or insignificant.

The ways in which scholars frame Islamic pilgrimage as sectarian is also problematic. *Ziyarat* is not a Shi'i or Sufi practice that is necessarily antithetical to *hajj*. Muslims also do not always visit sacred places due to sectarian affiliations. One exception is the graves of the Shi'i Imams, such as Imam Reza's shrine in Mashhad, which are rarely visited by Sunni Muslims. However, Sunnis visit the graves of Husayn, Ali, Fatima, Zaynab, and others who are part of the Imamate and its vast network of sites. Although the Fatimids (969–1187) memorialized religious practice as a matter of state policy, Sunni dynasties such as the Ayyubids (1187–1250) and Mamluks (1250–1516) followed, dedicating "thousands of sacred places to prophets, Companions of the Prophet, saints (*awliyā'*), holy people (*qiddīsūn*), martyrs (*shuhadā'*) and the righteous (*sālihūn*)."[26] As this book shows, *ziyarah* has been an Islamic practice from the beginning and one that has never been strictly Shi'i.

Islamic pilgrimages include visits to the tombs of Prophet Muhammad's relatives, companions, and followers, the graves of Sufi saints, individuals important to Muslims, Jews, and Christians like Abraham (*Ibrahim*), Mary (*Maryam*), and springs, mountaintops, rocks, and forests that are often associated with stories, miracles, dreams, and visions. In some cases, pilgrimages are inspired by visions of Prophet Muhammad, who visits people in a dream or a waking vision. As one example, Ahmad Reza Khan Barelwi (1856–1921), whose poetry is often recited by pilgrims, evokes the presence of the Prophet.[27] In other cases, the dead visit the living in a dream and reveal a secret, such as in the case of Sultan Satuq Bhugra-khan, who appeared before the Altishahr (Xinjiang) Sufi Muhammad Sharif one night and revealed the site of his grave, then helped Sharif find other graves "through his own interactions with other spirits."[28]

Ziyarat may be local, but they often involve long journeys, gathering networks of Muslims together from disparate communities around the globe to congregate in large numbers. Karbala often sees twenty million visitors in a year, many of them congregating during *arbaeen* and greatly outnumbering the pilgrims at *hajj*, which sees approximately two million visitors annually. The annual pilgrimage to Konya for Rumi's *'urs* (death anniversary) is also immense and transnational. *Ziyarat* often involves other special occasions, such as the *mawlids* (birthdays, or death anniversaries) of saints in Tanzania, when the blessing of the deceased is believed to be especially potent.[29]

Many Islamic pilgrimages are centered on the dead. Historically, the practice of visiting the graves of the deceased has often been focused on both helping the dead pass the test of faith and relieving their sadness at being deceased. As Renard explains, "Help from the community of believers enables the deceased to pass this crucial test, thereby alleviating the loneliness of the tomb, mitigating the sense of constriction the dead feel, and assuring an easier passage from this world to the next."[30] Among Muslims, the belief that the dead can sense the living is widespread and dates from the earliest days of Islam. Pilgrimage guides from the medieval period point to these traditions, which are not limited to graves, but also "mention sacred rocks, talismanic objects, and wells associated with saints and sacred episodes from Islamic and pre-Islamic history, sarcophagi in sacred caves, and saints' clothing."[31] This suggests that Islamic pilgrimage involves not only graves, but a wide array of objects connected to the bodies of the dead.

In addition to the belief that the dead can be helped in their state of transition, Muslims also believe that visiting the grave results in benefits for the pilgrim. The dead are believed to intercede on behalf of the living, offering a conduit to the Divine. Islamic pilgrimage practices focused on intercession from quite an early stage: "The traditional Islamic practices of *ziyārat al-qubūr* (the visitation of burial places) and reliance on intercessory prayers appear well established by the early tenth century."[32] Today, the belief that the living and the dead can communicate with each other is widespread, and is found among Muslims in disparate geographical locations. In Java, pilgrims often visit the graves of ancestors, relatives, and children. In Senegal, as well as in many other places with large Sufi communities, some Muslims communicate with the dead on a daily basis. Every morning at Serigne Abdoulaye Yakhine's mausoleum, disciples circle the tomb, reciting *dhikr* (the ritual of remembrance common among Sufis, also called *zikr*), and sing, but they also believe that the *shaykh* can hear them, that he speaks to them, and even that "they hold conversations" with their dead teacher.[33] In the Volga-Ural region of Russia, Muslims visit the graves of the dead, most often the saints buried in small cemeteries, which are called *zirat* – taken from the word *ziyarat*.[34]

Many Islamic pilgrimages occur at the local level, in smaller communities such as a village or town. In some cases, authority is constructed vis-à-vis an urban center such as Cairo, Qom, or Jakarta, but in other cases, authority may be independent of such places. Scholars have written extensively about local Islam and the communities that interpret Islamic texts and doctrines, translate them into their own cultural language, and negotiate various articulations of religious tradition with centers of authority. Although there are tensions between religious texts and authority on the one hand, and local or "popular" religion on the other, these are not necessarily diametrically opposed. Often the careful negotiation of texts, authority, and local tradition is involved. In the case of southeastern Morocco, for example, "Berber-speaking areas were crisscrossed with centers of religious learning based in *zawaya* or local mosques and manned by specialists with advanced theological training and mastery of classical Arabic."[35]

Islam is not monolithic. As one scholar notes, "preexisting cultural and religious patterns, together with local configurations of social and economic power, influence the ways in which universalistic texts, including the Qurān and Hadith, are interpreted."[36] Pilgrimage is but one of many areas in which these interpretations occur. In the seventeenth century, Wang Daiyu viewed the five pillars of Islam as parallel acts to the Five Constant Virtues, linking "the primary actions of Islamic religious commitment with the moral dispositions of traditional Chinese thought."[37]

Communities do not typically formulate pilgrimages without reference to texts; rather, they often construct their own traditions in creative negotiations with the texts identified by scholars as authoritative. As Paul Silverstein points out, "The scholastic dichotomy of 'popular' vs. 'official' (or 'scriptural') Islam constitutes a similar effort to map epistemological certainty onto a messy reality of shared religious belief and practice."[38] The pilgrims who travel to Karbala for *arbaeen* or visit local saints in Java, Bangladesh, Mali, and elsewhere may elevate local pilgrimages over *hajj*, bypassing the same sources that scholars identify as authoritative. In Bangladesh, Arabic texts are far less important than the key symbols produced through local practices rooted in the *desh* (homelands), which include a myriad of traditions ranging from the belief that dirt and soil from Sufi shrines contain *mortoba* (a kind of power similar to *barakah*) to the insistence that seven trips to the Ajmir shrine across the border in India is equal to performing *hajj*.[39] The tomb of Shaykh Safi in Iran was equated to the *ka'bah* and included circumambulation mirroring the *ta'waf* around the sacred structure in Mecca.[40] Scholars have often been inattentive to these more complex negotiations of Islam, in part due to the reliance on the model of Christian religious experience. Richard King has written extensively on this issue, arguing that the concept of religion is "the product of the culturally specific discursive processes of Christian history in the West" that has established Christianity as "the prototypical example of a religion and thus as the fundamental yardstick or paradigm-case for the study of 'other religions.'"[41] This seems especially true of ritual, including those associated with pilgrimage, for, as J.Z. Smith has written, the scholar is often "cool" on the question of ritual due to the "Protestant insistence" that affects so much scholarship.[42] The tendency to classify other people's religions according to Christian normative standards continues to be a problem in scholarship, as we shall see.

Typologies are useful academic tools because they help to sort a large amount of data into manageable categories. However, the typologies academics use for Islamic pilgrimage rarely accord with the realities of lived religion. One typology suggests six categories: devotional, instrumental, normative, wandering, initiatory, and obligatory.[43] Such a categorization classifies the Shi'i pilgrimage to Karbala as "devotional" and *hajj* as "obligatory," creating a hierarchy of importance that contradicts the ways in which many Muslims practice their religion. As one example, some Shi'i Muslims believe in a hierarchy of mosques following an order of priority beginning with the mosque in Mecca, "the Prophet's mosque in Medina, the mosque in Kufa, and the Aqsa mosque in Jerusalem."[44] However, Muslims have a wealth of motivations, experiences, and traditions. According to at least one *ayatollah*, "it is better to pray in the shrines of the Imams than in a mosque."[45] Typologies of ritual seldom address the complex experiences religious people have. *Hajj* may be both devotional and obligatory, or simply devotional, and for some it is initiatory, marking one's entrance into adulthood or status as a *hajji* or *hajjah*.[46] *Hajj* can also be part of a pious practice in which a Muslim completes the pilgrimage with a religious teacher in order to gain *barakah*.

The complexity of these religious experiences makes it imperative that we interrogate the academic typologies

associated with Islamic pilgrimage. Muslims go on pilgrimage
for a variety of reasons – a family obligation, the power of a
religious narrative, reports of a miracle, a belief in relics, or
the promise of healing. In other contexts, Islamic pilgrimage
is formed around other traditions, involving an "appropriation
and manipulation of meaning" that involves a complex negotiation of texts, history, and communities in the formation of
holy sites.[47] The *Qadam Rasul*, the footprint of the Prophet,
has antecedent traditions in Judaism and Christianity, and
footprints are also part of the pilgrimage cultures of Hindus
and Buddhists.[48] The fact that such traditions are found among
numerous religious groups suggests that Islamic pilgrimage is
often related to, or is in conversation with, complex cultural,
historical, and religious milieus.

Political histories also can play a prominent role in the formation of pilgrimages in Islam. This includes the avoidance of
certain places that are believed to be cursed because of their
historical connection to particular people and events. In the
Shi'i tradition, for example, the second Masjid al-Hamra is
believed to be "accursed" because it was built on the grave
of a pharaoh.[49] Other sites are avoided due to an unfortunate
event or location. Such complexities are part of the story of
Islamic pilgrimage, revealing how history often plays a role
in the formation of Islamic sacred space and in constructing
beliefs surrounding what is forbidden and what is pleasing
to God.

One way of thinking about Islamic pilgrimage is through
a key difference between many of the most important *hajj*
sites – Mecca, Arafat, Mina – and the sites of *ziyarat*, the
majority of which are graves (*ziyarat al-qubur*). The *hajj* is not
centered on visiting tombs or other commemorative buildings
and monuments; rather, it is a set of rituals largely focused on
the lives of Ibrahim, Hajar, and Ishmael.[50] At the same time,
pilgrims in Medina visit the graves of the Prophet and other
important figures, and many may reflect upon the Prophet's

farewell pilgrimage near his death during their own journey. It is true that many non-*hajj* pilgrimages are very focused on funerary architecture through the visitation of a large and diverse array of what Oleg Grabar called "commemorative structures," which include the Taj Mahal, Mamluk mausoleums, village cemeteries, tombs of Shi'i Imams, graves of Sufis, and other loci.[51] Among these are *qubbah*s and *gunbadh*s (domes), *turbah*s (tombs), *Imamzadeh*s (tombs of the Imams), *wali*s and *marbat*s (tombs of Sufi saints), *maqam*s (holy places), and *mashhad*s (places of witnessing, sometimes of a miracle).[52]

The details surrounding the focus of such pilgrimages – the dead – may or may not be as important as the popular legend associated with the saint or holy person. In some cases, the saint may not even lie in the tomb being visited. Such is the case of the grave of the saint named Badsha Peer (d. 1894) in South Africa: "Who lies buried in the grave that bears Badsha Peer's name does not matter as much as the fact that large numbers of Muslims accept his existence without question and that his shrine is part of a deep Islamic tradition with thousands of adherents."[53] The lack of a body at many sites calls into question the notion that Islamic pilgrimage can be organized in terms of sites that are associated with the dead, and those that are not. In addition to this fact, many sites are associated with miracles, visions, and other events unrelated to bodies or relics.

Many pilgrimage destinations, such as the places associated with Ibrahim and Hajar that are visited during *hajj*, show how typologies – even those focused on bodies and relics – fail to help in the understanding of Islamic pilgrimage as a broad and diverse phenomenon. Some pilgrimage destinations are marked by sacred architecture or Qur'anic personalities, while others are not associated with individuals identified as central Islamic religious characters. Many *ziyarat* involve political genealogies, pre-Islamic landscapes, and other places of local or regional historical importance. In Indonesia, *ziarat* include the graves of Muslim kings, nobles, and saints as well as the founders of *pesantren* (Islamic boarding schools) and natural sites such as caverns, mountaintops, and springs.[54] Javanese pilgrimages often tend to be syncretic, in accordance with the history of the island, which includes rich Hindu and Buddhist cultures, as well as the more recent Christian presence. Journeys to former Hindu or Buddhist temples and Christian churches would not be considered acceptable by some outsiders, but for Javanese Muslims they are very much part of their traditions and are considered Islamic.

Islamic pilgrimages often focus on distinct spaces within urban settings, such as homes, bazaars, and other vernacular structures that might not be recognized as "sacred" by an outsider, as a shrine or graveyard might be. A tomb might be located next to a home or a grave constructed within a learning institution such as a *madrasah* (religious school). At one time the Salihiyya quarter of Damascus, an area rich in tombs, graves, and other pilgrimage sites, contained nine *suqs*, thirteen *khans* (caravanserais), and nineteen *hammams* (public baths).[55] This is one example of the Islamic practice of understanding sacred space as being constituted by immense borders. Examples of this are found in Bosnia, India, Iraq, Iran, Pakistan, and Java, where large pilgrimage landscapes are dotted with smaller sites marked with graves, miracles, and visions. The dead are often part of these landscapes, but in ways that do not necessarily involve a tomb, grave, or mausoleum.

ISLAMIC DEBATES SURROUNDING *ZIYARAT*

While this book takes no position on the specific controversies surrounding correct behavior, what Muslims call *akhlaq*, it is important to understand that the debates surrounding pilgrimage involve numerous factors, including politics, theology, ritual, and concerns surrounding gendered and sexual identities. Despite these concerns, many of the world's Muslims visit the dead, pray at their graves, and believe in intercession (*shafa'ah*). These beliefs and practices are not new. According to tradition, during his lifetime Prophet Muhammad planted a date palm in a grave to relieve the suffering of the dead, suggesting he believed the two worlds created a kind of liminal space.[56] Another old tradition relates to the speech of the dead during funerals. "According to al-Bukhārī (d. 870), whenever men burying a pious person on their necks (*'alā a 'nāq*) need to stop, the voice of the deceased encourage them to proceed quickly. If they transport a bad person, his voice laments the destination."[57] Although some legal traditions contradict the idea of the dead having such agency, the common view was the opposite: "Once quickened by its spirit, the corpse returned, not quite to life, but certainly to a semblance of life."[58]

Pilgrimage architecture is one way in which the popularity of these beliefs can be seen. Muslims have constructed tombs since the early days of Islam. Pre-Islamic commemorative architecture was common in the Hijaz as well as many of the regions where Islam spread. By the late ninth century, the first tombs appear in the historical record – the Qubbah al-Sulaybiyah at Samarra in Iraq and the tomb of Fatima at Qom.[59] These early forms of grave veneration could come from pre-Islamic traditions or might have been part of an emerging Islamic ethic surrounding the honoring of the dead. Evidence for the former includes the fact that pre-Islamic Arabia had a cult of the dead. The Qur'an called these pagan structures, which were essentially upright tombs, *ansab*, and pagan Arabs erected tents called *qubbah*, a term, interestingly, adopted by Muslims as a name for the mausoleums, or domed graves, that dominate many of the *ziyarat* examined in this book.[60]

It is difficult to determine how early and frequently these tombs were visited. Records indicate that visiting burial sites emerged as a form of Islamic piety in Cairo, Damascus, and Baghdad from the tenth century.[61] As early as the eleventh century, large monuments were constructed in Afghanistan, including the Shrine of Imam-i Kalan in Sar-i Pul.[62] These tombs (and others) suggest that *ziyarah* is not only an early development but one that is geographically widespread. For some educated Muslim elites, the practice of visiting these sites may also be understood in the context of Islamic theology, which was deeply embedded in Greek philosophy. As Shahab Ahmed argued in his work:

> The idea of the cosmic economy of *barakah* proceeds directly from the Neo-Platonic logic of emanation that underpins the Avicennan cosmos – indeed, an ordinary Muslim's *ziyārah* to obtain the *barakah* that emanates from the tomb of a Sufi in a village or mountain pass in Morocco, India or Indonesia is precisely a *de facto* acknowledgement of and active participation in a cosmos organized and structured and experienced in Neo-Platonic, Avicennan, and Akbarian terms.[63]

Islamic texts both *promote* the visitation of graves and *prohibit* the practice, depending on which text one believes. *Ahadith* (sayings or actions of Prophet Muhammad; sing. *hadith*) suggest that Muhammad both favored and forbade *ziyarah*. He reportedly visited the graves of his friends and asked God to intercede on their behalf.[64] Scholars point out that his followers prayed for rain both at his grave and at that of his uncle 'Abbas.[65] At the same time, the practice of *taswiyat al-qubur* – leveling graves – is found in several *hadith* collections.[66] Despite this practice of destroying graves (the extent of which is impossible to determine), the Prophet's grave became a pilgrimage site and often served as a model for other pilgrimages, including many of those examined in this book. What probably happened is that when the Prophet died, grave visitation was already a common occurrence and contributed to the various opinions surrounding his own views on the practice. As Shoemaker notes, "one would suspect that the narratives of Muhammad's death in Medina developed alongside the emergent veneration of Muhammad's grave and the related transformation of Yathrib into the 'City of the Prophet.'"[67]

Since the Prophet's death, the proliferation of pilgrimage sites has included sites pre-dating Islam and the graves of early Muslims, places of miracles and visions, and tombs of saints, sultans, and martyrs. Qur'anic narratives featuring biblical figures play a role in many of these sites, figuring prominently in pilgrimages dating back to at least the twelfth century if not earlier. In Damascus, Mt. Qasiyun contained a cave believed to be where Cain killed Abel, as well as the place associated with other stories of Abraham, Mary, and Jesus.[68] These sites helped attract Muslims to the area, eventually helping it to become a major pilgrimage center.

For most of Islam's history, pilgrims have only had to worry about the dangers associated with robbery, warfare, and illness while on pilgrimage, not about being attacked by fellow Muslims. Attacks against Damascenes visiting Sayyida Zaynab's tomb, for example, were unheard of until the introduction of Wahhabism and its associated ideologies, which are only a few hundred years old. Modern Islamic puritan movements are responsible for the explosion of violence against Muslim pilgrims in places like Iraq, Syria, and Pakistan. In part, these conflagrations of violence are due to political forces, but they are also situated in particular readings of Islam that, although followed by a minority of Muslims, have a widespread effect on the safety of many pilgrimages around the world. Many of these readings can be traced to Salafism. A Salafi is someone who identifies with the early community, or *salaf*. The various ideologies inspired by Salafism seek a stringent form of Islam that restricts tradition to the practices of Prophet Muhammad and his companions. Anything that came after this period, such as Shi'ism or Sufism (*tasawwuf*), is considered innovation (*bid'ah*), although only some Salafis take decisive, violent action against these newer traditions. In some cases, these efforts to curb *ziyarat* have been successful in suppressing these traditions. In the nineteenth century, Muslim scholars issued pamphlets denouncing the visitation to *keremet* (graveyard) groves, resulting in an almost complete cessation of the practice in parts of Europe.[69]

Pilgrimage that falls outside of *hajj* is one of the practices considered *bid'ah* (innovation) by puritanical Muslims. Because *ziyarah* is often associated with Shi'ism and with devotional, mystical, and ecstatic Islamic traditions (known collectively as Sufism) more than with Sunni Islam, these two groups – Shi'i and Sufis (who may be Sunni) – are the ones often targeted by violence. Ibn Taymiyyah, an Islamic theologian active in the late thirteenth and early fourteenth centuries, argued that *ahadith* encouraging the visitation of graves were forgeries (*mawdu'*) and furthermore, that such acts could result in the worship of the dead instead of Allah – a transgression that results in *shirk*, or the association with something other than God. The Wahhabis, who closely follow the teachings of Ibn Taymiyyah, are largely responsible for attacks on pilgrims. The founder of the movement, Muhammad Ibn 'Abd al-Wahhab (1703–1792), personally demolished the grave of Umar's brother, setting a precedent for the destruction of other sites that continues today around the world.[70] In 1926, Egyptian pilgrims were attacked by Wahhabis, who also destroyed their musical instruments – deemed, like *ziyarat*, an un-Islamic innovation.[71] As we shall learn, Muslims often play music or recite poetry as part of their pilgrimages to holy sites.

Wahhabism and its associated ideologies are not limited to Arabia. In the nineteenth century, the Ahl-i Hadith, a minority movement in South Asia that is characterized as more literalist than the Deobandis, opposed pilgrimage to Prophet Muhammad's tomb and all gravesites.[72] Inspired by

Wahhabism, the Ahl-i Hadith also focused on the teachings of Ibn Taymiyyah, who situated himself in the legal school of Ibn Hanbal, an Islamic theologian active during the ninth century. Rather ironically, Hanbal "allegedly allowed people to kiss the Prophet's tomb for *Baraka*, and he himself drank the water in which Imām al-Shāfī's (d. 820) shirt was washed in order to obtain blessing."[73] Taymiyyah never prohibited all *ziyarat*; in fact, "He even permitted visits to the cemeteries of non-Muslims, as far as the Muslim pilgrims did not pray for them."[74] Nevertheless, Taymiyyah is often one of the main influences on those opposed to *ziyarat*.

Questions surrounding the legality of Islamic pilgrimages outside of *hajj*, and in particular of the visiting of graves that involve the intercession of saints, often focus on notions of "orthodoxy" that are highly problematic. As seen in the example of Ibn Hanbal, Islam does not have consensus on the question of pilgrimage. When these debates come up, each side typically claims a position of authority, utilizing a careful selection of texts to back up their stance. In Yemen, for example, the *sufiyyun* (or Sufis) refer to themselves as "the followers of the pious ancestors" (*atba' al-salaf*), while their opponents call them "grave worshippers" (*al-quburiyyun*) and "propagators of innovations and superstitions" (*ashab al-bid'a wa 'l-khurafat*).[75] Yemeni Sufis use the word *salaf* self-referentially, the very word that functions as a synonym for the Wahhabis, which suggests how claims of authenticity on both sides depend upon a language of tradition and authority that is often contested. Devotion often takes precedence over literal proscriptions. In Senegal, for the *murids* (Sufi disciples), "reading the holy words is less important than working for the *marabout* [ascetic; saint]."[76]

Today, concerns surrounding gender and sexuality, including the free mixing of bodies that are often a large part of pilgrimage, often play a central role in debates surrounding *ziyarat*. Bodies are often the focus of pilgrimage in Islam. Scott Kugle argues, for example, that Sufism, which we will define in this context as being a nonsectarian and common set of Islamic orientations, is a queered aspect of Islam populated with homoerotic desires and acts, queered bodies, and complicated gender identities. The "immediacy of religious experience with, through, and in the body" for Sufis (and Muslims in general) is an important part of the pilgrim's experience.[77] Saintly bodies of men, women, and children, even after death, are believed to have the power to heal, aid, comfort, forgive, and save. Pilgrims visiting these individuals might touch the tomb, or even lean their entire body on it, in an intimate embrace of the saint. This is certainly true of Shi'i whose tradition of saints utilizes a powerful "imagery of intimacy."[78] At many tombs men often perform emotional songs of lamentation and men and women weep openly. At Muslim shrines music and dancing is often quite romantic, with all-male performances focused on the love of the saint that may veer into the homoerotic.[79] At the vast majority of tombs, shrines, and other Islamic pilgrimage sites throughout the world, including *hajj*, men and women mix freely, sometimes in large crowds that are engaged in emotionally charged, ecstatic, or even sensual practices.

Islamic pilgrimages frequently offer spaces of agency and mobility for women and queered bodies (including LGBTQ Muslims), something that does not sit well with Muslims who oppose the mixing of men and women and seek the enforcement of heteronormativity. In Java, martial arts dances are traced to Sufi brotherhoods and often involve transvestite performers.[80] Such transgressions of patriarchal boundaries function as sites of anxiety that involve both gender and sexuality. Even the *hajj* has served as a locus for sensuality. In Khaqani's twelfth-century text *Tuhfat al-Iraqayn* (Gifts of the Two Iraqs), the *ka'bah* is likened to a bride and a heavenly virgin, as well as a king – a queered object.[81]

The political aspects of these debates surrounding pilgrimage can be quite interesting. Ironically, some of the same groups that criticize *ziyarat* have Sufic elements in their organizational structures. According to the Salafis, the lines between the *ahl al-sunna*, with whom the Salafis identify, and the *ahl al-bid'ah*, the "innovators" or corrupters of Islam, which includes the people who go on these pilgrimages, are clearly defined.[82] Yet Islamism, the politicized form of Islam that is popular in many countries, often blur these lines. The Islamist organization MUQ (Minhajul Qur'an, or Method of the Qur'an) has Sufi leanings, is led by a *maulana*, and follows a master/disciple model like Sufi orders (*turuq*), exemplified by Tahirul Qadi's self-identification as a "wali Allah," or friend of God.[83] Sufis (examined in Chapter 3) are also not exclusively supportive of *ziyarat*. The Salihiyya leader Muhammad Abd Allah Hasan (1864–1920), for instance, was strongly against local Islamic practices in Somalia, including the worshiping of graves.[84] These examples point to some of the challenges inherent in these debates over pilgrimage, where the sentiments for and against are not typically aligned in a sectarian fashion.

PILGRIMAGE AND ISLAM

Pilgrimage is a rich topic for study – a human activity that exists in some form in most human communities in the world. The anthropologists Victor and Edith Turner's work on Catholic pilgrimage in the 1970s largely inspired the field of pilgrimage studies. According to Victor Turner, pilgrimage is a journey to the "center" that is external to the mundane, involving a journey to a place that is somewhere *out there*.[85] Turner described pilgrimage as a physical journey "on foot or donkey or camel through rough country with danger of robbers and brigands, and not much in the way of food or shelter," during which the pilgrim moves from the "familiar" and "secular, mundane, every day, ordinary" to the "far place" that is "sacred" and "rare."[86] The Turners developed a useful, albeit overly simplistic, framework for thinking about pilgrimage. As anthropologists, they were interested in how religious pilgrimage functioned as ritual in society, as well as what it could reveal about the power of such journeys to transform an individual and create meaning. According to the Turners, pilgrimage is characterized by five elements: it is voluntary; it is ludic (pleasurable); it fosters independence and equality; it is often anti-structural; and it creates *communitas* – a kind of bonding based on human likeness.[87] The images of *hajj*, when more than one million Muslims pray, walk, and perform other rites, is a perfect example of this coming together of humanity, which may be one of the reasons that some scholars of Islam continue to privilege this particular vision of pilgrimage. It is, in many ways, an easy way to think about an incredibly complex and diverse human activity.

According to the Turners, *communitas* takes place in the second phase of a three-part structure that characterizes pilgrimage. The first part of pilgrimage is the pre-liminal stage (structures are stripped away and the journey begins), the second part is known as the liminal stage (immersion into the experience of pilgrimage), and the third is the post-liminal stage (reintegration of the transformed individual into society).[88] Much of pilgrimage scholarship has focused on the second, liminal stage, the rituals and experiences located at the pilgrimage site; and *communitas*, the "spontaneously generated relationship ... between human beings stripped of their structural attributes."[89] Less attention has been placed on the post-liminal phase, a subject to which a chapter of this book is dedicated. It is unfortunate that so little attention is placed on the pilgrim's after-journey, as if the story of pilgrimage ends as soon as *communitas* takes place.

In recent years, scholars have suggested perspectives on pilgrimage that depart from the focus on *communitas* voiced by the Turners. Some studies have challenged the idea that pilgrimage constitutes an affirmative journey that is wholly separate from everyday life.[90] Turner's center is determined by a journey that is described as "deliberate travel to a far place intimately associated with the deepest, most cherished axiomatic values of the traveler."[91] This becomes complicated when we look at virtual and cyber-pilgrimages conducted in one's home or other spaces located far from a sacred site. Even in physical pilgrimages, the center might be next door. In Touba, for example, Senegalese *murid*s look at the tomb of their founder as the center of the "community's *imaginaire* and symbolism."[92] Although modeled on the holy cities of Mecca and Medina, the city's cemetery is on the *qibla* axis of the mosque (the direction of prayer toward Mecca); the cemetery is believed to be "the Gate to Paradise; physical burial amounts to passage through the Gate."[93] The practice of participating in *hajj* remotely, from a distant location, is not solely a contemporary one. Lio Zhi (1670–1724) argued that Chinese Muslims who were not able to perform the pilgrimage to Mecca could participate in the sacred center through *Qurban*, a "ritual substitution" achieved by "making the *Qurbān* sacrifice equivalent in merit with the pilgrimage."[94] Today, Ughyur Muslims pray toward the *ka'bah* but other prayers and the recitation of the Qur'an are often performed facing the tomb of the saint, with one's back turned to Mecca.[95]

Pilgrimage to a local graveyard, which often constitutes *ziyarah*, is another practice that complicates Turner's model of the center. In Java, visiting the graves of one's ancestors and relatives is considered a form of *ziyarah*.[96] The use of portable items – common in virtual pilgrimages – challenges the notion of pilgrimage as being situated *away* from the individual's mundane or regular life. Shi'i often use items from pilgrimages, or associated with them, in rituals performed at home or within their local community. The increased mobility and expansion of technology that formulate a large part of modern life are two of the powerful reasons why religious people, including Muslims, have a multiplicity of options – some of which are explored in this book – for performing pilgrimage.

In addition to the negotiation of space, scholars of pilgrimage have discussed other aspects of pilgrimage. Alan Morinis and Nancy Frey have focused on the individual's experience, rather than the communal aspect of pilgrimage represented by *communitas*; John Eade and Michael Sallnow have looked at pilgrimage from the perspective of market exchange, in one of the many studies that have focused on the economic aspect of religious activity; Ruth Harris and others have opted to look at the material and bodily aspects of pilgrimage; and Erik Cohen has challenged the ways we think about tourism and religious pilgrimage, arguing that they are often inextricably linked.[97] My book contains no major critiques of these scholars and others. Instead, I am interested in making an argument for a particular way of understanding Islamic pilgrimage that is not tied to one theory but is enriched by looking at the work of numerous scholars. Pilgrimage in Islam is a network of rituals, traditions, languages, communities, and histories. This is in contrast to the presentation of Islamic pilgrimage as consisting of one tradition, or a superior tradition, which, as we shall see, is a view that is informed by the problematic history of the study of religions and, as such, needs to be challenged.

In the vast majority of scholarship on Islam, pilgrimage is equated with one subject – *hajj*, the great journey to Mecca undertaken by nearly two million Muslims each year. *Hajj* is an important tradition for many Muslims – a duty situated in theology, history, and politics. Identified in the Qur'an and the *sunnah* (the tradition of the Prophet), the *hajj* is described as a duty (*fard*) in several legal traditions. However, *hajj* is an optional journey for many Muslims around the world. Shi'i Muslims often substitute *arbaeen* for *hajj*. In Java, the cult of the saints in Yogyakarta is so powerful that it often replaces the more arduous and expensive journey to Mecca. As Woodward notes, "The *kejawén* belief that pilgrimage to the graves of

Sunan Kalijaga and/or Sultan Agung can be substituted for the *hajj* is often cited as an example."[98]

Mecca is the city, along with Medina, identified with Prophet Muhammad's mission, exile, and eventual return. Among the images associated with the city is the *ka'bah*, the black cubical building toward which Muslims face every day to pray that serves as a focal center of the pilgrimage to Mecca. Rebuilt in 605 by the Quraysh, this mysterious stone structure is believed to have been built by Ibrahim and his son – a foreshadowing of Muhammad's call to monotheism.[99] Today, it is a major religious center of Islam, replacing Jerusalem, which was the center of Muslim topography and religious identity before the process of Arabization took place. The *ka'bah* also "links the realms of heaven and earth," appearing in many eschatological texts and paintings.[100] For all of these reasons, the *ka'bah* and other holy sites associated with *hajj* are prominent in the religious imagination of Muslims around the world. However, the importance of *hajj* does little to explain the failure of many scholars to include other pilgrimage traditions in academic studies of Islam. As one study points out, "While the hajj, the pilgrimage to Mecca, is a universal rite in Islam, the *ziyara* – literally, 'visitation,' a notion that encompasses all venerated places such as graves and shrines of saints, trees, wells, and rocks – is also universally popular, but lacks the authority of the Qur'an."[101]

Limiting Islamic pilgrimage to the *hajj* points to some of the problems in the study of religion and, in particular, scholarship regarding Islam. Orientalism's prominent voice in scholarship focused on Islam is related to larger problems in the academic study of religion. The godfather of religious studies, J.Z. Smith, has argued that "'Religion' is not a native category. It is not a first-person term of self-characterization. It is a category imposed from the outside on some aspect of native culture."[102] Much of Western scholarship about "religion" is really Christian (Protestant) self-referentialism.

Take mysticism, for example, a subject of study constructed out of post-Kantian epistemology and post-Enlightenment thought that juxtaposes rational religion (Protestantism) with non-rational, experiential religion (mysticism, Catholicism, Islam). As Richard King has pointed out, scholars impose the Christian concept of mysticism on other religions. This practice is anathema to King, who remarks, "This is an astonishing statement to make – that the notions of God, communion, the soul and themes of a loving relationship between the two can be found in (actually imposed upon) all non-Christian experience."[103] Sufism, identified as a form of mysticism, is a broad category of religious traditions in Islam that has also been implicated in this line of thinking, with the differentiation of Sufi and non-Sufi (i.e. Orthodox Sunnism) reading "like a Protestant polemic against (or even caricature of) Catholicism."[104] Islam, as a religion with roughly 1.5 billion followers worldwide, encompasses a huge variety of rituals, languages, traditions, and sects, yet it is often presented in simplistic terms. The great variety of pilgrimages to small village shrines, tombs of poets, saints, relatives of Prophet Muhammad, and national heroes, as well as to natural sites such as mountaintops and springs, is one way we can counter these older presentations.

The focus on *hajj* is indicative of larger issues in the study of religion. Sunni Islam, which is often highlighted in academic studies of Islam, is viewed as a kind of Muslim Protestantism, as the correct historical and methodological sect that is superior to Shi'ism and other sects. Muslims who are not Sunni have at times been described as unorthodox, even Catholic. The construction of Islamic pilgrimage follows the same logic. Upholding *hajj* as the correct pilgrimage and relegating others as minor, insignificant, or heretical privileges is one reading of Islam. It also assumes that Sunni Muslims have only one pilgrimage, when in reality they have thousands of them. This presentation is largely due to the work of Western scholars whose dominance in the nineteenth century established a particular reading of Islam. As J.Z. Smith once wrote, "The focus on the 'other' as unintelligible has led, necessarily, to 'their' silence and 'our' speech."[105] This book helps give voice to those other traditions.

Idealized treatments of Islamic ritual, including pilgrimage, are common. In reality, *hajj* is crowded, difficult, and dangerous, but for those looking from the outside, including scholars, *hajj* paints a postcard of the romantic East. The fixation on the *hajj* is due in part to the links that Orientalists made between Christianity and Islam in the nineteenth century. As Mohammed Sharafuddin has argued, Romantic Orientalists like Robert Southey attempted to "confirm and consolidate a number of Christian beliefs" in his writings on Islam and this included the identification of Arabia (and Mecca in particular) with the fall of man.[106] For Orientalist scholars, Mecca fulfills numerous Western fantasies about the East.

The *hajj* also holds a privileged academic position because of its role as one of the five pillars of Islam. Even today, many texts present Islamic belief and ritual as essentially defined by these five "pillars": the *shahadah* (profession of faith), *salat* (prayer), *sawm* (fasting at Ramadan), *zakat* (charitable giving), and *hajj* (pilgrimage to Mecca). According to tradition Prophet Muhammad said, "Five things are obligatory upon the children of Islam: Witnessing that there is no god but God, rising for the prayer, and giving of charity, fasting in the month of Ramadan, and performing the pilgrimage to the house in Mecca."[107] The five pillars model, while a useful framing device for introducing Islam, is a woefully inadequate system for understanding the entirety of traditions practiced by so many people. While it is true that all Muslims subscribe to the *shahadah* – the profession of faith that expresses monotheism and names Muhammad as a prophet – the other pillars are followed differently (or not at all) depending on sect or tradition. For example, Isma'ilis have seven pillars, not five. Not all Muslims pray five times a day; Shi'i often combine their prayers into three daily supplications. For some Muslims, *hajj* is often accompanied by pilgrimages to places like Medina, Konya, Damascus, and Jerusalem, and, as we shall see, may be supplanted by other pilgrimages.

For scholars, the *hajj* may fulfill the romantic idea of pilgrimage as a journey that equalizes humans and places them in a collective mystic space. The familiar images of the pilgrimage to Mecca mirror this idealized vision of human pilgrimage – two million people gathered in one space, dressed in like manner to erase all social and racial divisions, praying together, walking together, and experiencing *communitas*, the sense of mystic togetherness that pilgrimage creates.[108] Certainly, for some pilgrims *hajj* fulfills this promise. When Malcolm X went on the great pilgrimage, he observed the true brotherhood that was absent in American society. While in Medina, he wrote, "The very essences of the Islam religion in teaching the Oneness of God, gives the Believer genuine, voluntary obligations towards his fellow man (all of whom are One Human Family, brothers and sisters to each other) ... the True Believer recognizes the Oneness of all Humanity."[109] As many studies have noted, "The experience of racial harmony at the *hajj* transformed him."[110]

The *hajj* is described as "one of mankind's most enduring rites," "a spiritual destination to millions of men and women around the globe," "a collective celebration," "an intensely personal experience," and "the religious apex of a Muslim's life."[111]

It is hard for other religious journeys to compete with such accolades, even though *hajj* is, as I have stated, one of numerous journeys in the rich world of Muslim pilgrimage. Over the past fourteen hundred years, Islam has spawned an impressive number of other pilgrimages. In Shi'ism alone, there are over fifty major sites visited by the followers of its various branches and thousands of minor sites. In most studies of Islam, these pilgrimages are not even mentioned, nor are journeys to numerous shrines in Morocco, the shrines in Syria, or tombs in India and Pakistan and Samarkand. Even Rumi's great tomb in Konya and the vast network of shrines in Iran and Iraq where relatives of the Prophet lie often do not merit a reference. The pilgrimage sites that dot the islands of Indonesia, trade routes of West Africa, and outposts of Central Asia are also neglected. For the vast majority of the world's Muslims, these are familiar places at the other ends of the world that, even when not visited, live in the collective religious imagination – in narratives, poems, and songs that cross continents and are written in languages from Persian to Bahasa. Turkish *ilahi*s (devotional songs) that refer to a saint's grave in Anatolia may find their way into a Javanese village and members of an East African Sufi community may have visited the town of Hacibektas in Turkey, the home of its namesake, a religious teacher and mystic.

Muslims visit shrines and tombs, homes and mosques, graveyards, rivers, forests, and mountains in Africa, Asia, and other disparate regions by the millions. Unlike *hajj*, these places are not mentioned in the Qur'an or the *sunnah*. Why do Muslims cherish these sites? Above all, the people and places associated with these locations are dear to the followers of Muhammad. When the Prophet died, Umm Ayman left us these words: "Know I not that he has gone to that/which is better for him than this world? But I weep for the tidings of Heaven/which have been cut off from us."[112] Muslim pilgrims long for these tidings, for the whispers of Muhammad that provide comfort in the face of poverty, terror, sadness, and heartbreak. These tidings are often found in the spaces and places visited by pilgrims, places that are believed to provide comfort, blessings, and healing.

ORTHODOXY, ISLAMIC MOVEMENTS, AND PILGRIMAGE

Islam has inspired numerous religious movements that are classified by some as *bid'ah* (innovation) and their followers as *kafir* (unbelievers). This book takes no position on the religious orthodoxy of these groups; that is, whether they are Islamic or not. I am intentionally nonsectarian in this project, reserving judgment on who is and who is not "Muslim." In the spirit of this approach, the concluding section of this chapter includes brief discussions of three movements identified with Islam – the Ahmadiyyah, the Nation of Islam (NOI), and the Baha'i – and their pilgrimage traditions. While some would object to my inclusion of these groups, it is nevertheless important to be inclusive, rather than exclusive, in this book. It is my hope that the followers of these traditions do not take offence at the limited space dedicated to them, for clearly a more extensive treatment of their pilgrimage traditions is needed.

The Ahmadiyyah (Ahmadi) movement was founded in Qadian, India, in 1889, by Hazrat Mirza Ghulam Ahmad, who declared himself the Mahdi (or messiah).[113] In Islam, the Mahdi typically appears at the end times. A central figure for Shi'i, Sunnis also believe in his coming. As John Esposito explains, "Although Sunni Islam, unlike the Shii, does not have a formal doctrine of the Mahdi, popular lore did accept the notion of a *mahdi* ('divinely guided one'), a messianic figure who will be sent by God to rescue the community from oppression and to restore true Islam and a just society."[114] Ahmad's claim to be the Mahdi and a prophetic figure put him in stark opposition to many Muslims who believe that no prophet can exist after Muhammad, resulting in the persecution faced by the Ahmadi since their inception.

Ahmadis have a form of leadership that is similar to the Isma'ilis (examined in Chapter 3). They have a leader who serves for his lifetime, is democratically elected, and is known for being accessible to his co-religionists.[115] Ahmadi Muslims go on *hajj* even though they are technically banned by the Saudi authorities from the holy city of Mecca, as they are not considered Muslims. Ahmadis also visit other religious places that are not held in as high regard as Mecca, but are nonetheless important. Among these are Qadian, where Mirza Ghulam Ahmad was born and which is the site of the original headquarters of the Ahmadiyyah; and Rabwah, where the headquarters were later moved and the site of the largest Ahmadiyyah mosque in Pakistan – Masjid-e Aqsa. The annual gathering in Rabwah, known as *jalsa salana*, functions for some Ahmadiyyah as a replacement for *hajj*, in part because Ahmadis are banned from entering the holy city of Mecca.[116] This is one of many instances where Muslims have a substitution pilgrimage for *hajj* that is seen as being as meritorious as visiting Mecca, or as a reasonable alternative due to political or financial circumstances.

It is plausible that the Ahmadiyyah are connected to the NOI, as its founder Wallace D. Fard was believed to be influenced by the group, or even an Ahmadi.[117] As Imam W.D. Mohammad remarked about his father's teacher, "I believe he was an Ahmadiyya, dissatisfied with the state of the world and devoted to the propagation of Islam."[118] The NOI is an American religious movement most commonly identified with Malcolm X, the charismatic African-American activist and political leader who was assassinated in 1965. A Black Nationalist movement, the NOI was inspired by the work of liberationists like Marcus Garvey and in many ways can be seen as a reaction to the abuses of African-Americans by North American whites and the political establishment. The NOI was founded by W.D. Fard in Detroit in the 1930s, then led by Elijah Poole (Elijah Muhammad), who taught that Allah came to North America "in the person of Wallace D. Fard," who then chose him as his messenger.[119] The Islamic tenet of the *Khatam an-Nabiyyin* (Seal of the Prophets), which insists that Muhammad is the last in a long list of prophets that begins with Adam, stands in stark opposition to the claims of the NOI. Other beliefs of the NOI, including the existence of a superior (Black) race and the casting of Caucasians as "white devils," are also seen as being antithetical to Islam. At the same time, many of the beliefs and practices of Islam are also present in the NOI, such as prayer, *hajj*, and the wearing of *hijab* by women. The liberational message of the NOI is also one that finds common ground in Islamic liberation theology. After the death of Malcolm X in 1965, the NOI split into two major groups, one of which became closer to Sunni Islam; in addition, a large number of African-American Muslims left the NOI and joined Sunni Muslim (and, to a much lesser degree, Shi'i Muslim) communities.

Mecca is an important part of the NOI's teachings. Elijah Muhammad completed the *'umrah* in 1952, along with his sons Herbert and Akbar, and facing toward Mecca "symbolized the beginning of a journey toward the restoration of black greatness."[120] The development of a number of pilgrimage traditions outside of *hajj* includes visits to the graves of important individuals in the NOI. For many years, an annual pilgrimage to the gravesite of Malcolm X in the state of New York has been arranged by the Organization of Afro-American Unity. While this is not specifically a NOI pilgrimage, many followers of the Nation participate, along with non-Muslims, political activists, and others who are admirers of Malcolm X. Another NOI pilgrimage is Saviour's Day, the annual celebration of W.D. Fard's teachings. According to one follower of the NOI, the annual convention in Chicago is like a modern pilgrimage, a "power-packed, wisdom-laden meeting of the minds of men and women bent on a single errand – to achieve for themselves, their families and own kind freedom, justice and equality under one leader … one religion, Islam, and one God, Allah."[121]

The Baha'i are similar to the Ahmadiyyah and the NOI in believing that their founder was a prophet, or, depending on one reading, the embodiment of an earlier prophet. Islam is clear that the seal of prophethood is represented in the person of Prophet Muhammad – in other words, that no prophet comes after him. The religion of the Baha'i has two founders. The first of these, known as the Bab, stood against the *ka'bah* and proclaimed, "I am the Qa'im whose advent we have been awaiting."[122] The Qa'im, or Mahdi, is the figure who appears at the End of Days. For Sunnis, this individual is unnamed (but sometimes referred to as the Mahdi) and for Shi'i he is the Twelfth Imam. Later, he also claimed to be a prophet and even to be a messenger of God, of the same station as Prophet Muhammad, bringing a new scripture and a new Shari'ah (Holy Law). The second founder of the religion is Baha'u'llah, who also claimed to be a messenger of God and a prophet like Muhammad. In this respect they are not like the Ahmadiyyah or NOI. These issues are what makes the Baha'i problematic in the eyes of many Muslims and in part explains their diminished legal status in Iran where they exist in fairly large numbers. In Baha'i tradition, pilgrimage, which is equivalent to *hajj*, includes visiting the House of the Bab in Shiraz and the House of Baha'u'llah in Baghdad. Since these are problematic given the political climate, Baha'i have substitution pilgrimages to the Shrine of Baha'u'llah in Acre and the Shrine of the Bab at the Baha'i gardens in Haifa. Pilgrimage rituals for the House of the Bab in Shiraz and the House of Baha'u'llah in Baghdad can be found in the *Tablet of Pilgrimage*. The *Tablet of Visitation*, along with individual prayers and recitations, are recited at Baha'i shrines and there is also circling of the shrines much like pilgrims on the *hajj*.[123]

All three of these groups identify with the tradition of Islam, either as a true iteration of the faith or as a continuation of the teachings of Prophet Muhammad. The Ahmadiyyah see themselves as true Muslims, the NOI as a religious and political movement that is part of Islam, and the Baha'i as the fulfillment of Islam's prophecy of the Mahdi, or messiah. The Ahmadiyyah, NOI, and Baha'i illustrate some of the challenges scholars face when addressing the topic of Islamic pilgrimage. Who is included, and why? What are the standards for judging who is and is not considered a Muslim? Is it appropriate for scholars to make these determinations? One theme that emerges from looking at these three communities is that they all seek to be close to holy figures through the act of religious pilgrimage. For Muslims, whether Sunni, Shi'i, or Ahmadi, the quest to be close to God is often contained within the journeys they undertake and the idea that an intimacy with Allah is more achievable in certain spaces. How we understand these spaces is an important part of the story of pilgrimage in Islam.

SACRED SPACE IN ISLAM

For many Muslims, there is no division between the world of Allah ("sacred space") and secular space. This is an important distinction when we talk about sacred sites such as those described in the following chapters. Although we might think of them as somehow separate from the everyday world – the street, the market, and the home – in Islam, everything is God's domain. As Karen Armstrong reminds us, in Islam:

> there is no essential dichotomy between the sacred and the pro-
> fane. The aim of the Muslim community was to achieve such
> integration and balance between human and divine, exterior and
> interior, that such a distinction becomes irrelevant. Everything
> must be made to realize its sacred potential. No one location,
> therefore, was holier than another – at least in principle.[124]

At the same time, certain places are believed to have an intense or special quality. These places are often connected to bodies whose presence offers pilgrims the possibility of grace, or in Islamic language, *barakat* – blessings.

Muslim pilgrims visit places that are believed to have an *intensified* religious power. This power may be due to a number of reasons, including "the occurrence of some miracle there, the appearance of a saint, or the performance of ritual acts."[125] The belief that God is everywhere is an important aspect of Islamic pilgrimage traditions that contributes to the numerous – and diverse – spaces in which pilgrims perform rituals. This is why Mecca is not the only religious center – it is one of many places that host Muslim pilgrims. This ordering of the world is based on the idea of *tawhid*, which is often described as the unicity of God or the connectedness of Allah's creation. A tradition of Prophet Muhammad reflects this belief: "God is beautiful and loves beauty."[126] The idea is that God created the world to reflect Divine beauty, which can be seen in everything from a rose to a complex architectural form. *Tawhid*, which requires the belief in the interdependence of all life, also helps to explain why substitutive rituals for *hajj*, what we might call virtual pilgrimages, are possible. In these cases, which I examine in the final chapter, the pilgrim often forms a connection to Mecca through a distant site, or even through a portable object.

A brief rumination on Islamic architecture helps us to understand this theology of connectedness. In the centuries following Prophet Muhammad's death, Islam developed a sophisticated theology of sacred space. Islamic cosmology is a complex unified system. In Islam, architecture is constructed along Divine lines, using the principles of geometry to create a portrait of unity that is often "composed of a series of interrelated spaces that are pictorially unified."[127] This is intentional; the whole or the parts are never privileged in the individual's eye, a device for ensuring that the unity of the cosmos remains in focus. Islam's sense of unity helps to present the ideas behind some of the sacred architecture involved in pilgrimage sites, but it does not explain why these places are more important than others.

Pilgrimage sites are often intimate spaces where the individual seeks communion with a saint or other holy person. The *ka'bah*, tomb, shrine, or other pilgrimage site can function as a threshold, a place where material concerns are momentarily released and the religio-mystical takes over. This is what takes place in Turner's vision of *communitas*. According to the Islamic hermeneutics of sacred space, the dome, an architectural design often featured at Islamic pilgrimage sites, represents a reintegration into the universe, "a realization of the balance of creation, marking the axial approach to the ultimate unity of the dome."[128] This is the ideal, of course, and what each pilgrim experiences is quite another matter.

In some cases, pilgrimage involves a desire to experience what others have experienced in the past. This is true for *hajj*, for many of the rituals are reenactments of the actions of Ibrahim, Hajar, and Muhammad. At Karbala, pilgrims reflect on Husayn's martyrdom at the place where he and his seventy-two companions were killed. Cosmology and the ordering of sacred space may be meaningful in these cases, or it may be secondary to the historical narrative at play. Sacred space is often politically cultivated, promoted, constructed, and negotiated, giving us the *ka'bah*, the Prophet's mosque in Medina, the great tomb of Husayn, and many other sites. Sufi shrines are also involved in political projects, such as when the body of Mawlay Idris was "rediscovered" during a time of political instability in which allegiances between Sufi nobles and ruling clans were being formed.[129] What this case and others suggest is that pilgrimage sites may be important cosmologically, but they also have important political functions that may shape the pilgrim's experience.

In some cases, the distribution of Islamic relics, such as Prophet Muhammad's hair and fingernails, his footprints, *hadith* traditions, and clothing, helped to establish Islam's territorial reach.[130] In other cases, bodies and relics functioned as important symbols of religious power. Their ability to confer blessings (*barakat*) was so powerful that bodies were stolen, or rumored to be stolen, as in the stories of the numerous attempts to remove Prophet Muhammad's body from Medina.[131] However, pilgrimage sites can also be organic, popularized by religious fervor and a strong desire to remember – what Muslims refer to as *dhikr* (remembrance) – a person or event from the past. Near the Syrian city of Aleppo there is a site called al-Husayn, so named because according to some traditions Husayn's head was placed in a field after he had been killed at Karbala. A few drops of blood stained the rock on which it rested and soon after miracles and visions were reported. According to narratives about al-Husayn, the rock was taken, then rediscovered, and finally it disappeared forever. Despite the absence of the rock, it is still a sacred place. This has everything to do with the collective memories of Muslims and little to do with the borders of Islamic empire.

These examples demonstrate that in Islam, sacred space can be a powerful part of the pilgrim's experience. From the Islamic perspective, Allah is both manifest (*zahir*) and hidden (*batin*). The manifest forms of God are apparent in the macrocosmic world seen in the Qur'an and in God's creation. The hidden aspect of God is found in the individual and his or her inner, most Divine self, what Sufi scholars refer to as the "hidden treasure."[132] For Muslim pilgrims, the evidence of God's presence is often more animated at Islamic pilgrimage sites. As the following chapter explains, the story of these sites begins with the cities of Mecca, Medina, and Jerusalem.

2

NASCENT PILGRIMAGE CENTERS: JERUSALEM, MECCA, AND MEDINA

Mecca, Medina, and Jerusalem are the oldest holy cities in Islam and were among the most popular pilgrimage destinations for early Muslims.[1] The first two of these cities are associated with the *hajj* and highlighted in most studies of Islam. Jerusalem often receives less attention, although its importance in the nascent period of Islam and in the development of early pilgrimage traditions is critical. In fact, Mecca did not become the center of Islam until after the Prophet's death and was originally one of three main centers – alongside Jerusalem and Medina – of early Muslim piety.

In the first decades of Islam, Muslims held Jerusalem in high regard. It is the city associated with the Jews and Christians, whose traditions are linked to many in Islam, as well as Ibrahim's patrimony and the site of the End of Days.[2] The literature that elevates Jerusalem, is know as *fada'il Bayt al-Maqdis* ("Praises of Jerusalem") and dates to the 'Umayyad period (661–750).[3] The Hijaz (the western part of Saudi Arabia that includes Mecca and Medina) did not become important until the Arabizing of Islam that began in earnest in the century following the Prophet's death when the *hajj* became associated with Ibrahim and Ishmael. During these early years, the Muslims had "a related focus on the sanctity of Jerusalem and the Jewish traditions of the Temple" that remained unchanged until the sacred geography began to transition to the Hijaz under 'Abd al-Malik.[4]

This chapter focuses on Mecca, Medina, and Jerusalem, cities directly connected to the development of the *hajj*, *'umrah*, and other pilgrimages documented in this book. These places are all inscribed with meaning, and are constituted as sacred through theological texts and early rituals connected to prophets, saints, and political figures. The sacred ordering of these three cities has changed over time; however, today they remain important destinations for Muslim pilgrims. The traditions associated with Jerusalem, Mecca, and Medina also tell an important story about how sacred space and the veneration of bodies are connected through the cities in complex ways. Starting in the seventh century, pilgrims often visited Jerusalem before *hajj* as a way to purify themselves before the journey to Mecca and Medina.[5] Several traditions encouraged visiting the three holy cities at one time: "The most famous of all is the tradition that combines the pilgrimage to Mecca and the visit to al-Medina with a visit to Jerusalem, praising and recommending prayer in the three mosques of these cities during the same year."[6]

Jerusalem, Mecca, and Medina are linked in numerous Islamic texts. Jerusalem and Mecca are both identified as part of pre-creation, much like the identification of the Temple in the Jewish tradition. Islamic scholars often point to the following *hadith*, which was transmitted by Aisha:

> Mecca is a great city which Allah, may He be exalted, elevated and elevated its holy boundaries; Allah created Mecca and surrounded it by angels a thousand years before he created anything of the whole world. After that he added to it Medina

and he added Jerusalem to Medina; then he created the world at one time.[7]

A second tradition connects the three cities to the afterlife, citing Jerusalem, Mecca, and Medina (as well as Damascus, an early capital of the Islamic empire) as the three cities of Paradise.[8] Another tradition identifies Mecca and Jerusalem with the sanctity of mountains, places that are worthy "for solitary pious men."[9] In the first five verses of *Surat al-Tin* (Qur'an 95), the "fig" and the "steadfast city" are believed to be references to the mosque of Jerusalem and the city of Mecca, creating a link between the two holy cities.[10] Later, Jerusalem was relegated to a lower status, seen in *ahadith* like this one: "Pilgrimage to Mecca is preferable to two *'umras*; one *'umra* is preferable to two trips to Jerusalem."[11] However, as we shall see, Jerusalem has retained much of the importance it held from the early days of Islam, in part due to the numerous Qur'anic personalities who are believed to be buried there, as well as the role the city plays in Prophet Muhammad's Night Journey, or *mi'raj*.

JERUSALEM

In the nascent days of Islam, Jerusalem was an important part of the religious life of Muslims. The influence of Jewish teachings on early Islam, the importance of Jesus (*Isa*) in Islam, the Qur'an's numerous references to the liberation of the Holy Land (which were references to Jerusalem and Palestine), and the prominent role the city plays in the story of the Prophet's ascension (*mi'raj*) contributed to the elevated status of Jerusalem. *Ahadith* surrounding Jerusalem reflect these facts: "The main issues reflected in these traditions are Jerusalem and its holy sites, the controversy among Muslim scholars concerning its religious status, the importance attached to it in cosmology and eschatology, the Jewish origins of the traditions concerning Jerusalem, and the circles involved in their creation and proliferation."[12]

Palestine was an important region for early Muslims, understood as having a topography that contained holiness, what the Muslims called *mubarak* or *muqadas* (sacred, blessed) and the Jews referred to as *qadosh* (holy, sacred).[13] The *qibla*, or direction of prayer, was originally Jerusalem. There are several possible explanations for this practice. It may be that praying toward Jerusalem was a tradition in vogue at the time, which was followed by other monotheists and adopted by Muhammad. Monotheistic movements outside Islam have been noted by numerous scholars, in particular the *hanif* movement. Another possibility is that directing prayer toward Jerusalem was a strategy for recruiting Hijazi Jews to Muhammad's message.[14] The prominent role of *Isa* (Jesus) in Islam, which included at least one tradition in which his name is mentioned in a version of the *shahadah*, also may have inspired the practice.[15] Other possibilities include the combined weight of these traditions, which may have helped to formulate the importance of Jerusalem in the religious imagination of early Muslims. The *qibla* was officially Jerusalem for a period of at least sixteen to eighteen months, perhaps longer.[16] The importance of Jerusalem goes far beyond the *qibla*. Indeed, archaeological records confirm that Jerusalem was central in the religious lives of Muslims, so much so that the body was oriented toward it at death – not to Mecca, as it is today.[17] The fact that several graves at Tell al-Hesi, a late medieval cemetery in Palestine, had its bodies oriented toward Jerusalem suggests that "the abrogation of the *qibla* of Jerusalem in favor of the *qibla* of Mecca did not have an immediate effect on burial practices everywhere in the world of Islam."[18]

Jerusalem plays an important role in the religious imagination of Muslims, initially as the center of prayer, then later as a holy city alongside Mecca and Medina. It is unclear whether the idea of Jerusalem as the cosmological "center" of the Islamic world was identified with the Rock or Al-Aqsa, or perhaps with a Jewish association with the Temple.[19] Early Islamic traditions point to "the three mosques," a possible source for the continued elevation of Jerusalem in later periods. According to one *hadith*, the Prophet said, "You shall only set out for three mosques: The Sacred Mosque (in Mecca), my mosque (in Medina) and al-Aqsā mosque (in Jerusalem)."[20]

Mecca was eventually fashioned into the religious capital of Islam, while Medina functioned as the center of the intellectual tradition. This was a process that took time and resulted in a hierarchy of holy cities that had changed radically by the end of the first century of Islam. At this point, Jerusalem remained an important symbol of identity, but Mecca effectively became the ritual capital. The formation of this "newly consecrated landscape of an Arabian – and Abrahamic – Hijāz" involves a powerful narrative about exile and return, to Medina and back to Mecca, formulated in conversation with the traditions of the early Israelites but articulated so that Islam remained distinct from Jewish traditions.[21] While this consecration of the religious landscape was taking place, Jerusalem was being relegated to a less prominent status, albeit one that was theologically and politically significant. Mu'awiya, the founder of the 'Umayyad dynasty, took his oath as the head of state in Jerusalem and called the city part of "the sanctifying land" (*al-ard al-muqaddissa*).[22] This consecration of the holy land would have a large impact on later pilgrimage traditions in Palestine, oftentimes through the identification of political figures with particular religious sites.

The role of Jerusalem in the ritual life of early Muslims is an important part of this story. Ibn Ishaq reports that "although Muhammad had originally prayed toward Jerusalem while he was in Mecca, he did so by placing the Ka'ba between himself and the Holy Land."[23] Yet, Mecca was not the original *qibla* – Jerusalem was. Clearly, Jewish traditions influenced early Muslim practice. In one tenth-century Islamic text, stories of Nebuchadnezzar and the great flood enter the tradition, evidence of the early inclusion of these traditions in Islam.[24] An entire genre of *hadith* literature known as *fada'il al-Quds* (*Fada'il Bayt al-Maqdis*) contains *ahadith* about Jerusalem that were at times supported by, or in conversation with, Jewish and Christian stories about the city. In Musharraf b. al-Muradjdja's volume of this literature from the eleventh century, he cites "the biblical episodes of the sacrifice of Isaac, Jacob's dream, and Deuteronomy 33:2 with exegetical 'proof' that the teachings of Moses prophesized the coming of Muhammad" along with "quotations from Isaiah and Jeremiah, as well as traditions about Joshua, King David, King Solomon and others."[25] Numerous other Islamic traditions reflect Jerusalem's importance as "God's favorite spot on earth, toward which he glances twice a day," as the extension of Paradise, and as the place for which heaven "longs."[26]

The Arabic name for Jerusalem is *al-Quds*, or "the holy." The city, alongside Mecca, is identified as the center of the world in several Islamic texts. The idea of the two centers is an interesting one, which may have its origins in the Israelite division between the northern and southern tribes (1000–586 B.C.E.), the Christian centers of Rome and Jerusalem, or even the status of Constantinople (the city that later became Istanbul) as a prominent center of Christianity outside Rome. It could also be a concept that emerged organically from an early Islamic milieu in which early Muslims were seeking connection to corresponding traditions and religious figures – including prophets – associated with Jerusalem.

The Qur'an contains one unambiguous verse (*mukhamat*) referencing Jerusalem that is found in Surah 17, verse 1, which states Allah took Muhammad from his mosque to al-Aqsa in Jerusalem. Ambiguous verses known as *ayat mutashabihat* require more intense exegesis. Roughly seventy places in the Qur'an contain ambiguous verses in reference to *al-Quds*, including 5:21, 7:137, 21:71, 21:81, 34:18, and 2:114.[27] More general references to the land of Israel are quite common: for instance, 5:21, "the sacred land" (*al-ard al-muqaddasa*); 21:171, "the land God blessed" (*al-ard allati barakna fiha*); as well as the land where the Children of Israel are safe (7:137) and the land toward which Solomon rides the wind (2:198).[28] It appears there was considerable early debate surrounding the question of where to place Jerusalem in relation to Mecca. For example, the opinions surrounding verse 2:114 suggest that "the position of Jerusalem was indeed placed in jeopardy from the second century on: a development which is made clear by the growing attempts of Muslim scholars to resist the equation of its status as a place of pilgrimage with that of Mecca and Medina."[29] Despite these attempts to relegate Jerusalem to a lower status, it has remained an important pilgrimage destination, a fact that is apparent today in its status as one of the most sacred cities for Muslims alongside Mecca, Medina, Damascus, Qom, Konya, and others.

Several early *ahadith* extol the virtues of Jerusalem. Among these is the Hadith of the Three Mosques, in which Prophet Muhammad reportedly said, "The saddles of the camels shall only be fastened for a journey to three mosques, namely the *ka'bah*, my own mosque, and the mosque in Jerusalem (*'Lā tushaddu al'rihāl illā ilā thalātha masājid, al-masjid al-Harām, wa masjid al-rasūl, wa 'l-masjid al-Aqsā*)."[30] The identification of the farthest mosque with Jerusalem is not unanimous; some Muslims believe the third mosque to be "located directly above Jerusalem or Mecca" while the Shi'i hold the mosque at Kufa as more important than the mosque of Jerusalem.[31] The tradition of the three mosques in Mecca, Medina, and Jerusalem is found in several *hadith* traditions, including one that suggests that praying in Jerusalem is worth a thousand prayers anywhere else.[32] This is the *hadith* that probably helped to establish the Muslim pilgrimage to Jerusalem. According to one tradition, "Visitors of Mecca, are, for example, said to be forgiven and elevated eight steps, whereas visitors of Medina are to be forgiven and elevated six steps, while visitors of Jerusalem are to be forgiven and elevated four steps."[33]

Jerusalem holds a special place in the hearts of Muslims for many other reasons, for its role in Prophet Muhammad's Night Journey, its symbol of the early expansion of the empire, and the city's role in the lives of prophets cited in the Islamic tradition, including Adam, Isa (Jesus), and Muhammad. The fact that several graves of these individuals, including Adam's, are believed to lie within the city's walls helped to sanctify the city in the eyes of early Muslims.[34] The importance of Ibrahim (Abraham) in Islam is also reflected in Qur'an 21:71, which creates a link between the Holy Land and Mecca.[35] Like Abraham, Jerusalem's role in the Prophet's life is very important. Al-Aqsa ("the farthest mosque") is the place from which Muhammad ascended on his heavenly journey. Karen Armstrong gives us this succinct account of his journey:

> The first account of this profound mystical experience is found in the biography of Muhammad ibn Ishaq, written in the middle of the eighth century CE. It tells us that Muhammad was miraculously conveyed from Mecca to Jerusalem in the year 620, in company with Gabriel, the angel of revelation. When he arrived at the Temple Mount, the Prophet was greeted by all the great prophets of the past, who welcomed him into their midst, and Muhammad preached to them. Then, he began his ascent to the divine presence, through the seven heavens; at each stage he met and conversed with major prophets: with Jesus and John the Baptist, Moses and Aaron and Enoch, and, at the threshold, he met Abraham, the father of Jews, Christians and Muslims. Muhammad did not therefore arrive on the Temple Mount as a solitary worshipper, but was warmly greeted by his prophetic predecessors.[36]

Al-Aqsa is identified in numerous ways – as the place where Muhammad ascended to heaven, the site of the sacrifice of Isma'il, the location of the Holiest of Holies of the Jewish temple, and the burial place of Adam. It is yet another reason why Jerusalem is so important to Muslims today.

The story of Prophet Muhammad's ascension to heaven, known as the *mi'raj*, provided an early story of pilgrimage that would prove to be a permanent fixture in the religious imagination of Muslims. Focusing on the Prophet's journey and his encounter with the Divine is something that was quite intentional in the construction of the mosque. The *axis mundi* verticality of Jerusalem is also an important part of Judaism and Christianity, where the temple is envisioned as the place at which earth reaches up and heaven reaches down until they are nearly touching. Inscriptions strongly suggest that 'Abd al-Malik was responsible for building the mosque, wanting to honor the Prophet's miraculous journey to heaven and to reflect the *hadith* about Jerusalem being an important pilgrimage site. It is not just the mosque that explains why Muslims visit Jerusalem as a matter of religious belief. The story of the Night Journey is the likely inspiration for the various pilgrimage traditions that evolved in relation to Jerusalem, influencing the network of pilgrimage sites that exist today. While the story of the Prophet's journey originally centered on Mecca and Jerusalem, as time went on other cities were added. As Isaac Hasson explains,

> For instance, it is related that on his way to the al-Aqsā mosque Muhammad stopped in Medina, Midyan, on Mount Sinai (Tūr Sīnā), at the graves of Moses (on the Red Hill), in Hebron, and Bethlehem, praying at each of these sites. The acceptance by many Muslims of the authenticity of this Tradition, with all of its various details, was an incentive to the believers to include these places in the pilgrimage route to Mecca.[37]

The influence of early Christian pilgrimage to Jerusalem on emergent Islamic practices is also important to note. Helena, Constantine's mother, popularized pilgrimage to Jerusalem. As early as the fourth century, Christian pilgrims were traveling to the city for the Encaenia (the festival commemorating the Church of the Holy Sepulchre), including "monks and apotactites from the provinces – in particular Mesopotamia, Syria, Egypt and the Thebaid – as well as lay men and women."[38] The influence of these Christian festivals on Islamic pilgrimage is an understudied topic, but it is likely that, like Jewish traditions, they influenced the ways in which Muslims thought of Jerusalem as a sanctified space.

In addition to the *haram* (the farthest mosque), which includes the Dome of the Rock and its sites (such as the Gate of Paradise and the Dome of the Ascension of the Prophet), and al-Aqsa, Jerusalem hosts other pilgrimage sites visited by Muslims. In the medieval period, the places in Jerusalem that Muslims visited during pilgrimage included fifteen different sites: Qubbat al-Sakhra (the Dome of the Rock), al-Balata al-Sawda (the Black Paving Stone), al-Maghara (the Cave), Maqam al-Nabi (the Place of the Prophet), Bab Israfil (the Gate of the Angel Israfil), Qubbat al-Silsila (the Dome of the Chain), Qubbat al-Mi'raj (the Dome of the Ascension of the Prophet), Qubbat al-Nabi (the Dome of the Prophet), Abwab al-Rahma (the Gates of Mercy), Mihrab Zakariyya, Kusri Sulayman (Solomon's Stool), Bab al-Sakina (the Gate of the Divine Presence), Bab Hitta (the Gate of Remission), al-Masjid al-Aqsa (the al-Aqsa Mosque), Mihrab Umar, Mihrab Mu'awiya, Bab al-Nabi (the Gate of the Prophet), Mihrab Maryam (the Tomb of Maryam, also known as the Cradle of Jesus), al-Mawdi Alladhi Jibril Alayhi al-Salam bi-Isba'ihi wa-Shudda fihi al-Buraq (the Place where Gabriel Drilled with His Finger and Tied Up al-Buraq), Tur Zauta (the Mount of Olives), and Mihrab Dawud.[39] Each of these places is significant for Muslims. The Bab Israfil is the place where Israfil will blow the ram's horn on the Day of Resurrection, Bab al-Nabi is where Prophet Muhammad is believed to have entered the *haram* during his Night Journey, and Mihrab Dawud is the room in which David saw a beautiful dove that, while escaping, caused him to see Bathsheba bathing.[40] Centuries later, these places remained important, and were often included in the large network of sites that Muslims visited when they traveled to Jerusalem. According to a mid-sixteenth-century guide to Jerusalem, additional places were added to the pilgrim's itinerary, some that reflected the activities of Shi'i and Sufi communities and others that built upon the traditions established in earlier centuries. One example is the grave of Shaykh Abu 'l-Abbas Ahmad al-Thawri on Mount Abu Thawr, whose "wādī and waters are from heaven" and whose grave offers its pilgrims "plentiful bounty."[41]

Today, popular pilgrimage sites include the Tomb of David, a mosque marking the burial of Samuel, another mosque marking the place where Jesus ascended to heaven, and the grave of Moses. The grave of Moses, known in Arabic as Nabi Musa (Prophet Musa), has been an Islamic pilgrimage site since the thirteenth century when the Mamluks created special endowments (*waqf*) to establish the site, a project that was continued under the Ottomans.[42] The grave was renewed as a pilgrimage site in the late 1990s under the Palestinian National Authority, which returned it to Muslim control and helped to encourage pilgrimage to Nabi Musa as part of a larger network of sites stretching from Jerusalem to Mecca. "It seems that the ancient *ziyara* of Nabi Musa was reintegrated with personal *ziyara* to Jerusalem, as well as with visiting other shrines in the land."[43] Nabi Musa is one of many sites that is important in the religious history of Muslims, as well as the political history of the landscape in which it is located.

Jerusalem's status as a pilgrimage city is thus important for many political, eschatological, and religious reasons. Conquered by Umar in 637, it remained in Muslim hands for

much of the past thousand years (except for intervening periods during the Crusades) until it was lost to Britain and other
powers after the collapse of the Ottoman Empire at the end
of the First World War. Politically, it is an important symbol
of extinct Islamic empires. Eschatologically, Jerusalem is the
city where the resurrection, the day of judgment, the second
and final exodus, and the gathering of the righteous will take
place.[44] For many Muslims, Jerusalem is one of many places
where a person can be close to the deceased whom they love
and hold dear. In some cases, these sites are believed to be
conduits for communication between the living and the dead.
Moses' shrine in Jericho and Abraham's tomb in Hebron were
often associated with the disembodied voices of the deceased –
believed to be prophets communicating directly with the pilgrims who visit them.[45] As we shall see, Jerusalem offers an
early case of the veneration of the dead that characterizes so
much of Islamic pilgrimage in the Holy Land and beyond.

MECCA

Mecca's importance in Islam is paramount. It is the city of the
Prophet's birth, his missionary activity, his exile and eventual
return; the site of the *ka'bah* and the Masjid al-Haram; the
home of Ibrahim, Hajar, and Ishmael; and the center of the
hajj. In the era predating Muhammad's life and mission, Mecca
was an important center of trade, commerce, and pilgrimage
for Arabs. In Islam, Mecca is believed to have been a holy
place before it became a city, founded in the late fourth or
early fifth century by a man named Qusayy.[46] Its sacred status
is due to the *ka'bah*, believed by Muslims to be the world's
first monument commemorating monotheism built by Ibrahim
and his Arab son Ishmael. In addition to Ibrahim's connections
to Mecca, the city is believed to host the graves of numerous
prophets. According to various traditions, seventy prophets

including Hud, Salih, and Ishmael are buried in the sanctuary surrounding the *ka'bah*, Noah (*Nuh*) and Shu'ayb are also buried there, and perhaps as many as three hundred prophets are interred in the holy sanctuary.[47] Much of the evidence suggests that Mecca was originally not part of *hajj*; rather, Arafat and Mina were the focus.[48] The families who controlled these cities in the early years of Islam shifted, a point noted by several scholars: "it was common knowledge that not the Quraysh but the Sufa, and later the Tamim, held the religious offices, the so-called 'permission' (*ijaza*) at Arafat and Mina."[49]

Mecca is also important to Muslims because it was the Prophet's home until he was exiled to Medina. According to Islamic sources, Muhammad's birthday (*mawlid an-nabi*) was celebrated in Mecca in the centuries following his death. In the thirteenth century, the account of Ibn Jubayr notes *mawlid an-nabi* as a small yet significant festival, a special day commemorated by people in the city.[50] It was not fixed on a special date, but celebrated "on all Mondays in the month Rabī'i, so four or five times," and accepted by religious elites, signified by the fact that the holy sites were open on those days.[51] Today, the Prophet's birthday is celebrated around the world and is a focal point of many pilgrimages, such as in the visitation of Sufi shrines that celebrate the *mawlid* (the Prophet's birthday), occasions that may go on for weeks.

For Muslims, Mecca is sacred because it contains the holiest of holies, the *ka'bah*. Although the larger city is holy, its sacredness is focused on the building that is the center of pilgrimage. The area surrounding the *ka'bah* is known as al-Masjid al-Haram and is, as the name suggests, "the forbidden (sacred, inviolable) mosque" – a space restricted to Muslims. Surrounding the *ka'bah* is a larger *haram*, or restricted space, marked by the *ansab al-haram* (stone boundary markers) that define a distinct Muslim space.[52] Non-Muslims are not permitted to cross this boundary and the holy city of Mecca is reserved exclusively for those who follow Islam. According to

Sunni *fiqh*, the larger *haram* includes an area of several miles, encompassing several sites visited on the *hajj* – Muzdalifa, Arafat, and Mina – whose boundaries (called *miqat*) mark the points at which Muslim space begins and non-Muslims are excluded.[53] According to the Shi'i *ulama* from the Ithna-Ashariyya (Twelver) tradition, the *haram* is defined as the entire city.[54] According to one *hadith* of 'Ali, "Just as Mecca is the *haram* of God, and Medina is the *haram* of the Prophet, Kufa is my *haram*."[55] This tradition is important in defining the sacred boundaries of a holy city as well as prescribing where prayers can be shortened, something that is important for Shi'i, whose recitation of longer supplications could put them in danger. As Liyakat Takim explains,

> The Shi'is shortened their prayers during their journey to the holy places. If, after reaching a holy place, they suddenly reverted to offering the complete prayers, their Shi'i identity would no longer remain covert as their acts would differ from those of the Sunnis. If their identity as the followers of the imams would be revealed, their lives would be endangered.[56]

The Qur'an makes numerous references to the great pilgrimage to Mecca, which according to Islamic belief existed as a pilgrimage site long before the Prophet was born. The second Surah in the Qur'an mentions the pilgrimage four times and includes references to the foundations of the *ka'bah* ("the house"), Safa and Marwa (the two hills between which pilgrims run to symbolize Hajar's search for water), the moon's role in determining the time of the pilgrimage, and the *hajj* and *'umrah* specifically.[57] Surah 22, Surah 3, Surah 5, and Surah 9 include three verses prohibiting pagans from having access to the sacred sites, as well as the proclamation 'Ali was instructed to make at Mina in 631.[58] The original *ka'bah* is believed to have been built by Adam and eventually destroyed in the flood, only to be rebuilt by Abraham and Isma'il, then taken over by pagans until Muhammad reclaimed it for monotheism. Originally the structure may have been a tent, as the early Arabs used the same name for the Israelites' tents as they did for the early *ka'bah*.[59] Like Jerusalem, this Jewish tradition also influenced early Muslim traditions in Mecca.

The *ka'bah* (the black box that stands in the center of the Masjid al-Haram) has been rebuilt and expanded many times since the beginning of Islam. The current expansion of the holy precinct includes facilities to accommodate the growing number of pilgrims that visit Mecca.[60] The current *ka'bah* is built of granite and draped in black cloth, standing fifteen meters tall, twelve meters long, and ten-and-a-half meters wide.[61] A black stone, which was covered in silver in the late eighth century, stands in the east corner of the *ka'bah*. The stone is said to come from Abu Qubays, a nearby mountain that overlooks Mecca, and was saved from the great flood that destroyed Adam's original *ka'bah* – thus symbolizing the perseverance of monotheism.[62] The *ka'bah* is the focus of the *haram*, the sacred space that includes the great mosque. While it is the center, several other important sites are found in the *haram*. These include the *hatim*, a wall that covers the area where Ishmael and Hajar are believed to be buried. This site is called *al hijr*, which means "the inviolable," and is linked to several stories involving dreams and mystical experiences. Prophet Muhammad is believed to have been visited by the angel Gabriel (Jibril) at this place, where he started his Night Journey.[63] Near the northeast side of the *ka'bah* is the well known as Zamzam, where water miraculously appeared for Abraham and his family. Zamzam water is believed to be special and drinking it efficacious, providing healing and blessings. Near this is a stone known as the "Station of Abraham" (*maqam Abraham*), which is believed to have his footprints embedded in it.[64] Qur'an 2:125 urges the Believers (Muslims) to pray at the Station, a free-standing stone that is believed to be a site of God's manifest signs.[65]

In Surah 22, verses 27–29, the Qur'an reads:

> Proclaim the Pilgrimage to all people. They will come to
> you on foot and on every kind of lean camel, emerging from
> every deep mountain pass to attain benefits and mention God's
> name, on specified days, over the livestock He has provided
> for them. Feed yourselves and the desperately poor from
> them. Then let the pilgrims perform their acts of cleansing,
> fulfill their vows, and circle around the Ancient House. All
> this [is ordained by God]: anyone who honours the sacred
> ordinances of God will have good rewards from the Lord.[66]

Another important verse is Surah 3:96–97, which reads:

> The first House [of worship] to be established for people was
> the one at Bakka [Mecca]. It is a blessed place; a source of
> guidance for all people; there are clear signs in it; it is the
> place where Abraham stood to pray; whoever enters it is safe.
> Pilgrimage to the House is a duty owed to God by people
> who are able to undertake it. Those who reject this [should
> know that] God has no need of anyone.[67]

Hajj is one of the largest mass pilgrimages in the world. Each
year, around two million people congregate in Mecca and
nearby sites to complete the rites of this pilgrimage, which
is viewed by many Muslims as a compulsory religious duty.
It takes place during the last month of the Islamic lunar calendar between the eighth and thirteenth days. This month,
called Dhu-l-Hijja, is the last of the lunar calendar. Pilgrims
perform a prescribed set of rituals: chanting the phrase known
as the *talbiyah*, "At your service, God, we are here" (*Labbayk-
Allahumma Labbayk*), circumambulating the *ka'bah*, running
between the hills of Safa and Marwa (repeating the actions of
Hajar's search for water), standing on the Arafat (when the
forgiveness of sins is requested), throwing pebbles at pillars

symbolizing Shaytan (Satan) (representing the expiation of sins), and sacrificing animals at Mina (reflecting the sacrifice of Ishmael).[68]

The rituals of *hajj* can also be understood as comprising ten steps, or phases: (1) the eighth day of Dhu-l-Hijja – putting on the *ihram* garments (two white seamless cloths), entering the sacred precinct of Mecca and reciting the *talbiyah*, and performing the *tawaf* or circling of the *ka'bah* seven times; (2) the eighth day – the night spent at Mina; (3) the ninth day – the gathering at Arafat for the day of standing; (4) the ninth day and morning of the tenth – departure from Arafat and night spent at Muzdalifa, and gathering of pebbles for the stoning of the devil in Mina; (5) the tenth day – the stoning of the devil at Mina, animal sacrifice, and removing of the *ihram*; (6) the tenth or eleventh day – return to Mecca, second *tawaf*, and running between the hills of Safa and Marwa; (7–9) the eleventh to thirteen days – the stoning of all three pillars and spending the night in Mina; and (10) the *tawaf* of farewell.[69]

When Muslims decide to go on *hajj*, they recite the *talbiyah*, which is repeated throughout the preparations. Before embarking on the journey, pilgrims enter a state of ritual purity that is also known as *ihram*, like the two white seamless cloths that men wear on *hajj*.[70] In the medieval period, pilgrims, who traveled to Mecca on foot or on an animal, performed the ritual ablutions (*ghusl*) at several stations before arriving at the city, practicing the state of *ihram* along the way, which, for men, included shaving all the hair, and for women, cutting off a few locks of hair.[71] Donning the cloth used to take place at the points of entry (*miqat*), but now pilgrims often wear it on the plane to Saudi Arabia.[72] This is preceded by an oath of intention (*niyat*), ablution, and depilation, which are all undertaken before wearing the special clothing.[73] The *ihram* is identical to the burial shrouds (*kafan*) of Muslims around the world. In some cases, pilgrims to Mecca keep their *ihram* to be buried in. Historically, the restrictions on dress were more stringent. According to Ibn Qudamah, the pilgrim could not wear "a shirt (*qamīs*), turban (*imā'mah*), trousers (*sarāwīl*), shoes (*khifāf*), hooded cloak (*burūs*), open garment (*qabā'*), covering (*duwāj*), long sleeves that cover the hands, or head covering."[74]

Maintaining a state of purity during *hajj* is very important. Any of the following violates *ihram* and requires an animal sacrifice (*dam*): cutting of the nails, use of perfume, sexual activity, arguing, or hunting.[75] The importance of purity (*ihram*) while on *hajj* is highlighted in the Qur'an, especially in Surah 9, verse 28, which addresses the Masjid al-Haram. During the medieval period, eunuchs (*aghawat*) were responsible for making sure men and women did not pollute each other, for even the touching of hands could invalidate the *hajj*.[76] Even more care was taken to restrict non-Muslims from entering sacred spaces. In some exegetical traditions (often called *tasfir*, pl. *tafasir*), the difference between the believer (Muslim) and the unbeliever, who is impure (*najas*), is an important one, for only the pure can enter the restricted (*haram*) space in which the *ka'bah* sits. Because this space has a particularly strong Divine presence, it is crucial that only the pure of body, mind, and heart enter its shadow. As Linda Darwish points out, Miqdad al-Hilli claims that the Qur'an used a rhetorical device to extend the rule for the Masjid al-Haram to all mosques.[77] Today, the practice of excluding non-Muslims from entering mosques is only enforced in some cases. The sanctity of the *haram* in Mecca helps explain why the *hajj* is often cited as the model of ritual for other pilgrimages. However, although the *ka'bah* lies at the center of Muslim life and organizes the daily prayer, numerous pilgrimages around the world may be substituted for *hajj* and, at times, Muslims even perform some prayers toward a grave or other site, at times with their back turned to Mecca.

Before entering the holy city of Mecca, the pilgrim must state his or her intention (*niyya*) and say, "Here I am, Lord, here I am!" thus announcing the beginning of the journey.[78]

Tawaf is the first major ritual of *hajj*, performed after the *talbiyah* is announced – a prayer announcing the arrival of the pilgrim. *Tawaf*, the circumambulation of the *ka'bah* performed seven times in an anti-clockwise direction, mimics the movement of the angels around the celestial throne. In the medieval period, the area around the *ka'bah*, called the *mataf*, was divided according to gender and white sand was spread over the women's section.[79] Pilgrims attempt to kiss the black stone during these rotations and raise their hands to their ears and say the *takbir* and *tahlil* prayers.[80] The spot known as Ibrahim's place, located directly across from the door of the *ka'bah*, has a rock believed to have an impression of Ibrahim's foot – an impression left in an ancient stepping-stone he used while building the *ka'bah*.[81]

Sa'y (or *sa'ee*) is the running between the hills of Safa and Marwa, an act repeated seven times. In the past, it was performed outdoors; today, pilgrims perform this ritual "in a large air-conditioned marble paved corridor" that connects the two hills.[82] It symbolizes Hajar's desperate search for water for Isma'il when Ibrahim left her and their infant son alone in the desert.[83] Completion of this rite is important for those performing *'umrah*, the lesser pilgrimage, as it is the point of departure for those not completing the rest of the *hajj* journey.[84]

Wuquf is the next major ritual and for many, a deeply emotional experience. It is preceded by a sermon (*khutbah*) at the Masjid al-Haram. The following day pilgrims travel to Mina on the Plain of Arafat, arriving there to listen to two additional *khutbah*s, and spending the hours between afternoon and sunset asking for God's forgiveness. This part of *hajj* is an intimate reenactment of Prophet Muhammad's farewell sermon. It also represents the struggle of Ibrahim against idolatry.[85] Shi'i Muslims have supplications in addition to the prescribed ones performed by most pilgrims visiting Mecca. The Prayer of the Day of Arafah (Arafat), a long prayer attributed to Imam Husayn, is traditionally recited whether one is on *hajj* or not. When pilgrims recite it, they are honoring the Imams as part of the larger pilgrimage. An excerpt of the prayer includes these words:

> O God, cause me to fear Thee as if I were seeing Thee, give me felicity through piety toward Thee, make me not wretched by disobedience toward Thee, choose the best for me by Thy decree and bless me by Thy determination that I may love not the hastening of what Thou has delayed, nor the delaying of what Thou has hastened.[86]

The day following *wuquf* is focused on the stoning of pillars (*jamarat*) representing Shaytan at Mina, in the most dangerous rite of *hajj*. This is the point at which many pilgrims release emotion, apologize for their sins, and make amends for the past, all with stones in hand. Like many *hajj* rituals, it is focused on the experiences of Prophet Ibrahim, in this case recalling "the instruction given to Ibrahim by the angel Gabriel to reject Shaytan's temptations to disobey Allah, by pronouncing the *takbir* (the formula Allahu Akbar, God is Great) and stoning him."[87] According to Islamic tradition, Shaytan appeared to Ibrahim three times and each time he told Ibrahim to disobey God's command to sacrifice Isma'il. Ibrahim's ability to resist these temptations and the belief that he threw stones at the devil is reenacted by pilgrims who throw pebbles and thus symbolically chase away their own temptations, regrets, and sins.

The sacrifice (*qurbani/kurban*) is the penultimate ritual of *hajj*. It commemorates the sacrifice of Ibrahim's son Isma'il. The sacrifice of animals is an act performed by pilgrims, as well as by those who celebrate the end of *hajj* elsewhere during the holiday known as Eid al-Adha. "The sacrifice of the animal is done the same day by Muslims all over the world on the tenth day of Dhū al-Hijja, observed by non-pilgrims as 'Īd al-Adhā, or the Feast of Sacrifice."[88] After the sacrifice and meal, a final *tawaf* of the *ka'bah* is made and the pilgrim becomes a *hajji* – one who has completed the *hajj*. Pilgrims typically leave Mecca after the completion of this step, but some go on to Medina to visit the graves of the Prophet and his relatives.

'Umrah is known as the lesser pilgrimage. It does not fulfill the requirements of *hajj* and is not a substitution for it, but is sometimes used as a practice *hajj* or as a way to experience aspects of *hajj* without taking the physical risks inherent in the full pilgrimage journey. There are some important differences, however. Pilgrims on *'umrah* typically wear the *ihram*, but they enter through the *'umrah* gate (as opposed to the gate of mercy reserved for *hajj* pilgrims), and then perform the *tawaf* and *sa'y* rituals.[89] *'Umrah* can be done at any time of the year and is especially encouraged during the month of Rajab.

The prescribed rituals of *hajj* (and *'umrah*) are well known to scholars of Islam. However, there is a wide array of lesser-known traditions that also take place near Mecca and Medina, including many that reflect particular liturgical practices and rituals. Due to the state religion of the Kingdom of Saudi Arabia, which is aligned with Wahhabism, many of these traditions are not widely known and are practiced in secret. Many tombs belonging to relatives of the Prophet have been destroyed by the Saudis, part of the campaign against *ziyarat* that is such a central part of the Wahhabi ethos. However, many Muslims know where these places are and they visit them, some even collecting sand (which they call *turbah*, a name for earth or tomb) for blessings. Many of these places are known to Muslims, are connected to figures like Umar, and are popular with families who have been in the region for centuries. Before the arrival of Wahhabism, the Hijaz was characterized by Sufi practice, much as Islam was in many other Muslim communities around the world. The strict control of the holy sites in Mecca and the surrounding areas has not yet vanquished these traditions, but has succeeded in driving them underground.[90] Among these traditions are the special prayers performed in Medina, which are often done silently, under the watch of the religious police who guard holy sites in the Prophet's city.

MEDINA

Medina is the city that received Prophet Muhammad when he was exiled from Mecca in 622. Originally called Yathrib, the city was renamed Madinah al-Nabi, the city of the Prophet. It remains a place associated with the life and mission of Muhammad and as the place at which his grave and many of those close to him are located. Medina, like Mecca and other sites in the Hijaz, increased in importance after the Prophet's death. As is the case with the original *qibla*, Jewish influences on Islamic traditions are also found in Medina. One such example is the Prophet's birthday which, according to Islamic sources, was inspired by the Jewish traditions of fasting known as 'Ashura that celebrated the victory of Moses and the Jewish people over the Pharaoh.[91] This is not to be confused with the Shi'i tradition of 'Ashura,' which commemorates the death of Husayn. The relationship between the Jewish and Islamic traditions is explained thus:

> The Jews commemorated this day without paying attention to the exact day of the week on which this rescue of Moses had taken place, but nevertheless the Prophet adopted this day. If 12 Rabi'i then does not fall on a Monday, this day still has to be commemorated, because according to consensus (*al-ijmā'*) this date is accepted as the birthday of the Prophet.[92]

From the beginning, the Prophet's grave was an important pilgrimage site in Islam. In the decades following his death, it became a site of veneration that was often equated with

venerating Muhammad himself.[93] Some early Muslims con-
tended that it was holier than the *ka'bah* and that visiting
the Prophet's grave was more important than performing the
hajj.[94] Substitutive pilgrimage is not limited to the Prophet's
grave at Medina, but this is perhaps the earliest case we have
of pilgrims visiting a site instead of the *ka'bah* and it being
viewed as equally or more meritorious in the eyes of God.

As mentioned above, many sites in Medina and Mecca have
been lost to the Wahhabi campaigns of destruction, including
the spot where the Prophet prepared food before the flight to
Medina.[95] However, numerous places associated with his life
and death, as well as those of his relatives, are still visited,
including the Prophet's mosque, his grave, and the graves of
many of his relatives. The mosque of the Prophet (*al-Masjid
an-Nabawi*) is an important symbol of the early formation of
the *'ummah* (community) and its survival while in exile from
Mecca. The structure incorporates one facade of the Prophet's
home, which, according to tradition, was chosen by Prophet
Muhammad's camel, which was "under the command of God"
and picked the spot for his home by flattening her chest upon
the ground.[96] Like the *haram* in Mecca, it has been altered over
the centuries. The Prophet's mosque was expanded by Caliph
al-Wahid in 702, then by the Ottomans in 1932, was further
modified by the architect Abdel Wahid el-Waki in 1986, and
is currently undergoing further renovations.[97]

Because the Prophet's mosque in Medina was his home, it
has a special place in the hearts of many Muslims. As Karen
Armstrong writes, "Muhammad and his wives lived in small
huts around the courtyard of the Prophet's mosque; public
meetings to discuss social, political, military and religious matters were held there. The whole of life was to be brought into
the ambit of holiness as an expression of *tawhid*."[98] Muslims
performing *hajj* often visit Medina after the completion of
their journey for a period of ten days in order to perform
fifty prayers – a tradition established by Muhammad, who

reportedly said that praying in his mosque was one thousand times more effective than praying anywhere else.[99]

Jannat al-Baqi (Garden of Heaven) is the burial site of Prophet Muhammad. Situated on the eastern side of the Prophet's mosque (Masjid an-Nabawi), the graveyard also contains the graves of Uthman (the third caliph), 'Abbas (the Prophet's uncle), Aisha (the Prophet's wife), Fatima (the Prophet's daughter), Hasan (the Prophet's grandson), and several others.[100] The prescribed actions for Sunni Muslims when visiting the cemetery include greeting the dead, reciting Surah Ikhlas seven times, Surah Fatiha once, and Surah Yasin once, although reciting the entire Qur'an (known as *hatm*) is encouraged.[101] Shi'i Muslims often visit the graveyard, because in addition to being the Prophet's burial place and that of his beloved daughter Fatima, it contains the tombs of the second Imam Hasan, the fifth Imam Muhammad b. 'Ali, and the sixth Imam Ja'far b. Muhammad, all greatly loved by Shi'i.[102] Shi'i recite a number of *ziyarat* prayers, for the Prophet, Fatima, and others. These supplications honor the saint as well as the larger family, with words like, "O Allah, do not make it my last visit to the grave of Your Prophet. If You take me away before that I bear witness in my death as I bear witness in my life that there is no god but You and that Muhammad is Your slave and Your messenger peace be upon him and his family."[103] Sufis also visit these graves, recite prayers, and some even recite *dhikr* (remembrance) under their breath. In earlier centuries, the tomb was known as *Rawda*, or garden, a word later used to refer to the area from the southern gallery of the mosque, from the Gate of Peace to the Prophet's tomb.[104] Later this term was used for the first area and the actual tomb was designated as *al-Hujra*, "the chamber."[105]

The traditions associated with the Prophet's grave became the standard for later examples of grave pilgrimage, including the practices of visiting early imperial cities like Damascus, Baghdad, and Cairo, all places with old and important cemeteries. Damascus became the capital of the Islamic empire shortly after the Prophet's death and evolved as a pilgrimage center focused on graves, "a landscape in which people were truly dedicated to living with and commemorating the dead."[106] Wives, relatives, and companions of the Prophet were buried around the city, in mosques, shrines, and graveyards.

Relics quickly became part of the Islamic funerary and pilgrimage traditions. Mu'awiya was reportedly buried in the Prophet's clothes and had clippings of Muhammad's finger-nails and strands of his hair placed over his eyes and mouth when he died, examples of the importance of relics in Islamic culture in the decades following the death of the Prophet.[107] According to one version of his burial, the hair and fingernails of the Prophet were "stuffed in Mu'āwiyah's mouth and nose in accordance with his bequest."[108] Such an intimate connection to the Prophet's body is not rare. Relics and their associated powers are commonly identified with Islamic sacred sites, often playing a role in the establishment of shrines, the for-mation of rituals, and the commemoration of the deceased at festivals and other occasions. The traditions associated with the Prophet's grave at Medina were later adopted and expanded to pilgrimages around the world, including those associated with the Shi'i, the focus of the following chapter.

3

SHI'I PILGRIMAGE: THE PROPHET'S HOUSEHOLD

FOUNDATIONS OF SHI'I PILGRIMAGE

Shi'i comprise the second largest group of Muslims in the world, consisting of several branches, including those found in large numbers in Iraq, Iran, Afghanistan, and elsewhere. The formative narrative in Shi'i religious identity is the Battle of Karbala, in which Prophet Muhammad's grandson Husayn was killed while fighting the 'Umayyad army. This event inspired a cycle of martyrdom narratives, Shi'i Islam's great tradition of liberation theology, and numerous rituals related to Husayn and other martyrs, including those involved with pilgrimage. Numerous accounts of this battle are found in both Sunni and Shi'a sources. In 680 (61 in the Islamic calendar, which begins with the exodus to Medina), Husayn refused to give allegiance to Yazid as the leader of the Muslims. He and a small band of men, women, and children challenged the entire 'Umayyad army on the plains of Karbala. The 'Umayyad army, which numbered somewhere between 10,000 and 100,000 soldiers, surrounded the small group. Husayn and the seventy-two men who accompanied him were killed, dismembered, and beheaded and the few survivors were marched to Damascus. Husayn's head was paraded about the town and then placed in the great mosque, to the great horror of the citizens of the city.

Shiʻi pilgrimage begins with the story of Karbala, an event largely focused on the sacrifice of bodies and the miracles associated with the martyrs. Stories about his head and its miraculous powers reflect the reverence Shiʻi Muslims have for the Prophet's grandson. According to one tradition, it was found and preserved: "After its discovery in ʻAsqalān, the head was cleaned up, perfumed, and transported to Cairo in a basket to be housed in the Husayn mosque."[1] Stories of Husayn's body include various claims about where his head and the rest of his body are interred, as well as miracles and visions associated with these parts of his body. They speak to larger themes in Shiʻism about the power of the dead and their ability to offer blessings. One place this is seen is in the transformation of Karbala as a place that begins with being cursed (as the site of Husayn's death) but becomes a place that is "blessed, honoured, and sanctified."[2] In fact, the status of Karbala is so high that it is believed to have been created and sanctified twenty-four thousand years before the *ka ʻbah* was erected, providing the rationale for Shiʻi to visit Karbala instead of completing the *hajj*.[3]

Karbala also functions as the primary political symbol in Shiʻism. The battle does not simply represent the death of Husayn but the cosmic struggle between good and evil. Karbala is an ideological narrative that sets history into motion. As Hamid Dabashi puts it, "The defining moment of Shiʻism – and with it Islam in general – is the doctrinal sanctity of *mazlumiyyat*, of having been wronged, subjected to tyranny."[4] Pilgrimage is an important part of *mazlumiyyat* because it is a practice that involves the intercession of the dead in the lives of those living under tyranny. Karbala involves several important Shiʻi figures in addition to Husayn, including his sister Zaynab, who reportedly gave a speech forty days after the battle at the site of his martyrdom, establishing the tradition of mourning known as *arbaeen* that occurs forty days after 'Ashura'. As scholars have pointed out, even if this connection is somewhat tenuous, Zaynab's praise of her brother and condemnation of Yazid are voiced in rituals today, including those conducted during pilgrimages.[5] In fact, her speech is often referred to as the model of *rawzeh khwani* (recitations of the story of Karbala) and the tradition of mourning at Husayn's grave, which, inspired in part by her words, is foundational in the pilgrimage to his shrine at Karbala that was established during the 'Abbasid period.[6]

Pilgrims who complete major pilgrimages to cities like Karbala and Najaf earn the title of *zaair*, a status similar to that of a *hajji/hajjah*.[7] Similarly, pilgrims who complete the journey to Mashhad are called *mashdi*.[8] The origins of these pilgrimages are probably found in the gatherings, called *majlis*, that occurred after the death of Husayn. *Majlis* occur in numerous forms at local Shi'i *masjid*s (mosques), at Hussainiyya and other centers, weekly supplications, and on special occasions such as the commemorations of the deaths of the Imams and their relatives, and at pilgrimage sites. *Ziyarat* guides, which include booklets and are also accessible through websites, help pilgrims navigate these sites. One online instructional guide includes these directions:

> As you see the shrine, empty your mind from worldly thoughts and think how Allah has blessed you with the opportunity to meet with such a great personality … Then kiss the entrance gate and while stepping in recite the following: In the name of Allah, for the sake of Allah, in the cause of Allah, and on account of the religion of the Messenger of Allah, blessings of Allah be on him and his children.[9]

Among the many pilgrimages associated with Husayn, the most important is to his grave, a journey that may take precedence over visiting the *ka'bah* in Mecca. The source of these traditions, including those surrounding Husayn, is found in reports from the Imams, which are preserved in written form. One such tradition from the fifth Imam Muhammad bin 'Ali al-Baqir regarding Karbala reads:

> Whoever visits the grave of al-Husayn bin 'Ali (a) on the day of 'Ashūrā, in the month of Muharram and persists in weeping at his grave, then Allāh the Glorified and Exalted will receive him on the Day of Judgment with the reward of two thousand major pilgrimages, two thousand minor pilgrimages and two thousand military expeditions. The reward of each major and minor pilgrimage and military expedition will be akin to having undertaken them with the Prophet of Allāh and the Rightly Guided Imāms.[10]

The time at which Shi'i rituals at the graves of the Imams became a common practice is unknown. Documents from the late 'Umayyad and early 'Abbasid period suggest a growing set of rituals associated with Husayn's grave that by the writing of Kulayni's *al-Kafi* (tenth century C.E.) included an established set of rituals, including liturgical texts and particular actions to be performed at the threshold to his shrine, at the foot of his grave, and at the resting place of the Imam's head.[11] In Sunni and Shi'i sources from the same period, references are made to public gatherings of Shi'i mourning Husayn. In many cases, Sunni documents reflect sympathy and even approval of some of these practices, probably due to the fact that visiting graves was popular among many Muslims.

Shi'i pilgrimages often include commemorations of the death anniversaries of the Imams and their relatives. Gatherings (*majlis*) include the enormous procession of pilgrims at Karbala as well as at other sites in Iraq, Iran, and Syria.[12] These rituals date from the twelfth century or earlier.[13] Banners called *alamat*, with symbols of 'Ali, Husayn, and others, among them the winged horse and sword, the latter of which was incorporated into Sufi symbolism, are often carried in these processions.[14] At times, these mourning rituals include the reenactment of the Battle of Karbala (called *ta'ziyeh*) in dramatic form, self-flagellation (*zanjir-zani*), and solemn chanting and prayer.

The development of Shi'i pilgrimage sites where the relatives of Prophet Muhammad (the *ahl al-bayt*) are buried, from simple graves to elaborate tomb complexes covering many acres, has often been tied to empire. In Pahlavi as well as pre- and post-Revolutionary Iran, politics has played a role in the subsidization, promotion, and control of pilgrimage sites. As one scholar points out:

> Although a traffic of pilgrims and religious scholars existed between Ottoman towns and territories with Shi'ite inhabitants such as Karbala, Najaf, Jabal 'Amil, and Persia prior to the creation of modern nation-states, the meaning of these holy sites to local citizens as well as pilgrimage to these sites have acquired new meanings ever since. During Pahlavi rule, the tomb of the eighth Shi'ite *imam al-rida* (hereafter Imam Reza) located in the northeastern part of Iran in Mashhad was restored and a complex comprising a library and museum was added to the periphery of the shrine, but after the Iranian Revolution, the site (known as *astan-i quds-i rasavi*), has been renovated to perfection, receiving about twelve million pilgrims annually; and the state has become directly involved in the managing and the politics of pilgrimage.[15]

The politicization of saintly bodies is not restricted to Shi'i Islam, of course, and scholars are attentive to the numerous examples of "discovered" bodies and the formation of state power. John the Baptist's head was suddenly discovered when the Muslims took over the Byzantine church that became the 'Umayyad mosque in Damascus. In Morocco, Mawlay Idris's body was rediscovered in the last years of the Marinid dynasty and functioned to "affirm the critical connection between bones, blood, and power in the formation of the body politic."[16] In Shi'i Islam, the performance of prayer, singing, and other rituals are often connected to current political trials: "Lamentations and wailing at the sacred sites are integrated with various forms of powerful invocations and complaints about injustices and violations of rights."[17] In large shrines in Iran, political items are often located in shrines. A souvenir shop in the grounds of the Shah Cheragh shrine and a museum attest to a mixture of politics and religious pilgrimage, complete with soldiers' relics from the Iran–Iraq War – prayer books, compasses, rosaries, and shoes.[18]

For the Ithna-Ashariyya (Twelver) Shi'i, who comprise the largest group of Shi'i in the world, the burial places of the Twelve Imams are among the most revered sites that Shi'i pilgrims visit. The Fourteen Infallibles – the Twelve Imams plus Fatima and her father, Muhammad – are the focus of Shi'i liturgy and pilgrimage.[19] These tombs and burial complexes are held in such high regard that, as has been mentioned, some believe a visit to Najaf or Karbala is as important as – or even more important than – the *hajj*.[20] Imam Ja'far Sadiq, the sixth Imam, reportedly said, "Whoever visits Husayn's tomb on 'Shura is like the one who performs the pilgrimage to Mecca."[21] Among the Shi'i these sites are not only viewed as substitutions for Mecca, but as part of a network of sites that are related to Mecca and Medina.[22] As Seyyed Hossein Nasr explains:

> The tombs of all the imams are considered extensions of the supreme centers of Mecca and Medina, and thus, pilgrimage to these sites, not to speak of the authentic *imam-zadehs*, or tombs of the imams' descendants, are strongly encouraged by the jurists and the official religious hierarchy and play a very important role in Shi'i religious life.[23]

Saints not included in the Fourteen Infallibles also constitute an important part of Shi'i pilgrimage. Sayyida Zaynab, the granddaughter of Prophet Muhammad and the daughter of Fatima and 'Ali, has minor infallibility (*al-'isma al-sughra*), "because she was raised by and with infallibles."[24] She also has a high status due to her presence at the Battle of Karbala and the bravery she showed to Husayn's enemies after the battle. Numerous individuals function as saints in Shi'i Islam, including relatives of Prophet Muhammad, martyrs in the Iran–Iraq War, and others who are connected to Shi'ism theologically, historically, or politically.

When Muslim pilgrims visit a tomb, a graveyard, or another site related to the dead, they often seek the *tawassul*, or intercession, of the person interred at the site. It is believed that the dead have the ability to listen and to grant favors. This notion of intercession is very specific: "Shi'a scholars explain *tawassul* during *ziyarat* as a means of seeking intercession with God through the holy personality being visited – for instance, asking an Imam to ask God to grant their requests; a distinction is drawn between this and actually asking the holy personality himself (or herself) to grant their requests."[25] Shi'i pilgrims often carry pilgrimage guides, or small books of supplications, that specify the prayers for particular shrines, in the belief that reciting them may result in a blessing, good health, healing, or even a miracle. Shi'i are not alone in these practices. Sunni Muslims, including those who would be considered Sufi, also recite prayers and ask for blessings at shrines and other locations.

Within the Shi'i tradition, certain individuals play especially important roles in theology, liturgy, and rituals, including pilgrimages. Among these are the Prophet's cousin 'Ali, Muhammad's daughter Fatima, their sons Hasan and Husayn, and their progeny. 'Ali, the Prophet's cousin and son-in-law, is the first Imam in the Shi'i tradition and the patriarch of the lineage from which the Imamate emerges, those Muslims related to Muhammad that Shi'i look to for moral guidance and as infallible religious authorities. Hasan and Husayn are the second and third Imams. As mentioned earlier in relation to Karbala, Husayn is the proto-martyr of Shi'ism and figures most prominently in Shi'i liturgy and pilgrimage, especially for Twelvers: "According to the Twelver Shiite worldview, the martyr *par excellence* is the third Imam, Abu Abdallah Hoseyn ibn Ali, whose epithet is *Sayed al-Shohada*, 'The Prince of the Martyrs.'"[26] Husayn's role as the proto-martyr and his spiritual primacy in sacralizing Karbala, the site of his martyrdom, were developed in the hagiographic literature (*maqathil*) that is still popular today.[27] In Iran, Iraq, and Afghanistan, pilgrimage sites are often connected to current political struggles that mirror the martyrs' sacrifices at Karbala.

Fatima is the most important female saint among Shi'i. She is often referred to by one of her honorific titles, such as Fatimah al-Zahra (Fatimah the Radiant One). As the Prophet's beloved daughter, the wife of the first Shi'i Imam ('Ali), and the mother of the second and third Imams (Hasan and Husayn), she figures importantly in the *ahl al-bayt*, the Prophet's family tree, which is the dominant organizing principle of the Twelver Imamate. Fatimah also has a privileged position in Shi'ism because she reflects Allah's Divine Light (*Nur*). According to one tradition, Fatima was created when the first humans asked God for a vision of Paradise. Allah created Fatima, adorned with a myriad of lights, on a throne, with a crown, rings in her ears, and a sword.[28] Symbolically, her crown represents Muhammad, her earrings Hasan and Husayn, and her sword 'Ali; however, Fatima's sainthood is not just predicated on the familial ties she has to her father, husband, and children, but on her essential nature as a leader.[29] As Karen Ruffle writes, "Fatimah's divine radiance is like a beacon that guides the Shia in their remembrance of the Imams and the Ahl–e Bait."[30]

Shi'i are known for their deep love for the Prophet and his family, but this adoration is not restricted to this sect. Fatima plays a prominent role in Islam. She is often evoked in the prayers and supplications recited at shrines and other sites and figures prominently in Sufi orders, including those identified as Sunni. One group that shows the strength of this tradition of love for the family is the Hadrami 'Alawis in Yemen, whose lineage is identified through 'Ali but who follow the Sunni Shafi *madhhab* (law school). They view "themselves as descendants of Prophet Muhammad and keepers of deeply rooted mystical secrets incorporated in the 'Alawī *tarīqa* (mystical path)."[31] These mystical secrets are focused on a love for Muhammad and his family.

Shi'i refer to Fatima as the "mistress of the women of the worlds" (*sayyidat nisa' al-alamin*) and as the progenitor of the Shi'i Imamate, her role in pilgrimage is critical. Fatima and Husayn provide intercession (*shafa'ah*) for those who remember them and the Prophet's family on special occasions, such as during the month of Muharram.[32] Intercession takes place at the tombs, shrines, and other sites prominent in Shi'i pilgrimage. Fatima is believed to descend to earth from heaven each time prayers are said for her son Husayn, at pilgrimage sites as well as at the Shi'i community gatherings known as *majlis*.[33]

BODIES AND PILGRIMAGE

Shi'i pilgrims frequently visit graves, tombs, mausoleums, and shrines that contain the bodies of the *ahl al-bayt* (the Prophet's family) or relics associated with them. Outside Karbala, a number of other sites are associated with Husayn's body, including his head, which numerous Muslim communities claim to have. As is often the case with relics, the location and history of Husayn's body is contested. As Lesley Hazleton points out:

> Hussein's head would have many resting places, its presence spreading along with the story of what had happened. Most say it is buried by the east wall of the Grand Mosque in Damascus, but some have it in a shrine near the main entry to the Al-Azhar Mosque in Cairo, while yet others maintain that it was spirited away to Azerbaijan for safekeeping. Some even say it was returned to Karbala.[34]

Visiting the places associated with the Imams and their relatives constitutes a large part of Shi'i pilgrimage, but like many other Muslims, Shi'i also go on *hajj* and *'umrah*, and visit sites associated with Sufi saints, often alongside Sunnis and others. The practice of visiting the graves of Prophet Muhammad's relatives does not preclude Shi'i from participating in other pilgrimages that are often framed as Sunni or Sufi.

Husayn's body is not the only contested body or relic in Islam. Zaynab, Husayn's sister, has shrines in both Cairo and Damascus. As early as the ninth century, claims were made that she was buried in Cairo, and later scholars expressed a lack of concern regarding where her body was interred.[35] The twentieth-century scholar Sayyid Muhsin al-Amin argued that "the importance of the shrine is only marginally related to its authenticity as Zaynab's final resting ground. Its greater significance lies in its role in attracting people, honoring Zaynab and the *ahl al-bayt* (the family of the Prophet Muhammad), and promoting piety as a model for good living."[36] In other words, historical facts surrounding a pilgrimage site are often less important than the religious imagination connected to a saintly figure. Saintly bodies typically inspire a rich religious imagination, "rooted in particular ways of imagining the place of human beings in the cosmos."[37] The bodies of Husayn and Zaynab are not the only examples of contested relics among

Shi'i Muslims. Numerous *mazar*s (tombs) located in China have served as popular sites for pilgrims despite their lack of a relic or body. As Minoru Sawada argues, "Although these nine mazars are not the real tombs of the Imāms, people consider them real mazars and go there on pilgrimage."[38]

The status of *ziyarat* in Shi'ism is of the highest order. The rewards for visiting the graves of the Prophet's relatives are great. Several traditions equate these journeys to *hajj*. For example, Husayn's son Abdallah (Abu Abd Allah) reportedly said, "What is incumbent upon us (*mā yalzimunā*) is what is incumbent in the *hajj*."[39] Virtually no theologian from a Shi'i school has prohibited pilgrimage, except to those sites deemed as spiritually dangerous – places where the graves of the enemies of the followers of 'Ali are located, or where pharaohs are buried. The pilgrimage sites that Shi'i visit are extensive, and, as Flaskerud reminds us, they are "sanctified," for the "journey is considered a pious act and is associated with religious merit, *savab*."[40]

Shi'i pilgrimages resemble other Muslim journeys, including those often described as "Sufi" in the scholarly literature, in several important ways. Like many Muslims, Shi'i emphasize the importance of the dead, visit their graves, communicate with them in dreams, and believe that the dead can intercede on the pilgrim's behalf, healing the body, bestowing a blessing, or sanctifying a life decision. As Liyakat Takim explains, "As in Sufism, Shi'ism locates the *baraka* on the dead as much as the living."[41] These similarities make apparent how difficult it is to classify Islamic pilgrimage.

Dreaming is important in Shi'i tradition, as it is in other Muslim communities. Dreams have a strong imagery featuring the bodies of saintly figures and are often connected to the founding of pilgrimages. In many cases, the history of a shrine, mosque, or other commemorative structure is "not based on verifiable material evidence, such as relics, but is often the product of a dream or a vision."[42] This is how the shrine for Husayn outside Aleppo was sanctified.[43] It is not alone. The Mashhad of Light over the grave of Sayyida al-Sharifa Maryam was constructed after a pillar of light was seen emanating from the site, which was unearthed and a tablet detailing the saint's genealogy discovered.[44] The tomb then became known as a place where pilgrims' prayers were answered.[45] In one report documented in Syria, an elderly woman dreamt of Sayyida Zaynab, who appeared with full veil and a glass of water, and told her that visiting the saint's tomb was the source of her "miraculous healing."[46]

Although some sites are an established part of Shi'i tradition, such as Imam Reza's shrine in Mashhad, some of the most important pilgrimages in the Twelver tradition arc visited by other Muslims. Sunnis visit Karbala and they certainly visit Sayyida Zaynab's shrine in Damascus. Both Sunnis and Shi'i visit the Prophet's grave at Medina, although the prayers recited may be different. The whole business of classifying these pilgrimages on the basis of sectarian identity, as discussed in the first chapter, is problematic. Pilgrimage in Islam rarely follows sectarian rules – even in the case of places dominated by Shi'i hagiography. At Sar-i Pul, the tombs of the greater and lesser Imams (Imam-i Kalan and Imam-i Khurd) survived long after Shi'i became a minority community in the region and are still held as important sites by many Afghans today, the majority of whom are Sunni.[47] In many Sunni majority contexts, Shi'i pilgrims have been tolerated for political or social reasons. Pilgrims visiting the Mashhad of al-Husayn in Cairo during the Ayyubid period, who were reported kissing the tomb and throwing their bodies onto it, were part of the lasting legacy of rituals established during the Fatimid period.[48] As such, their traditions were often adopted and incorporated into the wider social milieu. In many of these cases, it is unclear who established grave visitation and its associated rituals, because so much of this activity marks Muslim history.

MAJOR BRANCHES OF SHI'I AND *ZIYARAT*

The three largest groups of Shi'i are the Zaydis (Zaidis), prominent in north Yemen, the Isma'ilis (Seveners), and the Ithna-Ashariyya (Twelvers). Shi'ism is very focused on lineage, which is viewed as constituting sacred authority and establishing leadership of the community. The Isma'ilis and Twelvers (also called Imami) differ regarding the successor to Ja'far as-Sadiq, the sixth Imam. The Zaydis accept Zayd b. Ali b. Ali Talib as their Imam and, unlike other Shi'i, accept the legitimacy of the first three caliphs. The Isma'ilis believe that Ja'far's son Isma'il established a line of living Imams, maintained today in the individual known as the Aga Khan. The Twelvers follow the Twelve Imams and believe that the son of the eleventh Imam went into occultation and is the Mahdi, the messianic figure who will return at the End of Days.[49] These historical contingencies shape the pilgrimage practices of each of these communities.

The remainder of this chapter examines the pilgrimage traditions of these different groups, as well as others whose pilgrimage traditions are related to, or embedded in, Shi'ism. In the scholarly literature, more attention is given to the Twelvers, who have an extensive network of shrines and others sites in Iran, Iraq, Syria, India, and other countries. However, all Shi'i Muslims hold the members of Prophet Muhammad's family in high regard, granting particular honor to the offspring of 'Ali and Fatima. As caretakers of the Islamic *'ummah*, the members of the *ahl al-bayt* (the people of the house; Muhammad's family) are believed to hold special wisdom. Their ability to offer blessings, or *barakat*, a special power that is maintained in death, is a central part of Shi'i *ziyarat*. Pilgrimage is a particularly important activity for Shi'i due to this belief in the agency, or life-force, that survives the grave. They often point to the Qur'an, which says, "I do not ask of you any reward for it but love for my near relatives," when explaining their strong attachment to visiting the Prophet's relatives.[50]

The vast amount of scholarship on Shi'i *ziyarat* is focused on the Twelvers, and in particular, on their pilgrimage traditions in Iran, Iraq, and South Asia. Of course, Shi'i communities are found all over the world, but less is known about their practices in places like Yemen, Afghanistan, or Southeast Asia, where they exist in smaller numbers. Afghanistan, for example, has major Shi'i shrines and relics in places like Sar-i Pul and Mazar-i Sharif, although it is unclear whether these places function as pilgrimage sites today, or are popular relics of the past.

The scholarship on the Zaydis is scant in comparison to other Shi'i sects. The Zaydis diverge from the majority of Shi'i on the question of rulership, claiming Zayd ibn 'Ali, a grandson of 'Ali, as the rightful heir to the Imamate, as opposed to Muhammad al-Baqir and his son Ja'far.[51] Zayd attempted to topple the Bani Umayah (the 'Umayyads), a campaign his half-brother (and the fifth Imam of Twelver Shi'ism) Muhammad Baqir warned against: "Do not go out [against] the people of Kūfah as, verily, they are people of trickery and machinations – they killed your great grandfather, and betrayed your uncle al-Hasan and they killed your grandfather al-Husayn ... I fear for you my brother that you will tomorrow be crucified in the 'church' (*kanīsah*) of Kūfah."[52] Zayd was killed as his half-brother predicted. He was beheaded and crucified, and his body was put on display for four years, until it was finally burned and the ashes deposited in the Euphrates.[53] The story of Zayd's head mirrors the story of Husayn's – it was buried, rediscovered, exhumed, "anointed with unguents and perfumes," and then reburied.[54] This type of narrative – the destruction and resurrection of the body of the martyr – is common among Shi'i.

Historically, the Zaydi theology shared some similarities to the Kharijite belief that doing good and prohibiting evil is a duty for Muslims. Zaydis staged rebellions against early dynasties including the 'Umayyads and the 'Abbasids in protest at their decadence and immorality. The Zaydis differ from other Shi'i in several ways. They believe that any descendant of 'Ali could be Imam and that the first three caliphs, shunned by most Shi'i, are legitimate. The first Zaydi empire originated in 864, when Hasan ibn Zayd founded the Zaydi caliphate in Tabaristan.[55] They established a presence in North Africa, Arabia, Yemen, and southern Spain, but today are mostly found in Yemen, where a Zaydi state existed in some form between 893 and 1963.[56] The Jarudi Zaydi sect in Yemen is one of the most marginalized Islamic communities in existence due to their professed non-alignment with the majority of Shi'i Muslims, which includes mocking the concept of the twelfth Imam and calling those who subscribe to Iranian or Twelver Shi'ism "Ja'farized" (*taja"far*).[57] Such a statement differentiates the Zaydis from the transnational Shi'ism associated with Iran and its extensive influence over many Shi'i pilgrimage sites, including those in Lebanon, Iraq, and Syria.

Zaydi pilgrimage is an understudied academic subject. Historically, the sect has had a tradition of visiting graves and building large, commemorative buildings to house tombs, but the popularity of these practices among Zaydis is unknown. In burial, Zaydis preferred a boulder (*sakhra*) at the head of a grave over the more common tablets (*alwah*), sometimes marked women's graves with two stones, and allowed inscriptions as long as they were not ostentatious or marked by too much ornamentation (*zakhrafa*).[58] These traditions suggest not only that graves were visited but that there was some lenience as to their construction and style.

Zaydi architecture includes a number of types of mosques and tombs. Tombs were typically accompanied by a large mosque, such as the Great Mosque of Saharah, and were often located in mountainous locations, enclaves called *hijar* that allowed for a degree of protection.[59] The typical style of these tombs, called *qubbatayn* (sing. *qubbat*), is a domed shrine with a prayer hall, courtyard, and adjoining mosque.[60] The architectural decoration surrounding the graves of Zaydi Imams is extensive, much more elaborate than that surrounding mosques in other traditions: "While the ornamentation in mosques was restricted to the *mihrab* and its bay, these domed tombs are decorated all around, making it a shrine, admission to which is completely forbidden to non-Muslims."[61] The inner shrine or sarcophagus is where the *barakah* is concentrated and the site where pilgrims often felt they would receive a blessing.[62]

As far as scholars can surmise, pilgrimage has never been an established part of Zaydi practice in the same way it has been for other Shi'i communities. This is because in principle, the Zaydi Imams are considered scholars, not Imams in the tradition of the charismatic figures found among Isma'ilis and Twelvers. In fact, there are records of the wholesale destruction of shrines by Zaydis, who in India were responsible for destroying the *mashhad* of 'Ali b. Muhammad al-Sulayhi.[63] This suggests that pilgrimage traditions among the Zaydis were not uniform but, rather like much in Islam, represented by "plenitude and complexity of meaning" rather than a matter of doctrine or common experience.[64]

Isma'ilis, also called Seveners, who began as a missionary movement challenging the Sunnis, comprise the second-largest group of Shi'i in the world. The Isma'ili movement dates to the ninth century, to the idea of "the rightly guided summons" (*al-da'wa al-hadiyah*), a doctrine that was not institutionalized until the Fatimid caliphate (909–1171) and continued under the Nizari state (1094–1258).[65] Sainthood is an important part of Isma'ilism: "The Ismā'īlī anthropocentrism puts men, whose guide and true representative claimed to be the Imam of the Time (*Imām-i Zamān*), in the centre of theological discourse and creates in his image the real source of sanctity and divinity."[66] This concept of sainthood is situated in a strong belief in the Living Imam, who is the descendant of Husayn and the person invested with taking care of the Isma'ili community. In addition to foundational texts like the Qur'an, Isma'ilis follow the teachings of the Aga Khan, the living Imam. Isma'ili Muslims are called Seveners for a number of reasons. Besides their views regarding the number of Imams, Isma'ilis believe that the seven days of creation are related to prophetic cycles, with the seventh day symbolizing "the triumph of Isma'ilism."[67]

Historically, Isma'ilis have performed the rituals of *hajj* and visited tombs of several of the Imams. As with other Muslims, pilgrimage practices are often determined by how near one's community is to tombs and shrines, as well as the teachings followed regarding *ziyarat*. For example, the Da'udis, a subset of Isma'ili Shi'i, are known to "make the *hajj* pilgrimage to Mecca and pay equal attention to visiting the shrines of the Imams 'Alī b. Abī Tālib and al-Husayn b. 'Alī, at Najaf and Karbalā."[68] There is great diversity in the pilgrimage practices of Isma'ilis, whose communities are found in many places around the world.

Visiting the Living Imam is also an important practice for many Isma'ilis. When the fourty-seventh Imam Aga Ali Shah discouraged physical pilgrimages to tombs, some Isma'ilis began to focus their pilgrimage practices on *didar* (glimpse), the physical or mystical "seeing" of the Imam. In 1910, the Persian Nizaris began differentiating some of their traditions from those of the Twelvers.[69] As Farhad Daftary explains, "They were also discouraged from joining the Twelvers at their mosques or on special occasions, and from participating in the Shī'ī mourning rituals of Muharram because the Nizārīs had a living and present (*mawjūd va hādir*) Imam and did not need to communicate with any of their dead Imams."[70] *Didar* is a prominent practice in contemporary Isma'ili communities, resting on admiration and love for the Imam and his representation of Muhammad's prophetic legacy. The beatific vision experienced when gazing on his face is likened to a physical pilgrimage in its transformational effect on the individual.

Today, not all Isma'ilis reject shrine pilgrimage in favor of *didar*, however. The Bohras, a sect of Isma'ilis primarily found in India (with smaller communities in fifty other countries), visit a variety of shrines that include the tombs of the holy five (*panjatan pak*) and Islamic prophets, Isma'ili missionaries, and family members.[71] Bohras are named after their twenty-seventh leader, or *dai*, Daud bin Qutubshah, and are led by a male class of clerics, although at least four tombs and one shrine containing female saints are part of the network of sites in India visited by Bohra pilgrims.[72] Bohra Isma'ili pilgrims perform ablutions and rituals that are similar to those seen at other Islamic shrines, including those visited by Twelver Shi'i. These include being clean, donning a modest garment over one's clothes, reciting supplications, and touching the shrine in hopes of a blessing. In the case of the shrines in Gujarat:

> The devotional ritual is simple and requires no presence of a cleric. The pilgrims enter the mausoleum bare-footed and with heads covered, bending forward from the waist down, moving their right hands between the floor and the forehead signifying a respectful greeting (*tasleem*). In front of the tomb, as a mark of humility and respect, they half prostrate (*sajdo*) themselves by going down on their knees and touching the ground with their foreheads and then kissing the four sides of the tomb. They offer rose petals and lilies, placing them on the tomb; cash contributions are put into the shrine box; and they read a prayer (*dua*) and a chapter of the Koran (*Yasin*), usually making small requests.[73]

Isma'ilis are also active in Central Asia, a vast area that includes Afghanistan, Tajikistan, and Uzbekistan, all places with a strong pilgrimage culture that includes Isma'ili shrines. The Isma'ili community in Tajikistan includes numerous saints (*awliya*) and shrines (*qadamgah*), focused largely in a region occupied by the Wakhis that borders Afghanistan.[74] The foundational myth of the Wakhan Isma'ilis claims that Imam 'Ali, with his sons Hasan and Husayn, defeated a pre-Islamic king named Qah-Qaha, bringing Islam to the region.[75] For Isma'ilis, 'Ali is the foundation of Sufism and is described as "the king of sainthood" (*Shah-i wilayat*); he is identified as the individual who serves as the model for all mystics, whether *shaykhs*, *murshids* (guides; teachers), *pirs* (elders; teachers), *darvishes* (members of a Sufi order; teachers), or *faqirs* (renunciants; ascetics).[76] As in many Sufi communities, in Isma'ili Gnosticism one does not need to be a descendant of 'Ali to be a saint, but they must embody the qualities of Muhammad, 'Ali, Hasan, and Husayn.

Several types of shrines are visited by Wakhan Isma'ilis, including piles of stones, springs, trees, remnants of buildings, and tombs.[77] A common type of shrine is the *astan*, or "doorway," found in each village and composed of trees or stones, but there are also the more typical *mazar*s for saints, *qadamgah*, the "stepping places" where saints left their holy footprint (*qadam-i mubarak*), and the "house of orders" (*far-man-khana*), a home shrine in which relics are placed, ranging from bodily relics like hair to Isma'ili religious texts.[78] Pilgrimages to these shrines may take place at any time but are more common during Islamic holidays and seasonal festivals, a practice common among Shi'i communities. Wakhan Isma'ilis commonly visit shrines to petition the saint for help, aid, or healing, and also to obtain comfort after a nightmare.[79]

Iran, a country dominated by Twelver Shi'ism and its associated shrines, features Isma'ili traditions that complement more dominant pilgrimage practices, such as the end-of-summer visit to Naw Hisar. This commemoration of Imam Abu 'l-Hasan's encounter with Imamquli, who became a great poet and stands as the most famous person from Dizbad, a tiny village in the northwestern corner of Iran, is marked by the telling of the story of the Imam and a picnic lunch at the spring where blessings are believed to be centered.[80] Isma'ilis also participate in the spring pilgrimage to Abalu to visit the shrine of a poet named Qutb al-Din, whose tomb the pilgrims touch with their right index finger while praying silently.[81] These pilgrimages are not necessarily distinct or separate from those of other Iranian Shi'i communities, who often undertake these journeys together, representing a collapse of the sectarian divisions that can result in shared pilgrimages.

Muslims who follow the Twelve Imams compose the largest group of Shi'i, existing in large numbers in Iran, Iraq, Saudi Arabia, Afghanistan, and Bahrain, with smaller numbers in many other Muslim-majority countries as well as minority communities in North America and Europe. They are referred to as Twelvers or Ithna-Ashariyya because of their belief in the Twelve Imams, relatives of Prophet Muhammad who serve as the living representatives of his wisdom and grace. According to this branch of Shi'ism, the Imams are important historically and eschatologically, a view based on the relationship of Prophet Muhammad's cousin 'Ali (who married the Prophet's daughter Fatima) to the Twelfth Imam, who is "also known as the Mahdi (Messiah), the Imam-e Montazar (Expected Leader), and the Sahab-e Zaman (Lord of the Age)."[82] The Twelfth Imam is the culmination of this lineage – of 'Ali and Fatima – representing the end of suffering through the arrival of the messiah who will commence a time of justice and redemption.

The history of Twelver Shi'ism is an extensive subject that is not covered in detail here, except for those institutions involved with *ziyarat* (pilgrimages). Followers of this branch of Shi'ism have distinct pilgrimage traditions, including the visitation of tombs where the Twelve Imams and their relatives are buried as well as other sites that are frequented by Jews, Christians, and other Muslims. The importance of the familial line on which all this rests is expressed in numerous traditions, such as the commemoration of the birth and death anniversaries of the Prophet's relatives as well as the visitation of their tombs. As discussed above, the visitation of graves predates Islam and has continued during and after the Prophet's lifetime. Shi'i Muslims visit the gravesites, tombs, and mausoleums of religious figures, some of whom are saints and others who are important historically or politically. This is something Shi'i have done from the beginning, inspired by already existent Muslim practices but taking on a new importance with the establishment of Safavid Iran in the sixteenth century. At this point, cities and towns containing tombs increased in importance due to the participation of Shah 'Abbas in the sanctification of *imamzadeh*. As Heern notes, "As a public pronouncement of his Shi'i religiosity, he made the pilgrimage from Isfahan to Mashhad on foot, which was a critical step in developing Mashhad as a pilgrimage center."[83] 'Abbas also established Isfahan as an important educational center, a move that helped lead to its sanctification as a pilgrimage center.[84]

Imamzadeh refers to the large tombs in which the Imams are buried. A Persian word with numerous meanings, it is often translated as "the tomb of the descendant of an imam."[85] Oleg Grabar, the great historian of Islamic art, understood it to mean "sons of an Imam."[86] In Iran, which boasts numerous Shi'a sites, *imamzadeh* is often explained as "the place of the Imams." *Ziyarat gah mogaddas*, a Persian phrase, often refers to the places where the relatives of the Imams (and, by extension, Prophet Muhammad) are buried. Alternatively, major sites are simply called by their proper name, such as "Imam Reza," or as "the *haram*." *Imamzadeh* also can refer to the small shrines that can be found in Shi'i-majority countries like Iran and Iraq. Numbering in the thousands, these sites are found in large cities as well as small villages and commemorate everyone from regional saints to family members and fallen soldiers. Much like in Sufism, *Imamzadehs* may not be marked by a tomb or grave. They may consist of non-corporeal objects like "sacred trees, wells, and footprints" that are associated with a holy person.[87]

Shi'ism is a tradition that has many mystical, or Sufi, resonances within it. The history of Sufism is one that is, according to many scholars, deeply embedded in Shi'ism, so much so that the *awliya* (the Sufi saints known as the intimate friends of God) *are* the Imams.[88] In one text, the friends of God are described as the lovers of the Imams, mirroring the language found in Sufi texts about the Beloved.[89] As Hamid Dabashi has pointed out, the history of Shi'ism has included efforts "to incorporate Shi'ism and Sufism into a third narrative space and craft a new transcendental language."[90] Today, these efforts are seen in pilgrimage sites, which function as spaces of mystical contemplation for Muslims who may identify as Shi'i, Sunni, or Sufi.

In the Twelver tradition, holy cities include Mecca, Medina, and Jerusalem as well as Kufa, Karbala, Mashhad, Najaf, and other cities intimately connected to Shi'i history. Kufa, located in modern-day Iraq, is one of the holiest cities for Shi'i Muslims. As Liyakat Takim explains:

> It is reported from as-Sadiq that if people knew the merits of the mosque in Kufa, they would even crawl to get there. It is said to be a place where one's desires can be fulfilled. Over a thousand prophets are reported to have prayed there. Shi'i devotional literature maintains that even the Prophet prayed in this mosque when he ascended to the heavens and that the twelfth Imam, the Mahdi, will pray in it when he reappears.[91]

Kufa is important for a number of other reasons, including its association with Muhammad, later prophets, the Imams, and the End of Days. The following story about Prophet Muhammad demonstrates how the city's privileged position came to be:

The sources identify Masjid al-Kūfa as the main Shī'ī mosque for the entire city and emphasize its importance through an anecdote about the Prophet's ascent to heaven (*mi'rāj*). In the account, as the Prophet is being carried by Jibrā'īl (Gabriel), he is informed that they are passing above Masjid al-Kūfa where every prophet or servant of God had performed prayers. Muhammad asks for and is granted the same privilege.[92]

Particular sites are also connected to earlier prophets and the Mahdi, creating a link between the pre-Islamic past, Muhammad's prophecy, and the future redemption through the messiah. The Masjid al-Hamra is connected to both Yunus (Jonah), as the site of his tomb, and the Masjid Ju-fi is the place at which the Mahdi performs prayers.[93]

By the eighth century, Kufa had over fifty holy sites, "part and parcel of a broad network of religious spaces frequented by the nascent Imāmī community."[94] The Imami tradition also delineated approved sites and those that were prohibited or accursed – friendly or hostile.[95] Early in Shi'i history, supplications and rituals were developed in relation to Kufa. Many of these traditions have survived to the present. Specific prayers should be recited at the various pillars inside the mosque at Kufa and the interior of the mosque is believed to be the place where 'Ali will judge humans and where, at the seventh pillar, Allah offered Adam a chance to repent.[96]

Karbala, also in modern-day Iraq, is of course of paramount importance as the place where Husayn was martyred at the Battle of Karbala in 680. Other pilgrimages often refer to Husayn and Karbala as the center of the Shi'i *ziyarat* practice. As Renard explains, "Originally centered on Husayn, the ritual has gradually broadened to include the whole family of Imams and all their fellow martyrs. When Shi'i pilgrims visit the tombs of other Imams, such as that of the eighth Imam, Riza, at Mashhad, they keep the image and story of Husayn in mind."[97] The soil (or sand) of Karbala is believed to have special qualities, such as the ability to heal the sick and restore sight to the blind. In addition, Shi'i are encouraged to pray on tablets made from the sand (although some traditions also cite Najaf as the source of this special soil), place it in their graves, and eat it.[98]

The Iraqi city of Najaf, alongside Qom in Iran, is one of the two most important cities of Shi'i religious scholarship. The city has a long history of education and is home to one of the world's oldest Islamic schools, a *madrasah* that was founded in 1057 by al-Tusi (d. 1068), a renowned Islamic philosopher.[99] Najaf has an elevated status as the burial site of 'Ali. Ayatollah Sistani has stated that the reward for offering prayers in 'Ali's shrine is equal to two hundred thousand prayers.[100] Najaf also is the site of the Wadi al-Salam cemetery, where many Shi'i hope to be buried, so much so that the city is a funeral capital with thousands of funerals taking place each year in the cemetery that lies adjacent to the city of Najaf.[101] Like many Islamic relics, 'Ali's body is contested. Not all Shi'i believe that 'Ali is buried at Najaf. Afghans claim his body lies in a mosque at Mazar-i Sharif in Afghanistan.[102] According to Afghans, the white doves that congregate at the mosque at Mazar-i Sharif represent the presence of 'Ali at the site.

Mashhad is the second-largest city in Iran. Its name refers to the status of the city as a shrine capital and means "a place of witnessing or martyrdom." It is where the tomb of Imam 'Ali b. Musa al-Rida (d. 818) is located. The shrine was first developed by the Timurids in the fifteenth century, then later by the Safavids in the sixteenth century under Nadir Shah (d. 1747), who chose it as his capital.[103] Like Najaf, Mashhad has a tradition surrounding burial, founded on the belief that burial near an Imam will bring blessings. Shi'i Afghan immigrants have moved to Mashhad in huge numbers over recent decades, hoping to be buried near the Imam in the hopes that his proximity will bring blessings, healing, and a clear passage to heaven at one's death. Mashhad is not just

Figure 3.0 Shrine of Imam Reza, Mashhad, Iran (photo courtesy of Alireza Baghoolizadeh).

about pilgrimage in this life, but "burial and salvation in the hereafter."[104]

The *imamzadeh* at Kufa, Karbala, Najaf, and Mashhad represent a few of the larger, more monumental pilgrimage sites, places where various male relatives of Prophet Muhammad are buried. Samarra, Kazimayn (Baghdad), and Qom are also important cities for pilgrims. Shi'i often visit the graves of women, including Zaynab and Ruqayya at Damascus, Fatima at Medina, and Masoumeh Fatima (Imam Reza's sister) at Qom. Both men and women visit these graves, often entering the male and female parts of the shrine separately, at other times being part of a crowd of men, women, and children. These are often emotionally charged spaces, reflecting Muslim piety, a long history of oppression, diasporic realities, and the narrative of martyrdom that is so central to Shi'i identity. In one account of Masoumeh's tomb at Qom, men face Mecca, call on the saint for forgiveness, health, or healing, and touch the bars that encase the tomb, which are believed to emit the *barakah* of the saint to the pilgrim.[105] Female saints include unmarried women such as Abesh Khatun and Bibi Dohkhtaran, both buried in Shiraz.[106] The power of female saints is not reserved for women's issues. Men visit the shrine of Sayyida Zaynab, the Prophet's grand-daughter, for a variety of ailments. As Edith Szanto documents in her work, one Syrian gentleman lost his voice and was told he would never speak again, but after reading the *ziyarah* prayer, clinging to the tomb, and praying, "*Allahuma salli 'ala Muhammad w'āli Muhammad!*" repeatedly, he was cured.[107]

The operative themes in all these spaces are martyrdom and the power of the dead to help the living. As Christiane Gruber reminds us, "In Shiite milieux in particular, the legitimacy and symbolic power of martyrdom has often been derived through analogics to the politico-religious mission and tragic death of Imam Hoseyn at the Battle of Karbala in 680 CE."[108] What does this mean, exactly? For one thing, the power of this story casts its aura over many types of sites, from enormous tomb complexes to memorials that exist on a single wall, like the one I was shown in Isfahan in 2004. A wall of a single room in a *madrasah* had been made into a kind of temporary memorial for a son lost in the Iran–Iraq War. The martyr's father, a cleric living at the *madrasah*, pointed out a newspaper clipping in which his son's sacrifice was noted. This was a sanctified space despite the absence of a body or relic.

In Shi'ism, the pilgrimage to tombs is also politically connected to the Husayn paradigm, in which an almost endless variety of experiences and people are aligned with the death of Husayn, his revolution (*thawrat al-imam al-Husayn*), and the meaning of his death. In Iran, memorials to the 1979 Revolution and the Iran–Iraq War are everywhere: "Images of martyrs like Motahhari and Beheshti were placed on stamps and posters and were often painted in the form of huge murals at cemeteries or on the sides of prominent buildings. Symbols of struggle and martyrdom also became centerpieces of *meydans*, or squares at major intersections."[109] Political

Shi'ism is also part of contemporary pilgrimages, including sites that do not feature a holy person, as in the case of the memorial wall described above. The Martyrs' Museum in Tehran is a commemorative monument to those who died in the Revolution (1979) and the Iran–Iraq War (1980–1988). There are no Imams buried here and no bodily relics of the Prophet's family. Instead, the museum features relic cases (*ganjinaha-yi asar*) filled with an almost endless array of objects including "small Korans and Koran stands, laminated portraits of Khomeini (sometimes bloodied), prayer beads and clay tablets, rosaries, rose-water flasks, rings with carnelian stones, shirts, weapons, hats, helmets, headbands, bandannas, ear-warmers, personal letters, poetry, robes, shirts, handkerchiefs, identity cards, eyeglasses, photographs, watches, medals, currency, bags, shoes and cassette tapes."[110]

Some shrines are more important than others, such as Imam Husayn's large tomb complex in Karbala and Imam Reza's shrine in Mashhad. Visiting these sites is often highly meritorious; however, some Shi'i believe that the length and difficulty of the journey is most important – a belief patterned on the journey of Imam Husayn. Pilgrims who visit certain shrines may earn an honorific title that is akin to *hajji/hajjah*. The reasons for this are complicated, probably resting on the long distances some Shi'i Muslims had to travel to reach Mecca, the growing importance of the Imamate politically, and, above all, the importance placed on the bodies of the Imams and their ability to sanctify the landscapes in which they were located:

> In the 19th century (and to a lesser extent among the older generations today), it became customary to designate persons who had visited the Shrines at Karbalā and Mashhad by such prefixed titles as Karbalā'ī and Mashhadī, in parallel to the designation of *Hājjī* given to those who had performed the pilgrimage to Mecca (the *Hajj*).[111]

The architecture of *Imamzadeh* and other major tombs in Twelver Shi'ism is typically Persianate, a style that includes *aineh kari* – mirror work – that adorns the inside of these buildings. Fractured pieces of mirror are organized geometrically, reflecting the Shi'i prohibition on praying in front of one's image and focusing the pilgrim on the shimmering display of light that dominates the walls surrounding these tombs.[112] According to scholars, the Light Verse (Surat an-Nur, Qur'an 24.35) is particularly apropos here.[113] Divine light, which is associated with Prophet Muhammad, his family, and numerous saints, is often an element in Muslim shrines and pilgrimage spaces, including those found outside Shi'i communities. In Java, a poem inside the *qubbah* (domed mausoleum) of one shrine impresses on pilgrims "that they are within a sacred enclave pervaded by Prophetic light shining through the meditation of al-'Attās."[114]

As one enters a shrine, the prayer of visitation (*ziyarat-Namah*) that often hangs above the entrance is recited.[115] Pilgrims often have a prayer book containing special supplications for the Twelve Imams and assorted relatives, including figures such as Imam 'Ali, Imam Husayn, 'Ali Akbar, the representatives of the Mahdi, Fatima Ma'suma, and Zaynab. Often a short biography of the saint's lineage is provided, followed by a prescribed prayer (*namaz*). As an example, in one *ziyarat* prayer guide 'Ali is described as the "brother of Your Prophet, successor of Your Prophet," and "a hand to his courage and the crown of his head."[116] The instructions for prayers follow, with a supplication, the proper number of *rak'a* (prayer cycles), and more supplications, which include the words "Peace be on you, O Commander of the Faithful and on Abu 'Abd Allah al-Husayn for as long as I am alive and the nights and days endure. May Allah not make this my last visitation to both of you, may He not separate me from the two of you."[117]

Figure 3.1 Box of *turab*, shrine of Sayyida Ruqayya, Damascus, Syria (photo courtesy of author).

The rituals performed at these Shi'i pilgrimage sites include these prayers, which are believed to result in the saint's intercession in the life of the pilgrim, as well as in healing and sometimes miracles (*mojizih*).[118] Often, Twelver Shi'i pray with a small tablet called a *mohr* or *turbah*, which is typically available at the mosque, shrine, or other pilgrimage site. These tablets, made from the clay of Karbala or Najaf, are a way of connecting the pilgrim to Prophet Muhammad's family and, in particular, the offspring of 'Ali and Fatima who make up the Imamate.

A variety of prayers, supplications, and petitions are offered at shrines. In one report from Iran, women were seen to whisper vows near the grave, cling to the bars of the tomb, asking for forgiveness (*al'af, al'af*), practice silent prayer and meditation, and circle the tomb.[119] In another case, at a *zaynabiyyah* (a gathering place for prayer) in Shiraz, a number of supplications were recited: "*du'a faraj* would be recited at the end of the reading of a pilgrim prayer, *ziyarat nameh*, at the end of a *sufreh*, and at the end of a longer *du'a* in which one asked for mediation."[120] Pilgrims often kiss the casing (*darih*) that encloses the tomb. When leaving a shrine, pilgrims walk backwards as a sign of respect.[121] At some shrines, sweets and nuts are distributed as a sign that prayers have been answered.[122] Shi'i Muslims often purchase religious souvenirs at these sites, some of which carry the blessing of the saint or holy person. While these objects are a focus of a later chapter, it is worth mentioning here that the continued sanctification of pilgrimage objects is quite common in this tradition of Islam. Objects that have an association with a sacred person or site may have a role in annual commemorations of a saint, or in weekly or daily prayers. Votive gifts from *Imamzadehs* and other Shi'i sites are an example of this. "The image gift may function as a personal souvenir, as well as stimulating the religious awareness of a local interpretive community. Moreover, a wall hanging purchased from sanctified pilgrimage site is believed to enhance the potential power for mediation in a particular ritual location."[123]

Although Twelver Shi'ism is strongly focused around the family of the Prophet, the *ahl al-bayt*, and their offspring – especially the Imams – Shi'i also visit local shrines and the tombs of poets, teachers, philosophers, and other individuals whose relationship to Shi'ism may be tenuous. Not all pilgrimage sites frequented by Shi'i are tomb complexes with courtyards, mirror mosaics, and other accouterments. In some cases, simple graves are important pilgrimage destinations. These are not always distinctly Shi'i sites, as they are also visited by Sunni Muslims, providing one of the many examples of the often fluid and dynamic nature of pilgrimage. In contrast to the massive tomb complexes of the Imams, some of these graves are open to the sky, while others consist of mini-mausoleums, often with a prayer-room (*namaz-khana*).

The visitation of graves is not the only Shi'i pilgrimage tradition. For instance, the place called al-Husayn (or the Shrine of Husain), near Aleppo, Syria, is where Shi'i claim Husayn's head was placed after the Battle of Karbala, leaving a drop of blood on a rock. Called "the Drop" (*al Nuqta*), a shrine was built at the site.[124] The rock, which disappeared, was recovered and vanished once again, rumored to be stolen by the enemies of Husayn. Miracles and visions surround this site as they do at other sites around the world, some visited by Shi'i, but also places attracting a diverse population of pilgrims, gathered together in anticipation of a blessing, miracle, or other divine event.

Since the Iranian Revolution in 1979, many Shi'i pilgrimage destinations have become politicized. In Iran, the democratization of Shi'i religious art is tied both to the need to validate the ideology and goals of the Revolution, and to the religious ideals that are embedded in much of the society. In addition to billboards, posters, stamps, and other cultural materials, new pilgrimages have emerged that support the Islamic state and reify Shi'i beliefs surrounding martyrdom, revolution, and the promise of redemption that will come with the reappearance of the Mahdi. One example is the use of portraiture at war cemeteries, in which photographs of the dead and other items are placed on their gravestones. This post-Revolutionary type of grave reinforces the idea of an Islamic Shi'i state through tokens of sacrifice, relics, and memorializing photos: "The display sometimes appears as a collage of photographs and notes inscribed with poetry, prayers, personal letters and small objects, turning the cases into sites for personal commemoration."[125] Pilgrims visiting these graves are often the relatives of the dead, whose visits include prayers, the laying of flowers, and other devotional acts. No one related to Husayn is buried at these sites, but his person looms large because he is the proto-martyr; all later martyrs are related to him. One of the most impressive of these examples is the tomb and shrine of Khomeini, which is located near the Behesht-e Zahra. As Aghaie explains, pilgrims visiting this shrine perform the same set of rituals as they do at the tombs of the Imams: "Each year during the nights of *Moharram*, mourning rituals have taken place at Khomeini's shrine complex. These mourning rituals, organized by different *hey'ats*, have included *rowzeh* sermons, processions, chants, *sineh zani* (flagellation of the chest), and even *zanjir zani* (flagellation with chains)."[126] Processions for Muharram offer another opportunity for Shi'i imagery to be displayed and democratized for the public in a form that utilizes recognizable forms and characters. Karbala is revived and re-sanctified in posters and murals that are often combined with Revolutionary slogans.[127] In some cases, these processions are part of pilgrimages to a graveyard, tomb, or other site.

Not all sites in Iran are overtly political, however, and some are not strictly Shi'i. A large number of ethnic, linguistic, and religious groups live in Iran, including various tribes, religious minorities like Jews, Christians, and Zoroastrians, and other communities, whose influence on pilgrimage is quite evident. In some cases, these communities share particular sites (a topic examined in a later chapter), but in other cases, the confluence of non-Islamic and Islamic traditions are in force. Scholars' study of the Bakhtiari tribe, for example, reveals that community rituals are not necessarily usurped by larger Islamic practices. In some cases they are combined, as in the case of the Bakhtiari men who say prayers under the statues of stone lions, and women who visit stone lion statues to pray for a baby boy whose character resembles that of Imam 'Ali.[128] The presence of lions in Shi'i traditions is extensive and is an important part of the cult of saints. For Shi'i, lions play a central role in stories of the Imams, including several narratives that detail paintings of lions being turned into living animals, a sign of the miracles associated with the Imamate that helps to explain why their graves are important centers of *barakat* (blessings), for the Imam has the "ability to affect objects around him."[129]

'ALAWI AND ALEVI PILGRIMAGE

In addition to the three groups of Shi'i discussed above, several movements that are related to Shi'ism survive in small communities, including the 'Alawis and the Alevis. These groups, who get their name from Imam 'Ali, are distinct yet are often confused because of their close geographical proximity and their mixture of Shi'ism with other religious and local traditions. Religious scholars do not typically place these groups within Shi'ism, describing them as heterodox or even extreme, using the word *ghulat*, a pejorative term used for Muslims whose positions "were regarded as unsophisticated exaggeration of what came to be regarded as proper Shî'î views."[130]

The 'Alawiyyah, known commonly as the 'Alawis, have their origins in ninth-century Iraq where the founder of 'Alawism Ibn Nusayr lived.[131] The majority of 'Alawis are found in Syria and Turkey. Scholars have been unsure about which sect of Shi'ism to associate them with because of their complicated theology and rituals. A central belief in 'Alawism is the idea that Light Souls were materialized into human bodies – a condition aided by 'Ali – which may be redeemed, eventually considering themselves equal to God: "Thus the Light Souls were given the possibility to ascend once more to the seven paradises and return to God, on condition that they understood God's true nature, the *ma'nā*."[132]

'Alawi pilgrimage is directly connected to the belief in Light Souls, which are believed to be "reincarnated in unchanged form, thus guaranteeing the continuous presence of the saints and the sacred on earth, rendered visible by the shrines of Prophets (such as Mūsā, Yūnīs, Miqdād, etc.) in the Hatay region."[133] The 'Alawis name each pilgrimage site after a particular saint, *shaykh*, or prophet, and pilgrimages are directly related to either the belief in the reincarnation of souls or the transmigration of souls.[134] Obviously, this differs greatly from the Twelver belief in visiting shrines for saintly intercession, healing, and blessing, which is not to say that these elements are completely absent from 'Alawi *ziyarat* but that the 'Alawis have their own distinct beliefs related to the rewards of pilgrimage. 'Alawi rituals that are similar to those of other Muslims include kissing the tomb, lighting candles, reciting prayers, and attaching pieces of cloth to objects, although 'Alawis often tie them to trees or to someone's body, as opposed to the more common practice of tying them to the outside of the tomb.[135] 'Alawis believe that the *barakah* of the saint extends to the shrine's surroundings, to both animate and inanimate objects, which explains the practice of tying a sick person's clothes to a tree near the shrine, eating soil from the shrine's surroundings, and lying on the saint's grave.[136]

Khidr (the figure so common in Sufi traditions) plays a prominent role in 'Alawi shrines in Turkey, representing the different places at which Musa (Moses) encountered him, places associated with water and vegetation such as springs and olive or laurel trees.[137] The *khidr-ziyara* at Samandag in southern Turkey, which sits on a beach and is cleansed by the waves each night, is important because, according to 'Alawi tradition, it is the site where Khidr (called *Hizir* in Turkey), Moses, and other prophets met, a representation of the belief that Khidr is the "epiphany of 'Ali" and thus the site is considered equal to Mecca.[138] According to another 'Alawi tradition, the rock contained in the shrine is where Musa fell asleep after crossing the sea, and awakened to find Khidr standing at the rock waiting for him.[139] In some of these shrines, tombs lie at the center, which pilgrims circumambulate and where they offer prayers for dream-quests, surrounded by walls with images of Imam 'Ali, Arabic prayers, and the green pieces of cloth often found at other Islamic pilgrimage sites.[140] Sunni Muslims and Christians also visit these shrines, and in some cases 'Alawi sites are managed by a Sunni, illustrating yet again how Islamic pilgrimage often defies classification along sectarian lines.[141]

The importance of this shrine and others is due in part to the role that 'Ali's assassination plays in 'Alawi history. The 'Alawis avoid performing rituals in mosques because 'Ali was killed in a mosque in Kufa, which is why they have constructed shrines as an alternative space in which to conduct prayers and to "*take the place* of mosques in their customary worship practices."[142] Due to this event, shrines are more important than mosques for the 'Alawis.

The Alevis represent another movement inspired by Imam 'Ali, albeit one that differs greatly from the 'Alawis. Scholars have struggled with whether to understand the Alevis as part of Sufism, Shi'ism, or as a separate tradition altogether: "To name just a few competing stances, one position identifies Alevism with Sufi traditions in Islam, another derives the community's traditions from non-Islamic sources, and yet another situates Alevism in line with Twelver Shi'ism."[143] Originally the Alevis were nomadic, which may explain the amalgamation of Islam and other practices that characterize their traditions.[144] When they settled in Anatolia (between the eleventh and fourteenth centuries), the Alevis encountered challenges based on the differences between their religious practices and those established by Seljuk and Ottoman standards of Islam.[145] Today, they differ from the Turkish Sunni Müslümanlik, the latter characterized by a literal belief in the Qur'an, mosque attendance, and the five pillars, whereas the Alevis self-identify as following *Alevi'nin Šartlari* (the Alevi code), defined by the saying, "Be master of your hands, tongue, and loins."[146] This moral code reflects both general Islamic principles as well as the moral code (*edep*) associated with Sufism.[147]

Alevis and Bektashis, the Sufi order based on the doctrines of Hajji Bektash Wali, were at one time two distinct social groups – the Alevis settling in rural areas and the Bektashis in cities – but today the term "Alevi" is often used to describe both groups.[148] They have similar beliefs and rituals, including those that are focused on pilgrimage. Both groups participate in Sufi traditions including *dhikr* (remembrance) and *sama* (audition, which in this case involves the performance of music to honor Allah). Hajji Bektash, like many saintly figures, is also connected to Khidr.[149] For Alevis, *hajj* is optional, and is considered less important than making people in the community happy.[150] Historically, Alevis have had their own *hajj*-like pilgrimages, which may be part of the reason why the journey to Mecca is optional. During the sixteenth century, under the Ottomans, Bektashi Muslims visited the shrine of Seyyid Gazi, one of two great pilgrimages: "The shrine of Seyyid Gazi hosted the annual sacrificial festival of the Abdals, known as 'the great pilgrimage' (*hācc-i ekber*), one of two annual Bektashi festivals mentioned in the hagiographies of Haci Bektas."[151] For Bektashis, pilgrimage is an activity that is believed to take place in one's soul, a belief that may be based on the Alevi focus on purity and prayer, which is expressed in numerous rituals including the *cem* ceremony.[152] This ceremony, a combination of music, dancing, and singing, is explained as an expression of the Prophet's journey to heaven, which is often cited as the prototype of the inner pilgrimage.[153]

Cemevi – Alevi places of worship – are quite different from mosques, often including symbols that hold meanings distinct to Alevism. One example is the lighting of candles, objects that symbolize saints and their divine light.[154] In addition to the pilgrimage of one's soul and the symbolic pilgrimage contained within the *cem* ritual, Alevis also have pilgrimage sites that are quite popular. Among these is the town of Hacibektas, the burial place of Hajji Bektash Wali.

Figure 3.2 Shrine and museum of Hajji Bektash, Hacibektas, Turkey (photo courtesy of author).

Like many sites in Turkey, it is controlled by the *Diyanet*, the governmental body that controls religious matters according to a particular vision of Islam influenced by Kemalism and Sunni practice. Despite these influences, the town of

Figure 3.3 Triptych of Imam Ali, Hajji Bektash, and Kemal Ataturk (photo courtesy of author).

Hacibektas and its tomb, which is open to the public as a museum, still attract pilgrims from near and far. Near the shrine is a marketplace that features numerous items reflecting Alevism, its dominant figures including 'Ali, Husayn, and Hajji Bektash, and, in the case of the triptych shown in figure 3.3, the careful negotiation of Alevi traditions and Kemalism.

As with many traditions that fall under Islamic pilgrimage, the lines between Shi'i, Sunni, and Sufi are often blurred. The cohabitation of Shi'ism, local tradition, and Sufism that is evident with both the 'Alawis and the Alevis is indicative of larger trends in Islamic pilgrimage, which often does not follow sectarian lines. The religious journeys made by Muslims are rarely exclusivist – a fact that is also evident in Sufi pilgrimages, the focus of the next chapter.

4

SUFI AND SHARED PILGRIMAGES: CONTESTATIONS OF IDENTITY

SUFISM OR ISLAM?

"Sufism" is used in Western academia to refer to the wide set of beliefs, attitudes, and practices describing Muslim devotional and contemplative traditions. It is based on the Arabic word *tasawwuf*, which has a complicated etymology. The word has its origins in one of the following three terms – *suf* (wool), *saf* (pure), or *safwa* (elite) – referring to the wool garment early Sufis wore, the purity of their hearts, or the status of Muhammad's most devoted followers.[1] The word "Sufi" was first "used by and for Mu'tazilites and ascetics with Shi'i tendencies" in the eighth century, when three individuals from Kufa were identified as Sufis, and this was followed by the usage of the word for al-Baghdadi (d. 910) and his students.[2]

Some two thousand definitions of "Sufi" exist in Islamic works alone.[3] Scholars have often defined Sufism incorrectly as a sect alongside Sunni and Shi'i Islam. Sufi orders exist in great variety and may be either Sunni or Shi'i, an identification that is often tenuous. However, even in these cases the sectarian orientation of an order does not always determine which sites pilgrims visit. 'Abd al-Ghani Nabulisi (d. 1731), who spent time in both the Qadariyya and Naqshbandiyya

orders, made several *ziyarat* journeys that included visiting
the companions of the Prophet, 'Alid (Shi'i) martyrs, and
Sufi *shaykhs*, suggesting Sufis have little concern for sec-
tarianism when it comes to pilgrimage.[4] Naqshbandis, who
follow a Sunni teacher, often visit sites readily identifiable as
Shi'i. These examples and others represent the challenges to
scholars, including me, in organizing Islamic pilgrimage into
categories that do not risk collapsing under academic scrutiny.

Sufism is typically presented as an Islamic form of "mysticism," a distinct category of religious experience distinct
from normative practices. This description is problematic
for a number of reasons. For one, Sufism may include a
particular devotional expression that is not necessarily distinct from "normative" Islam. The majority of the world's
Muslims do "Sufi things" such as reciting extra prayers
and visiting graves. Sufis are difficult to identify because
Sufism is rarely a self-referential term. Muslims who follow
a particular teacher (*shaykh*) or perform certain devotional
practices may utilize a Sufi vocabulary, using words like
dhikr and *ziyarat* frequently, but they would not necessarily
call themselves anything but a Muslim.

Despite the continued practice of describing Sufism as a
sect or a distinct community of Muslims, it is really more of
a set of attitudes and practices. Ahmet Karamustafa describes
the central practices of the Sufis of Baghdad in the tenth
century as including separate communities, group travel,
distinct prayers, the performance of music, the recitation of
poetry, initiation practices, and particular sartorial choices
such as the wearing of white robes.[5] This excellent historical
description evolved over time to include more practices. By
the thirteenth century, the elements of Sufism also included
an allegiance to a teacher, devotional rituals such as *sama*
(audition) and *dhikr* (remembrance), retreat (*khalwah*), the
purification of one's soul (or heart) through prayer, and pilgrimage (*ziyarah*).[6] Many of these practices were adopted by

Muslims functioning outside of a Sufi order, and today are seen widely in places like Indonesia, where *dhikr* is heard over a loudspeaker in some villages, and in Sri Lanka, where female *shaykhas* offer blessings in home shrines. For these reasons, we must be careful in using Sufism/Sufi in a way that belies or ignores these realities.

Many of these Sufi attitudes and practices are also reflected in Shi'ism. Islam is marked by much cross-pollination between different intellectual traditions, so it is not surprising that the lines between these are often blurry. Sufism is often described as the result of piety movements – a reaction to the empire and wealth that characterized Islam in the first century after the Prophet's death. Shi'ism is also a reaction to the new political reality of this period. The connections between the two movements is most noticeable in the sixth to ninth centuries, but after the eighth Imam Reza there appears to be a separation due in part to the Shi'i participation in political life and the Sufi tendency to disassociate from political life.[7] This does not mean that Sufi orders are not, at times, politically involved. The Nahdlatul Ulama movement in Indonesia, which has over fifty million members, is aligned with the Naqshbandiyya and Qadiriyyah orders.

The belief in *ziyarat* and in the power of the dead is shared by Sufis – including Sunnis – and Shi'i. Sunni orders, those whose members follow a Sunni *madhhab* (law school), may also be closely aligned with Shi'ism. Members of the order led by Habib 'Umar in Yemen often visit the tombs of the Ba 'Alawi family, and many of the religious teachers associated with the order are *sayyids*, illustrating how the devotion for the Prophet's family, seen in many Sufi orders, has deep Shi'i resonances.[8] The relatives of this family – those relatives of the Prophet who settled in the Hadramawt Valley in southern Yemen – have an extensive cult of saints that reaches all the way to Java, where the descendants act as caretakers (*al-qa'imun bi-l-maqam*) of tombs.[9] Historically, the tombs of the *ahl al-bayt* have been frequented by Sunni and Shiʻi pilgrims in Damascus, Cairo, and elsewhere. "Commemorating the ʻAlid dead did not begin with the Fatimid dynasty," and while the Fatimids promoted pilgrimage to these sites, *ziyarah* was already an established practice.[10]

Pilgrimages associated with saints, teachers, and mystics in Islam are often quite large. In Senegal, members of the Mouridiya order visit Touba, the capital of the founder of the *tariqah* (order), in large numbers, over one million a year.[11] The members of this order number over four million, nearly half the population of Senegal, suggesting once again that the definition of Sufism as a minority or sectarian orientation is deeply problematic.[12] At the tombs at Tarim in Yemen, pilgrims pray for rain and lay basil at the heads of gravestones, practices that are popular and ongoing.[13] Konya boasts millions of visits a year, more than *hajj*. All of these examples suggest that Muslims have numerous practices, which may or may not be tied to a Sufi *tariqah*. This is why Sufi identity is a thorny subject, difficult to define, and, as Ahmet Karamustafa argues, "essentialising approaches that postulate an unchanging core to all Sufi phenomena have certainly occupied a prominent place."[14] It may be best simply to describe these phenomena as "Muslim."

Some scholars have suggested that those who do not participate in Sufi traditions or who are hostile to them are alienated from Islam. This argument is based on the idea that Sufism reflects the practice of Islam before wealth, empire, and decadence corrupted the tradition following the first generations after the Prophet's death. This concern for Islam is not new. Ibn Khaldun argued this point in the fourteenth century. "Ibn Khaldun was also of the opinion that the first three generations of Muslims automatically and naturally practiced *tasawwuf*, which, since it was so widespread, did not require a special designation."[15]

Using Sufism as a category in this chapter is thus somewhat arbitrary. It is intended to allow the reader to think about *ziyarat* in complex ways while being attentive to the differences among Muslim communities. Sufism pervades Muslim life. The best strategy for dealing with these realities is to remember that Sufism is not a category for Muslims; rather, it is a way for scholars to think about a wide field of traditions and experience. Shahzad Bashir describes it as "an analytical horizon" and reminds us that "it is not, in its origins, an internal term but a descriptor employed by Western observers to refer to a diverse array of intellectual and social phenomena relating to those who have called themselves Sufis."[16] It is, in many ways, an unsatisfactory category of meaning.

Islam's focus on sainthood, which has an informal, public process of sanctification, is largely responsible for the huge number of pilgrimage traditions in which we see Muslims participating. As one scholar describes it, "Saints become saints by acclamation."[17] The term "friend of God" is sometimes used to describe saints in the academic literature, reflecting the intimate relationship that the saint and Allah share. The term *wali*, whose root comes from *wala* (to be near) and *waliya* (to govern), translates to "near, friend, protector, or helper."[18] The presence of a religious figure or saint at a site, often through his or her body/relic, is important because of *barakah*, the blessing that Allah bestows on the followers of Islam. In the case of *ziyarat* this power "sanctified a location through the presence or apparent presence of a saint and his personal effects, which became devotional or ritual objects."[19] Pilgrimages to the resting places of these individuals include large tombs, which were sometimes built against the wishes of those they honor. The saint and poet Rumi famously requested to be buried under the blue sky, but was interred in a large tomb, and Shaykh Safi asked to be "buried in a graveyard west of Ardabīl," but was instead interred in his *zawiyah* (place of retreat), which was expanded after his death.[20]

Sufism is often defined in terms of orders (*turuq*), the organizations through which Sufis claim allegiance to a particular lineage of teachers. These guides are often referred to as *shaykhs* (*shayhkas* for female teachers). Sufis go by a number of terms in languages including Arabic, Persian, Urdu, and Bahasa. They include "*marabūt, darvēsh, faqīr, pīr, walī, murshid, Shaykh, majdhūb*, and *qalandar.*"[21] Sufi saints are most often referred to as *awliya*, or the friends of God. Great variety exists within Sufism. In some cases, Sufis are not referred to as one of the *awliya* but by their proper names, or by endearing terms such as *maulana*, "my friend," the common name for Rumi.

Pilgrimage revolves around *barakah*, the sanctifying powers or blessings associated with a prophet, Sufi teacher, *shaykh*, or saint. Recognizing that someone has this quality, which has been defined as "a supernatural power of divine origins," is a way of identifying the Sufi with Prophet Muhammad and is often reflected in statements such as he or she "walks in the Prophet's footsteps" or is a "descendent [*sic*] of the Prophet" (even if the individual is not).[22] The line of transmission (*silsilah*) that originates in the family of the Prophet is carried forth in Sufi lineages. There is a mystical quality to this lineage because the gifts of the Sufi teacher, *shaykh*, or saint are a reflection of Prophet Muhammad's gifts to the world, a reflection of the idea that Allah's blessings are bestowed upon those associated with the Prophet's family and his followers. The love for the Prophet's family can be seen in the love for the Sufi, which is often expressed in performing the same rituals as a *shaykh* did in the past. These acts are not only efficacious (in training the heart to love God) but they show allegiance to the Sufi order. As Nile Green writes, what was done historically is often repeated by successive generations. "In view of the *sajjada nashins*' role as professional mystics, Shah Sa'id was described by Sabzawari as devoted to the different forms of Sufi meditation (*dhikr, muraqaba*). In the mid-1770s, Sabzawari also reported that the shrine's *khanaqah* (lodge) was still the residence of a large number of dervishes as well as local notables (*umara*), who would regularly gather to sit in circles repeating the characteristic loud chant (*dhikr-e jahr*) of the Naqshbandiyya."[23]

As we have seen, pilgrims often travel to a location other than Mecca. Although major sites like the *ka'bah* are dear to Sufis, other cities, towns, and villages also function as sacred centers. They are linked to the hereafter, often through a tomb or cemetery. The case of Touba in Senegal is one example, and is believed to provide a connection to heaven that transcends the "various compartments of the universe."[24] Within Senegal, there are numerous religious centers – Yoff, Cambérène, Tivaouane, Ndiassane, Tiénaba, Médine-Baye, and Médina-Gounas.[25] These places often serve as symbolic substitutions for Mecca, especially for those who cannot afford the *hajj*.

An individual embedded in a Sufi order, studying under a teacher, being part of a community, and working on his or her spiritual development, hopes to gain some of the wisdom of his or her teacher. As Tanvir Anjum explains:

> The Sufi Shaykhs were considered to be the embodied sources of *barakah*, i.e. (spiritual blessings or sanctifying powers). With the development of the *silsilahs*, the Sufi Shaykhs assumed a central position not only in the *silsilah* in doctrinal terms, or in a *khānqāh* in physical terms, but in the entire process of spiritual development and training of a disciple. The Sufi doctrine of *suhbah* (literally meaning companionship) explains it well. The company of a Sufi Shaykh is considered to be a source of spiritual development of a disciple, and is preferred to seclusion.[26]

The *khanaqah* where the teacher resided often became part of a pilgrimage site. For example, lodges (which are also called *tekke* in Turkish) are often located next to graves of famous

Sufis. Sufi groups and local saint traditions may be distinct, yet in support of each other. In Yemen, the link is so close that an attack on the one is viewed as an offense to the other.[27]

In some cases, a Sufi is not part of a *tariqah* but has accrued status due to a genealogical lineage. This is different from the chain of transmission (*silsilah*) that determines the history and leadership of a *tariqah* and instead relies on one's family connections to a particular *shaykh* or other important individual. In Mali, the people known as *ahl Arawan* (the people of Arawan) claim to be descendants of the founding saint of the town, Sidi Ahmad ada Agga, who was a relative of Prophet Muhammad.[28] In South Africa, Badsha Peer is only tenuously connected to a line of Sufis and so he was linked to the Chisti line through the celebration of the death of Chisti saints.[29] These examples suggest that there is a great variance in the ways in which Sufi identities are formulated and legitimized. This lack of formality may also show itself in ritual, when pilgrims participate in less than idealized ways. These examples of "contextual literacy," where the relationships between pilgrims and texts are more important than the texts themselves, are seen in Java, where pilgrims may not understand the Arabic liturgy but are "familiar with the limited evocational base from which the texts emerged."[30] In other words, it is enough that the proper names and a few Arabic words are recognized.[31] This enables the pilgrim to relate to the saint in community with other Muslims, employing a common religious language that crosses linguistic and cultural boundaries.

Sufi writings often argue that Muslims should develop a heightened attention to the world, seeing signs (*ayat*) in nature, reflections of the Divine in the world that surrounds each of us. For many Muslims, the world is an endless series of signs and messages. Muslim pilgrims often visit shrines and other places connected to a natural feature such as a mountain, river, or tree. In Turkey, small pilgrimages are often made during Hidrellez, the festival that commemorates Prophet Hizir, to small shrines with sacred springs.[32] Islamic cosmology provides an intense reflection on the Islamic ethic of sacredness – that it is everywhere and present at every moment. As Karen Armstrong writes, "mosques can be full of lights; birds can fly around during the communal prayer. The world must be invited inside the mosque, not left outside."[33] At the same time, certain sites are marked with *barakah*, a quality associated with individuals whose wisdom, visions, and miracles (*karamat*) are known through a variety of texts including hagiographies, poetry, and music.[34] In other cases, entire landscapes are believed to be special, imbued with a special sacred quality, such as the area surrounding Damascus known as the Ghuta, which is known as the "place over which God spread the span of Gabriel's wings."[35] Medieval Syrian pilgrimage guides reference the holiness of al-Sham,[36] due to God "commanding His angels to protect it with their wings and His Prophets and righteous saints to watch over it and extol its virtues to the believers."[37]

Miracles are often associated with the saints that pilgrims visit. In some cases, these miracles are associated with the saint's lifetime, often as part of a spiritual state that included "inspirations and illuminations."[38] One Javanese site, Tembayat, is the burial site of Sunan Bayat, who reportedly announced the *adhan* (call to prayer), which, because of his holy qualities, was heard over one hundred miles away.[39] In most cases, miracles reflect the traits of a particular saint, functioning as ideological narratives that emphasize the ideal qualities that Muslims should acquire.[40] Miracles may also be connected to the longevity of a saint, such as Ahmad Yasavi, the twelfth-century Central Asian Sufi who lived in a small pit: "He lived in all 120 years, or some say 133 years, and for the rest of his noble life he never left that honored pit, but remained like those who are in their graves, encumbered with exertions within that narrow enclosure."[41]

Sufi hagiographies contain all kinds of stories about miracles, dreams, and other magical happenings that mark the landscape of pilgrimage. As Nile Green writes, "One important contextual function of such texts therefore seems to be as saintly charters for maintaining the prestige of a given shrine by demonstrating the wisdom and miracles (*karāmāt*) of the saint in question. Sufi hagiography was in such ways also a reflection of local geographies of pilgrimage."[42] Stories of dreams are common in these texts and in many cases link a Sufi to one or more pilgrimage sites. In some cases, miracles were realized through a saint's appearance in dreams.[43]

Dreams are also prominent in Shi'i traditions, which presents interesting questions about how we categorize Sufism in relationship to mystical Shi'ism, or for that matter Sunni Islam, which identifies dreams as a form of prophecy.[44] In Shi'ism, Prophet Muhammad's family often appear in dreams to everyone from a Sufi teacher to a young child. "Members of the Ahl-e Bait often appear to Shia in dreams and as apparitions, providing solace, advice, and information about the future."[45] Does this mean that all Shi'i are Sufis because they believe in these prophetic dreams, or that Sufism is a category of religion that is impossible to define? Again, these questions suggest that it is extraordinarily difficult to separate Sufi experience from other Muslim traditions.

If we take Sufi pilgrimage to mean those activities that fall outside of *hajj* and *'umrah*, this leaves us with a very broad definition that encompasses the majority of Muslim religious pilgrimage traditions. Numerous scholars have argued this point, stating that Sufism is simply the form of Islam practiced by the vast majority of the world's Muslims. This opinion is supported by historical evidence that documents longstanding pilgrimage traditions outside sites in Mecca, Medina, and Jerusalem, as well as devotional practices associated with these early centers of pilgrimage. Muslims often recite extra supplications, conduct *dhikr*, and perform other rituals in these cities, as we saw in Chapter 1. However, these practices are not necessarily new. Jerusalem has a long association with devotional practices of individuals we would now call Sufi but who were known as *zuhhad*, "whose custom it was to seclude themselves in the environs of Jerusalem (apparently in imitation of Christian hermits)."[46]

The tendency among scholars has been to describe Sufi pilgrimages as supplementary to *hajj*. However, much like the importance placed on Karbala by Shi'i and its ability to be a substitute for *hajj*, Sufi pilgrimages are not simply extra rituals but can serve as substitutes for Mecca. Such is the case of Tembayat in Java, which not only is modeled after the *ka'bah* (one cannot have light in its inner chamber since there is no light in the *ka'bah*) but is a substitute for it.[47]

> Since the distance between Indonesia and Saudi Arabia is considerable, one can assume that the majority of Indonesian Muslims will never be able to make the *hajj*. That is why several Indonesian locations are considered to be cosmic centers that possess the same degree of spiritual power as can be encountered in Mecca. For example, Javanese Muslims believe that climbing up and down Mount Ciremai in Kuningan three times contains spiritual strength equal to performing the *hajj*.[48]

Such a tradition is unsurprising given the mixture of religious traditions in Indonesia – Hinduism, Buddhism, animism, Christianity, Islam – and the history of Sufism in the archipelago. While Islam was brought to Indonesia by Muslim merchants, from the thirteenth century onwards it was largely spread through "wandering *sūfis* and scholars" whose ideas contributed to the formation of pilgrimage, for "There were highly intricate crisscrossings of scholars within the networks, by way of both their studies of Islamic sciences, particularly *hadīth*, and their adherence to Islamic mystical brotherhoods (*tarīqahs*)."[49]

VISITING THE FRIENDS OF GOD

Scholars of Islam use "saint" to refer to a wide field of Muslims, including great teachers, famous ascetics, and individuals associated with visions or mystical events. Using the term carries the risk of translating Islam into a Christian tradition. It also glosses over important facts, such as that Muslims do not have a unified system for evaluating sainthood and no singular word refers to a special category of humans who are close to God. Muslims may refer to a saint by their name, by a term of endearment, or by *shaykh*, *pir*, or another title. As Bryan S. Turner argues:

> Arabic terms of marabout, darvīsh, sufi, walī cannot be translated into the Christian term 'saint,' because the history, institutions and cultural frameworks of these religions are distinctive. The centralized, complex and stringent process of canonization is crucial to the Christian understanding of saintship. Precisely because no such centralized, ecclesiastical machinery exists in Islam, there is no official or homogeneous terminology of maraboutism (saintship in Islam). When the western anthropologists talk about Islamic saints, they use the term as a shorthand for a diversity of roles.[50]

Sainthood in Islam is a complicated affair. There is no defined process like we find in Catholicism's institution of canonization. For Muslims, sainthood is determined by numerous agents, including supernatural abilities, institutions of political power, genealogical lineages, mystical knowledge, and great intellect. As Alyson Callan writes, "Legitimization of saintly authority occurs both at the level of the individual and at the level of a wider power base," and is affected by the saint's uniqueness as well as his or her relation to "globally shared esoteric knowledge," the saint's possession of supernatural abilities, relationship to a lineage, and blood ties to the Prophet and his family.[51]

Wali (pl. *awliya*) is one of the words commonly used to refer to saints, or what some scholars call the "friends of God." However, a *wali* may or may not be a Sufi, depending on the definitions being used for the two categories of individuals. A *wali* may perform miracles, or they may not, and as one scholar points out, "In a strictly morphological sense, the walî is not necessarily a Sufi."[52] *Wali* takes on different meanings depending on one's cultural and religious community. In Pakistan, a number of historical and religious individuals are featured in Sufism, and are the focus of pilgrimages, as well as appearing in poster art. They are established by popularity: "A saint, who is recognized and respected as such by *vox populi*, that is to say by public consent, is called *wali* (pl. *awliya*)."[53] In Java, *awliya* does not refer to poets and mystics in the tradition of Rumi, Rabi'ah, and Hafiz, but to the nine founders of Islam in Indonesia. These nine individuals are considered the first religious council and are different according to where one is in Java, representing local shifts in tradition that reflect hagiographical differences.[54] These variations determine some of the variety in pilgrimage traditions we see in Java.

In many places, the concept of sainthood is not situated in Arab-Muslim understandings of Islam, but rather in an indigenous culture far removed from historical centers of Muslim power, such as Cairo, Qom, and Mecca. In Indonesia, the cult of the saints associated with the Yogyakarta sultanate is imbedded in Javanese Islam, resulting in a language that is more Javanese than Muslim, and more animist, Hindu, and local than transnational. Some of the terms commonly used for "Sufis" are not even employed in Indonesia, while in other cases Arabic words exist in Indonesian form. *Kramat* is the Bahasa word for "the religious attainment of saints" and *kramatan* refers to "a holy grace or shrine," while *berkah* is a cognate of *barakah*, the Arabic word often used for blessing.[55] These examples show how complicated the vocabulary of Sufism is.

To illustrate this point further, let us take the example of the *wali*, who is often referred to as a saint. The *awliya Allah* are thought of as companions of God – those individuals who are loved by Allah. The friends may be associated with miracles or visions, and often have the gift of clairvoyance (*firasat*), but they are rarely martyrs. In some cases, a *wali* may be sanctified by his relationship with a political leader, an act that in turn legitimizes his authority or the *tariqah* with which he is associated. Such is the case of Baba Tahir and Sultan Tughril, one of many examples of the cohabitation of Sufism and politics.[56] The friends of God have great power. As Omid Safi writes, *awliya* may even cause their "ill-wishers to go blind, mute, or drop dead," as in the case of Ahmad-i Jam who struck one man with muteness, caused another to drop dead, and blinded a woman.[57]

The visitation of *awliya* is the central Sufi practice focused upon in this chapter; thus, it is important to understand how and why certain individuals gain this status. Devotion (*iradat*) is a central part of Sufi practice, and, in pilgrimage, it survives the death of the *wali*. During their lifetime, saints' religious powers are available to their followers and once the saint dies, this power remains accessible at his or her resting place. Shrine visitation became an important practice for many reasons. Among these is that without the reverence for the bodies of the dead, the power of the *tariqah* would be lost and the saint would be forgotten. In the Chisti context, mystical uses of shrine visitation were common. In one case from the seventeenth century, a graveside meditation (*dhikr-e-kashf-e-qubur*) was capable of revealing a saint's spiritual states, and even more casual meetings of Sufis at graves might elicit a mystical experience.[58]

Narratives about the *awliya* are located in Sufi hagiographies and extra-Qur'anic texts that range from poems to biographies. It is often the case that pilgrimages are situated in family histories connected to Prophet Muhammad, or that he is featured in a narrative about a sacred site, appearing in a dream or vision. In other cases, another figure dominates the stories surrounding a *wali* and his or her shrine. Al-Khidr, also known as Khizr or "the green one," is one such figure. Associated with many saints, he is the unnamed companion of Moses cited in the Qur'an (18.59–81) who is at times related to Elijah (Ilyas), St. George, a Hindu figure, and others.[59] Khidr is often described as the most loyal follower of Allah and is associated with countless Muslim figures, pilgrimages, and sacred places.[60]

Visions of Khidr are very common in Islam and are often attached to sacred sites and saintly figures. In fact, they are so common that sightings of Khidr are believed to be connected to all saintly figures, owing perhaps to the belief that he is active today, "still alive and flying continuously around the earth."[61] As discussed in the previous chapter, Khidr is very popular in the 'Alawi tradition. In these cases, Khidr, who is called Hizir in Turkey, is connected to dreams in which he appears at a wide array of sites ranging from those dedicated to Sunni Imams to 'Alawi saints.[62] Khidr is referenced in numerous Muslim communities around the world. In Indonesia, the saint Kalijaga is believed to have been initiated into Sufism by Khidr, a point made by Albertus Bagus Laksana: "There is no shrine associated with al-Khadir in Muslim Java, but his role as the teacher *par excellence* of the highest level of Islamic mystical knowledge is secured in various Javanese texts."[63]

The majority of *awliya* are men. However, there are many cases of female *awliya*. Rabia al-Adawiya is one of the most prominent of these. Like other saints, she is known for her piety and dedication to the contemplative life, as well as numerous visions and miracles. Among these are the dream of Rabia's father in which Prophet Muhammad announces her religious superiority and the lantern that floated above her head, which emanated a holy radiance.[64] Her grave was a focus of veneration, as is the case with many Sufis, and survives today.[65] As Rkia Elaroui Cornell points out in her dissertation, the location of Rabia's grave, which is in Basra, is often confused with another Rabi'a (Rabi'a bint Isma'il of Damascus) who is buried in Jerusalem.[66]

Female saints are not only located in the past. In Sylhet, Bangladesh, living female saints known as *firani* (*fir* is the Sylheti cognate of *pir*, a common word used for male saint) are associated with pilgrimage sites known as *mukam*s (shrines), the Bangladeshi version of the Arabic *maqam*, or tomb/shrine.[67] In Konya, the site of several tombs of female saints, independent Sufi teachers unaligned with Sufi orders run by men serve as *ana*s, or mothers, who guide women in *dhikr*, the mystical chanting or meditative practice common among Sufis.[68] Bangladesh and Turkey are but two examples of the involvement of women in pilgrimage, either as the focus of *ziyarat* or in the role of shrine guides. Iran has a strong shrine culture as well, embedded in a mixture of Shi'ism, Sufism, and local tradition that is, in the words of one scholar, characterized by "a coexistence" that was often the furthest thing from antagonistic, and was part of "the process of reinterpretation and transformation" that marks so much of Islamic history.[69] In Syria, women known as *'alawiyya* (a female descendant of 'Ali and Fatima) perform rituals and ceremonies and act as go-betweens for the pilgrim and the saint.[70] These individuals provide special access to the saint.

The determination of who is a saint or Sufi is one complicated by local practices and traditions. Rumi, Hajji Bektash, and other *awliya* are important saints in Turkey. In Iran, Iraq, and Syria, the cult of saints that pilgrimage revolves around includes the relatives of Prophet Muhammad (the *ahl al-bayt*) as well as others. In Indonesia, saints include Sufi teachers, ancestors, parents, children, and infants. In Java, the descendants of the Ba 'Alawi, the Prophet's relatives, are often connected to pilgrimages, representing the diaspora of his large and extensive family.[71] This "extension" of the cult of saints includes the beliefs that parents, even when dead, serve as mystical guides and that children, who are without sin, are unified with Allah – constituting a sainthood that is completely removed from the institution of *turuq* (Sufi orders) that defines Sufism in most scholarship.[72] Furthermore, numerous Muslim sites, which are often classified as "Sufi," are related to prophets, not saints. The tombs found in South and Southeast Asia known as *nau-gaz*, which are up to 175 yards long, provide one example of how diverse Sufi pilgrimages are and questions the very definitions of "Sufi" that are often given.[73] Given all of these facts, I have chosen to include a wide array of individuals who may be considered saints, Sufis, both, or neither. This provides a way to illustrate the rich culture of pilgrimage among Muslims without being trapped by the amorphous categories I have pointed out thus far.

TOMBS AND MAUSOLEUMS

Pilgrimage to shrines housing relics and the bodies of the relatives of Prophet Muhammad, teachers, *shaykhs*, mystics, political leaders, and others are so common in Islam that it would be impossible to catalogue every site. The popular saying of Egyptian Muslims, "God has forbidden the earth to consume the bodies of the saints," reflects the importance that Muslims place on the dead.[74] In Iran, followers of Shaykh Safi believed in this so strongly that his son's ablution water was viewed as "imbued by beneficial effect, as *tabarruk*" (blessed).[75] Many pilgrimages involve visiting a relic of the

Prophet, such as a hair, a piece of clothing, or a sandal (*na'a al-nabi*), objects many wished to be buried with and that were believed to emit *barakah*. The veneration of the Prophet's sandal is documented in historical records and other sources in the Maghrib, Egypt, Syria, and Turkey, suggesting that the practice of visiting the Prophet's relics has been widespread for quite some time.[76]

As we have seen, the belief that the body of an individual remains powerful after death is widespread in Islam. This is not a belief restricted to Shi'i or to Muslims who practice traditions associated with Sufism. For many Muslims, the saint, *shaykh*, or other venerated individual is "virtually alive, not only in spirit but in body as well."[77] And the saint's body is not the only location of power. Numerous sites include a sacred field of space radiating from the grave or tomb that encloses a large landscape with *barakah*. In Bangladesh, even the natural wildlife that surrounds the shrine (often called a *majar*, from the Arabic *mazar*) is considered holy. The black soft-shell turtles attached to the shrine of Sultan-ul-Arefin Bayzid Bostami are special because it is believed "that these turtles were brought and introduced to the Bostami pond by the Sufi himself."[78]

The tradition of constructing tombs is not restricted to saints. In many cases Muslims visit the graves of important teachers and intellectuals, ancestors or companions of the Prophet and his relatives. Damascus alone is the site of the graves of three of Muhammad's wives as well as Bilal ibn Hamama (the first *me'edhdhin* – that is, the first person who gave the call to prayer), Abu al-Darda, Fadala ibn Ubayd, Sahl ibn Hanzaliyya, and other companions of Muhammad.[79] These tombs are found in many places including graveyards and *madrasah*s that were often, but not always, associated with Sufi *turuq* (orders). The construction of tombs in *madrasah*s was done, in part, to discourage the practice of praying at a grave, out of fear that it might lead to "idolatry of the dead."[80] Of course, Muslims ended up doing this anyway, disregarding the concern of the *ulama* who wanted to regulate prayer and guarantee their position in society through the *madrasah*.[81] The *madrasah* was composed of the *iwan* (an open hall), *khalwah* (lodgings for students and teachers), and the *junayna* (courtyard), but typically had a number of ancillary attachments – a library, a Sufi monastery, an orphan's school, and a tomb.[82] As was often the case for places that hosted pilgrims, Syria includes a wide variety of tombs and other structures that suggest just how rich pilgrimage culture has been since the early centuries of Islam. One survey of Hama suggests the incredible diversity of shrines, graves, and tombs that exists:

> the maqām of Zayn al-'Abidīn, the maqām of Ja'far al-Tayyār, the tomb of Jonah in the Hasanayn Mosque, the tomb of Ham the son of Noah, the maqām of David, the tomb of the Emīr Sārim al-Dīn al-Nābulsī, the tombs of soldiers who fought with Salāh al-Dīn (Shaykh Muhammad Nahār and Shaykh Suweyd), the tombs of famous Muslim scholars (Abū al-Layth al-Samarqandī, Shaykh 'Alwān Abū Muhamad 'Alī b. 'Atīya, al-Shīrāzī, Shaykh Khallūf, al-Birmawī, al-Sālūsī, al-Muzaffar, Shaykh Ma'rūf, Umays al-Qaranī, Shaykh 'Ambar, Abū al-Wafā al-Hawrānī, Shaykh 'Abash, Sayyida Nafīsa, Shaykh Abū al-'Adīmnāt, Shaykh Hasan, Shaykh Mas'ūd, Shaykh Maknūn, and Shaykh Bashīr), the mazār of al-Husayn, and the maqām of 'Abd al-qādir al-Kīlānī.[83]

Shrines also function as social centers and places of rest, conversation, and community. In the case of the Tijani *zawiyah* (a space where Muslims do *dhikr*, the ritual remembrance of God) in Fez:

> "visiting" Ahmad al-Tijani may mean different things and includes a variety of activities. Some visitors position

themselves in front of the tomb, touching the railing and murmuring prayers, while others sit on the floor in front of the tomb. For some of the women the *zawiya* is a place to meet or take naps in one of the corners. Some of them do not seem to be interested in visiting the saint at all. Instead of going to the tomb, they sit or lie down and chat with other visitors while their children run around and play. Others seem to be just there out of curiosity.[84]

Muslim pilgrims often seek spaces in which they can perform devotional practices, but this is not always the case. Pilgrimage is also a social activity and at times a form of tourism.

In some cases, there is a history of devotional practices, commemorative architecture, and other evidence of a piety movement or contemplative community that is no longer active or has waxed and waned. One example of this is found in Indonesia, where the existence of approximately 1,500 Islamic funerary monuments, or tombstones, suggests that visiting the dead is a part of Muslim-Malay tradition dating back at least several hundred years.[85] The tombstones, which have more than 400 decorative elements, are found all over the archipelago, and at one point were highly decorated; a selection of the Malaysian ones were gilded and encrusted with precious stones.[86] The origins of these stones are probably Hindu or/and Buddhist, adopted by Muslims, and, like other traditions in Indonesia, reflect the poly-religious nature of Indonesian Islam. The fact that so much time and expense was dedicated to gravestones suggests that visiting graves is an old and widespread practice, which still exists today. The declining popularity of these stones corresponds with the introduction of more conservative schools of Islamic thought in the seventeenth century that continued with the spread of Wahhabism, whose followers "would oppose grave markers such as *batu Aceh* with their mixture of Islamic and pre-Islamic features and sophisticated decorations."[87]

Many Sufi pilgrimages are focused on visiting a dead body or relic, which are often but not always connected to Prophet Muhammad. The body of the saint is identified with Allah's blessings – *barakat* – as well as with the love of the Prophet and, by extension, his followers. The importance of the body is often linked to Mecca and to the *ka'bah* as the center of the Muslim ritual. The saint's body is typically buried so his or her head is directed toward Mecca, a practice that identifies the *axis mundi* to other Muslims, who are buried in this way. In some cases, the saint's body is also surrounded by flowers, candles, gifts, and other offerings. In one shrine in Pakistan, elaborate rituals are involved with these items:

> The grave's head faces west, towards Mecca. It is decorated with flowers and with intricately embroidered *chaddars*. At its foot are two containers of salt. People prostrate themselves at the foot of the grave or its sides, kissing its edge and tasting a pinch of salt. The area around the grave is carpeted. Two *hafiz* recite the Qur'an day and night through a microphone. They arrived when the *pir* was very ill and now reside permanently in the *darbar*, disrupting the deep silence of the valley with their continuous praying.[88]

Pilgrimage sites, which include shrines, tombs, and other structures, often house a relic of Prophet Muhammad. In Kandahar, Afghanistan, pilgrims visit a shrine that houses the Prophet's cloak. In a room adjoining Rumi's grave in Konya, pilgrims line up to see the Prophet's hair, bending down to inhale a sandalwood scent through a small opening, an action that is believed to result in a possible blessing. The footprint of the Prophet is called *Qadam Rusul* and is housed in shrines known as Qadam Sharif or Qadam Rasul Allah.[89] In India, these shrines are often called *qadamgahs* ("foot spaces") and not only house the footprint of the Prophet, but also may include the footprint of another Muslim figure like 'Ali, the Prophet's cousin and son-in-law.[90]

Shrines containing footprints are quite common in Islam. Often originating in distant lands, the stones containing body prints mark sacred territory far outside of the Mecca–Medina axis.[91] Footprints (and handprints) are found in various locations besides India, including Egypt, Turkey, Sri Lanka, and Iran. Like other relics, they are loci of *barakah*, constituting "commemorative places, such as shrines, portative holy objects, such as copies of the Qur'an and the sandal of the Prophet Muhammad."[92] The footprints of the Prophet are not only found at shrines, but are also housed in museums (such as the one at Topkapi Palace in Istanbul), serve as the foundations of mosques, and are included in the tombs of sultans and other politicians (Sultan 'Abd al-Hamid I, for example), all of which constitute pilgrimage sites.[93]

Footprints in Islamic pilgrimage are a widespread phenomenon. In India, numerous copies were made of these footprints and used ritually, suggesting that even a semblance of the original is valued.[94] Numerous festivals attracting both locals and pilgrims from afar feature a footprint. In India, these occasions include the period before the Prophet's death (*Barah Wafat*), during which the "Blessed Foot" is fanned, as if it were a living member of a royal family, and performance of the sandal ceremony, during which:

> A sandalwood paste is placed on a model of the Prophet's steed Buraq which is then carried in procession to the place where the footprint is kept. On reaching the spot where the footprint is kept, the fatiha [the opening chapter of the Qur'an] is recited, and each of the devotees rubs a little paste on the footprint. As vows are sworn, offerings are made to the footprint.[95]

For Shi'i Muslims, who believe that Prophet Muhammad's *barakah* is especially powerful in his lineage, the footprints of the Imams and their relatives also dominate many pilgrimages. At Qadamgah in Shiraz, the footprint of Husayn's brother 'Abbas is the focus of circumambulation, around which pilgrims pray and listen to religious sermons.[96]

Of course, not all relics are related to Prophet Muhammad or his family, even tangentially. One case is the Bangladeshi living saint Shuli Firani, who having had a vision of a stone in her belly that coincided with the miraculous appearance of a stone then built a *makam* (tomb or shrine) to protect it.[97] The stone, which was placed with other miraculous items that healed the pilgrims who visited the small shrine, became a center of prayer, fasting, and Qur'an recitation.[98] The focus of pilgrimage is also not necessarily focused on a saint, living or dead. In China, pilgrims visit tombs and graves at important times like *mawlid* (a birthday celebration, usually of the Prophet Muhammad), during the month of Ramadan, and on Fridays after prayer; they offer prayers and also honor the dead in particularly Xinjiang ways such as through practice of the "pole fixation," where a pole is tied with colored flags (*'alam*) to honor the saint and scare away evil spirits.[99] This region, referred to as *Altishahr* by its people, is full of such sites, as well as larger tombs more reminiscent of a *masjid* or shrine complex.[100] There are also examples of pilgrimages that refer to another place. In Pakistan, "memorial shrines" are far removed from the body or relic. In these cases, pilgrims visit the *dargah* (shrine) in order to pay respects to the individual to which it refers.[101]

Pilgrimage does not always involve a built structure. Sufi texts often focus on contemplation of the world that surrounds humans – the sky, earth, forests, streams, and fields of flowers. This meditation on the natural world is reflected in pilgrimage practices. In Bosnia, the landscape is sacred, dotted with holy sites that include tombs but also springs, hills, trees, and caves, sites of ritual activity that are "conceived of as sources of personal blessing (*bereket*), fortune and luck (*hair, sreca*), and the good life."[102] The Ajvatovica pilgrimage is the site of a miraculous spring attributed to Hajdar-dedo Karic, who spent forty days praying to Allah and on the fortieth day dreamt of two white rams colliding, awaking to find a large rock split in half – behind which was a hidden spring.[103] In another Bosnian example, outdoor prayers for rain are sometimes held at sacred sites completely unrelated to a *wali*. These ceremonies (*dove za kisu*) are held at sacred nature sites (*doviste*) ranging from hilltops to lime trees.[104]

A number of rituals associated with pilgrimage are part of *tasawwuf*, or Sufism. These include *sama* (audition) and *dhikr* (remembrance). *Sama* is often performed at pilgrimage sites, as is *dhikr*, and *khalwah* (retreat) may take place at or near tombs, shrines, and other spaces associated with Sufi teachers and saints. Rituals vary quite a bit. The grave of the Javanese saint Sunan Bayat is often slept upon as part of the pilgrimage, a practice less commonly associated with Islamic pilgrimages than circling the tomb, kissing it, and offering prayers to the dead.[105] The Sufis associated with the Hadramat 'Alawi of Yemen visit the graves of their ancestors and the tomb of Prophet Hud, among others; however, in other orders, *ziyarat* may involve ancestors and prophets, but also natural sites, such as mountains, rocks, and springs.[106]

Sama (also spelled *sema*) is a performative act. The musical tradition known in Turkish as *ilahi*s (songs of praise) is associated with Naqshbandi Sufis. For those who participate in it, it is viewed as an audition, or *sama*, for Allah, a way of honoring the love Sufis have for God, the prophets, and saints. The form of *sama* associated with Rumi – a kind of whirling dance – is related to his order and, in particular, with Konya, the city where he is buried. In particular, Sufis believe that Rumi's teacher Shams taught him the dance, which today serves as the hallmark of his order's practices and is often identified with the city of Konya. Interestingly, during his lifetime the whirling was strongly criticized. As one scholar notes, "In fact, some people in Konya complained about Rumi's *sema'*, believing that, it was either not permitted in Islam or caused disturbances and noise. Nevertheless, Rumi predicted that the people of Konya would love and need *sema'* in the future."[107]

Sama is often performed at Sufi shrines during pilgrimage. The large musical performances commonly associated with Sufis in Pakistan and India are one example. These communal gatherings may feature male or female singers and the music performed, such as Qawwali, is immensely popular in South Asia, sold in stores, and even featured in popular music (the late Nusrat Ali Khan was featured in a popular song by the Cranberries, an Irish band). The public type of *sama* seen today is quite different from the tradition that existed four or five hundred years ago, when it was often restricted to practicing Sufis. In these cases, a particular room or space was used, such as the Persian *maydan-i sama*, and only true believers were permitted to participate in the various types of *sama*, such as *tajawud* (*sama* of the body), *wajd* (*sama* of the heart), and *wajud* (*sama* of the spirit).[108] Music was also played, and continues to have a role in these traditions. Sufi poetry, which is often reflected in *ilahi*s, can tell stories about the visitation of graves, tombs, and other sites. *Ilahi*s and other devotional songs are performed at the site of graves and other holy places, principally by Naqshbandis, whose song lyrics often mention saints and other holy people they wish to visit.

Dhikr is another important Sufi practice that means "remembrance," referring to the remembrance of Allah. Described in various ways – as spiritual exercises, chanting, or contemplative recitation – the practice of *dhikr* constitutes a repetition of words and phrases that are intended to become "part of the utterer's inner constitution."[109] When performed as part of pilgrimage, it is considered especially worthy in the eyes of Allah. Among some Nubian Muslims, *dhikr* is performed often, including at shrines: "In addition, individual Nubians often went to a shrine in the vicinity and made a vow to the saint to whom they promised a *karāma* (vow fulfillment) in return for favors. This frequently involved a dhikr following a communal feast."[110] In other cases, Muslims may perform *dhikr* inside the shrine, in a prayer room, or at a graveside, all places that they feel are religiously efficacious.

ZIYARAT

As we have seen, the pilgrims who visit Sufi tombs and other sites are diverse – Sunnis, Shi'i, nonsectarian Muslims, and others. Because Sufism is not a sect but an orientation or set of practices, it is challenging to distinguish these pilgrimages from others. For some, Mecca is considered a Sufi site, along with the other places visited on *hajj*. In fact, the Qur'an suggests that at Muzdalifah, the halfway point between Mina and Arafat, a ritual of *dhikr* is required.[111] Qur'an 2:200 refers to this tradition. *Dhikr* – the Islamic notion of "remembrance of Allah" – should be in the hearts of the believers during the entire journey, at every step and with every breath. In fact, Muslims often perform the contemplative and pious traditions identified with Sufism while on pilgrimage. Pilgrims visiting Mecca and Medina for the *hajj* might perform supplemental prayers or gather for *dhikr* in a clandestine setting such as a hotel room. These activities are carried on today despite the prohibitions against them that are rooted in the Wahhabi movement of the eighteenth century. As Khaled Abou El Fadl reminds us, the Wahhabis "criminalized all forms of Sufi chants and dances in Mecca and Medina, and eventually in all of Saudi Arabia."[112] However, this does not mean that people have not found alternative ways of participating in these traditions.

The tombs and shrines associated with particular orders (*turuq*, sing. *tariqah*) constitute many of the sites associated

Figure 4.0 Pilgrims at Islamic shrine, Hyderabad, India (photo courtesy of Alex Shams).

with Sufi, or Muslim, pilgrimage. In these cases, the follow-ers of an order often visit a deceased teacher or saint. These places are numerous and diverse, located in Africa, South and Central Asia, China, the Middle East, and Europe.

A dervish in the Naqshbandi order may travel to East Africa to visit a saint's grave associated with another *tariqah*. Mevlevi Sufis typically visit sites far beyond Rumi's great tomb in Konya and indeed far beyond the borders of Turkey. The allegiance to a particular order does not preclude one from visiting the graves of those outside one's immediate community, in part because Sufis often have transnational relationships and in part because they seek guidance and blessings from numerous individuals.

Muslims may visit the graves, tombs, and shrines of the *awliya* (friends of God) at any time but they often make these journeys in order to be present during special occasions, such as the *'urs* (death anniversary) of the saint, Ramadan, or the Islamic New Year. Many of these pilgrimages are grand affairs with large numbers of people, ceremonies, and distinct rituals that are related to a particular shrine, *tariqah* (Sufi order), or local community. Every year in Konya, thousands of pilgrims attend the *'urs* for Rumi, which is one of the larger examples of such gatherings. Smaller pilgrimages are also common, such as the *hawl* (death anniversaries) in Java that commemorate the death of a holy person or revered scholar.[113] In some cases, "visiting" a place may involve a transitory practice, such as the "drive through" visits common in Uzbekistan, when visitors drive by a cemetery, giving *sadaqa* (charity) to people sitting alongside the road.[114]

South Asia is populated with Muslim shrines that are visited by Sufis and others, including Hindus. In India, mausoleums, graves, lodges, and other places associated with a Sufi are visited as a part of pilgrimage. In the case of Mu'in al-Din, his mausoleum, meditation center, and places associated with his life are visited – including the place where he died, which is now a *khanaqah*.[115] Each year at the shrine of the seventeenth-century poet Shah Husain, an elaborate festival of lamps (*mela chiraghan*) commemorates his death and is attended by a wide segment of people from Lahore and beyond.[116] As is the case with many Sufi pilgrimages, the pilgrims to Shah Husain participate in a large variety of activities – prayer, music, dance, and *dhikr*.

At pilgrimage festivities the lines between Sunni and Shi'i are often very blurred, or simply do not matter. At the shrine of Lal Shahbaz Qalandar, the drumming is understood as the *azhan*, or call to prayer, and the accompanying dancing is believed to be a performance of 'Ali's circling of the Prophet, who identified him as his successor.[117] This does not keep Sunni Muslims from participating, however. In addition to the blurring of sectarian identities, multiple religious traditions are often present at pilgrimage sites. These include numerous shrines in India where Hindu gods, heroes, springs, and trees were then identified with Muslim saints, providing a way for Islam to encompass sacred spaces that would otherwise be excluded from *ziyarat*.[118]

As mentioned earlier, Sufi pilgrimages are not always focused on a particular *tariqah*. In many cases multiple Sufi communities, and those outside these communities, visit a tomb of a religious figure who is often an important part of political history. Such is the case of Hajdar-dedo Karic, credited with bringing Islam to the Balkans and identified as a scholar, founder of a mosque, and *wali*.[119] Like many Muslim pilgrimage sites, this mosque is associated with healing and miracles. The oldest tomb in the mosque collects water in a pit that is used for healing and blessings and the mosque is reportedly impervious to fire, withstanding several arson attempts during the Second World War.[120] In Tajikistan, the Kyrgyz visit numerous graves that are not connected to mystics, but to martyrs who defended their land from Mongol soldiers, Qing warriors, and Red Army officers.[121] These pilgrimages are political events that involve Sufi beliefs like the bestowment of blessings (*bereke*) from the dead and the importance of saying prayers (*du'a/pata kyluu*) at shrines (*mazar*).[122] In these cases, traditions are embedded in national history and in particular in the current social position of the Kyrgyz and their status as ethno-religious outsiders in national politics.

As discussed so far, what pilgrims do at sacred sites varies significantly. This includes liturgical practices. Prayers and supplications exist in great variety in Islam, ranging from the daily *salat* (the prescribed daily prayers) to the recitation of prayers like *du'a kumayl* that Shi'i say on Thursday evenings. In Java, *salat* and *donga* (*du'a*) are important parts of pilgrimage – especially efficacious during nighttime – at shrines, caves, graves, and other sacred sites.[123] Prayers may be said in Arabic or the vernacular language, which is most often Bahasa. *Donga* may be memorized and recited on many occasions, but may also be collected into mystical manuals called *primbon*, which are used for activities ranging from waking up in the morning and starting one's day to more serious events such as asking for forgiveness or undertaking a pilgrimage.[124]

While prayer and supplications, *sama*, and *dhikr* are often part of shrine activity, outside of these rituals there is a vast assortment of ways in which the pilgrim relates to the saint, the body, and the larger social community. For example, at the shrines of female saints in Konya, people light candles, place wishing stones on the tomb, tie beads and cloth pieces to trees, press their bodies against the walls of the building enclosing a tomb, circle a grave, throw money at a tomb, and pray.[125] At the mosque of Hajdar-dedo Karic in Bosnia, pilgrims recite the Qur'an (*hatma dove*), sing songs (*ilahija*), say prayers for Ottoman and Bosnian martyrs (*tevhid*), and perform *dhikr* (*kijam zikr*).[126] The burning of candles is a practice that can be found centuries earlier. At Panchakki in India, pilgrims used oil lamps to burn sandalwood, camphor, and myrrh in honor of saints.[127] At the shrine of Mu'in al-Din Chisti in Ajmer, India, pilgrims rub their forehead at the shrine's entrance.[128] The inscriptions that surround the tomb not only praise the saint but also relate him to the beauty of the space, praising "the saint as a precious pearl, a reference to the pearl-like quality of the tomb's marble fabric and dome."[129] Pilgrims prostrate to his tomb and kiss it, throw rose petals over his grave, and tie strings to the pierced-marble screens that surround the tombs that are removed once the prayers are given.[130] Places associated with other Muslims are also important stops, such as the cave where Mu'in al-Din's friend and fellow Sufi Qutb al-Din did his meditation.[131] In China, pilgrimage traditions include devotional singing, dancing, wrestling, tightrope walking, and a wide assortment of offerings like horse tails, dolls (*qorchaq*), goat horns, and talismans.[132] For some, these traditions are considered outside the Islamic tradition because they originated elsewhere. However, for these pilgrims they *are* performing Islam.

SUFI AND SHARED PILGRIMAGES: MUSLIMS AND NON-MUSLIMS

Sufi pilgrimage poses a challenge to scholarly typologies and categories, a point made at the beginning of this book. Javanese pilgrimage is one case that resists categorization. Many of the practices and traditions associated with Java are Islamic, but they are also Hindu, Buddhist, animist, or some combination. Pilgrims may perform a local type of meditation, read the Qur'an, and honor a Javanese ancestor all at once. The Indonesian case suggests that Islamic pilgrimage is fluid, dynamic, and often multi-traditional. In other contexts a Muslim person may be considered a saint by non-Muslims, such as in the case of the hero spirits popular among the Christian Maris and Mordvins of Russia, who both venerate Sultan Keremet.[133]

In Yogyakarta, the local sultanate constitutes the cult of saints and their state buildings function as shrines that contain religious power. The descendants of the sultans are the former Hindu and early Muslim rulers of Java. Politically and ritually, the power of the sultan is expressed in state ceremonies that release certain amounts of power that are determined to "maintain the stability and prosperity of the kingdom."[134] In this case, the saint is not a Sufi teacher or mystic like Rumi, but a member of the royal family associated with this region of Java. In this part of Indonesia, the sultan is the representation of "the Divine on earth, expressing God's norm of earthly existence via perfection of the arts, architecture and etiquette in Kraton culture."[135] The *kraton*, or palace, is the mystical center of this power, a structure that contains heirlooms (*pusaka*) of the saints but is also a cosmological representation of the universe.[136]

Pilgrimage to the *kraton* is an important and popular tradition for many Javanese Muslims. This is a palace, not a Sufi *tekke* or grave, yet it is believed to be equally sacred – its status tied to the sultan. Pilgrims believe that the power present in the structure is fluid, emanating at different times and places – although Thursday night is considered particularly important.[137] This is significant because it is the same day that Shi'i and various Sufi traditions gather to pray. In the case of the *kraton*, "On Thursday evenings hundreds of people from all over Java spend the night walking around the palace, hoping to obtain a bit of the power of the sultan."[138]

The indigenous Javanese religious tradition known as *kejawén* is characterized by Muslim practices that have an independent, non-authoritarian flavor. *Kejawén* Muslims pray, but typically not five times a day; they fast, but often not during Ramadan; and they honor specific utilitarian objects, usually swords and daggers, that are believed to be powerful.[139] Similar to some other Sufi traditions, the followers of *kejawén* often do *ziyarat* at night, believing the nights preceding Tuesday and Friday to be most auspicious.[140] These are, not coincidentally, the same nights that Shi'i Muslims often say their prayers. Thursday nights are traditionally the times when Sufi orders gather to say *dhikr*. What is particular to the Javanese case is the combination of Javanese and Islamic calendars: "When certain days of the Javanese week (that has five days) coincide with the Islamic seven-day week, it will be considered a good time for *ziarah*. In cycles of thirty-five days, certain favorable combinations occur."[141]

In addition to the Hindu ancestors of the Muslim sultans who rule Yogyakarta and surrounding areas, Buddhist influences can be felt in Java. In the case of Tembayat (Sunan Bayat, also known as the Adipati), the narrative surrounding the saint mirrors that of the Buddha, with an abandonment of riches, devotion to meditation, and performance of miracles.

> After being called to embrace Islam repeatedly, the Adipati left his riches and power behind and devoted himself to prayer, meditation and the preaching of Islam. Already during his lifetime Sunan Bayat became a famous religious teacher who regularly performed miracles. He gathered a great following of students around him, who immediately after his death built him a great tomb, after which Sunan Bayat's fame grew even more.[142]

As discussed earlier in this chapter, the *'urs* (death anniversary) of a saint is often the focus of *ziyarat*. In South Africa, the *'urs* of the nineteenth-century saint Badsha Peer is an occasion for pilgrimage, with attendants ranging from pilgrims to locals seeking entertainment and selling trinkets and souvenirs.[143] The rituals at a 2002 *'urs* included devotional singing, skin and body piercings, prayers, music (*sama*), the Sundal procession (which includes attendants carrying sandalwood paste and covers for the graves at the shrine), and the laying of an elaborate flower decoration of over 1,500 carnations on the *chadar* (cover) that adorns the grave.[144] These traditions are not South African, but South Asian, part of the Indian communities from the continent that live in the country today. Much like the *hajj*'s pre-Islamic origins, Sufi pilgrimage is often inspired by other traditions. In South Africa, the influence of Hindu dance on performances like *ratieb* and *khalifah* (the striking of the body with sharp instruments) and of Christian rituals (such as candle lighting) on Sufi practices is well documented.[145]

Hinduism is seen in many Islamic traditions in India and Pakistan, including those connected to Muslim shrines and pilgrimage. In the case of the Madariya Sufis, the adoption of Hindu practices includes the rubbing of ashes on the body, the wearing of chains to suppress sexual desire, the ingestion of opium, and other *sannyasi* (Hindu ascetic) practices as well as the actual participation of Hindus in Sufi pilgrimages, something that is seen across India and Pakistan even today.[146] In addition to the influences on Muslim practices, Hindus also share shrines with their Muslim neighbors. Shared pilgrimages can be contentious, even violent, but more typically they illustrate the many ways in which diverse communities come together, even when their religious motivations are different or even antithetical.

In Uzbekistan, Muslims visit tombs, Sufi lodges, cemeteries, and natural sites. Defining the sacred involves a complicated negotiation of different traditions. "While the actual form of the site can vary (e.g. a water source, tree, stone, mosque, mausoleum, the saint's tomb), most sites consist of at least a tree, a water source, and a tomb, all of which are considered sacred because of their affiliation with the site and miracle stories (*karomatlar*) about the interred saint."[147] As the case of Uzbek pilgrimage shows, Islam is influenced by and often embedded in numerous communities. Official Islamic practice is often dictated by the political elite, but it is not necessarily followed by the masses. As one example, many shrines in Turkey are both shared and Sufi. According to one study, "We find out that while Alevis and Sunnis express different reactions toward 'official' Islam and the state's role in propagating such values, Sufi shrines serve as a sectarian melting pot where both Alevi and Sunni women go and pray to the saints."[148] These places are also visited by non-Muslims. As Jens Kreinath has pointed out in his work, the majority of shrines in Hatay, Turkey are visited by Sunnis, Alevis, Orthodox Christians, and Armenian Christians.[149]

Pilgrims in the Abrahamic traditions – Jews, Christians, and Muslims – share numerous religious personalities, resulting in sites that are often trans-religious. The hills and mountains surrounding Damascus were part of a sacred landscape filled with caves and other sites associated with Christian figures.

Under the Muslims, it became a large, shared religious space used by Jews, Christians, and Muslims: "For the Muslims and Christians of Damascus, Maghārat al-Dam (the Grotto of Blood) was a pilgrimage, and in Jewish tradition the family of Seth settled on Mt. Qāsiyun, where the family of Cain resided in Damascus, where Cain slew Abel."[150] In some cases, these sites were adopted by Muslims, and in others, already existing geographical features were re-imagined. The 'Umayyads did not have to import a large number of relics because they were already present in churches, sanctuaries, and grottos.[151] A cave on Mount Qasiyun was associated with Gabriel, Adam, and the Seven Sleepers, another cave with Khidr, and a third with Moses, while stones and boulders included imprints of the footsteps of Prophet Muhammad and 'Ali, and another stone was believed to be Aisha's mirror.[152]

Religious traditions that predate Islam – Zoroastrianism in Iran, and in Asia Hinduism, Buddhism, and animism – were all present before Muhammad's mission. In Iran, Zoroastrian and Muslim (Shi'i) pilgrimage traditions have a number of striking similarities, but there is also a tradition of shared sites, especially in the Kerman and Yazd provinces such as Seyh-Ali-Baba in Se-Gus and Zeyarat-gah-e Baba-Kamal at Baba Kamal, Sahrestan-e Kerman.[153] Islamic pilgrimage has adopted many sites that were previously part of another community, then re-named the saint and the tomb as Islamic, often associating it with a famous or important Muslim. The Christian cult of the saints in northern Anatolia is one area rich with the adoption/re-naming of saints:

> By the beginning of the fifth century, shrines once dedi-
> cated to St. George, St. Theodore, and the Prophet Elijah,
> and now known as shrines of Khidr, formed a new north-
> south pilgrimage route between Sinope on the Black Sea,
> passing through Elbistan to either Aleppo or Mosul. These
> sites included a Khidr-Ilyās monastery in Sinope, a Khidr

mountain in Merzifon, a *zāwiya* (dervish lodge) near Corum linked to the cult of Khidr and a column in the main mosque of Sivas where people brought sickly children in the hopes of finding a cure.[154]

As detailed in Chapter 2, Palestine also contains many places that are pilgrimage sites for Jewish, Christian, and Muslim communities. Political changes, appropriation, desacralization, and re-appropriation have an effect on pilgrimage:

> Shrines, when not secularized or abandoned, are often simply adopted; they may change their nominal affiliation, the powers they memorialize may be transformed in name and in character, and the population which frequents them may either be distinct from that of the earlier worshippers, or, if the same, have changed sectarian affiliations, but the same places, and often the same buildings, are frequently 'rebranded' and reused.[155]

The remainder of this chapter focuses on shared sites that are identified as Islamic but involve other traditions – Hinduism, Buddhism, Judaism, Christianity, and others. Defining these sites is a difficult problem. Consider the Javanese site of Tembayat, which includes offerings of flowers and frank-incense at a site dominated by Hindu stylistic details, the participation of Christian and Confucian Indonesians, and the inner shrine, modeled on the *ka'bah*.[156] Tembayat and other sites present an important methodological question regarding how scholars think about rituals and traditions that involve different religious actors and whether these cases are syncretic or multi-religious or "Sufi." In at least one case, the Islamic saint Khidr, the mysterious companion to Moses also known as "the green man," is identified as a *version* of St. George.[157] One of the sites associated with these two figures is identified as the place where St. Theodore slew a dragon, a church, a cult center for Khidr, and the resting place of a Sufi saint.[158] Whether this represents a case of adoption and re-naming of a site, or is a continuation of succession in which Khidr functions as a form of St. George or St. Theodore and later becomes part of a sixteenth-century Sufi saint, is unknown. This makes the question of whether the *zawiyah* of the latter figure is a shared site or a Sufi shrine an open-ended one. One scholar suggests Khidr is a "protean figure," allowing for the adoption of the site by numerous communities.[159]

The question of whether these places are "shared" is difficult to answer. In some cases, Muslims have adopted sites and the personality associated with them. At other times the rituals performed at sites are part of Islamic traditions; that is, a community's own practices. They may not be part of *sunnah* – the Prophet's practices – but to a group of Muslims, they *are* Islamic. Western China and Central Asia have many cases of this, such as the numerous Uzbek shrines that contain the horns of mountain goats, which are believed to have protective powers.[160]

Pilgrimage sites can be points of contention. At the Muslim shrine of Nizamuddin Auliya, differing beliefs over burial practices have created conflict. The Hindu cremation ground *Samshan ghat* is not only believed to be the residence of "Hindu ghosts" that occupy the site, it also interrupts the saint's powers, which include the blessing available to Muslims buried at the shrine.[161] At Adam's Peak in Sri Lanka, Buddhists, Hindus, and Muslims all believe that one footprint or another marks the site, a conflict of traditions that results in different paths up the mountain. Muslims often cite Adam's fall from Paradise in reference to the mountain, suggesting that the place marks the spot where Adam fell from heaven, leaving a footprint, but other sources claim it is the place where Adam is buried.[162]

The 'Alawi sites in Turkey can function as points of contention because of history, politics, and identity. One site is held sacred by the 'Alawis because it is believed to hold the bodies of two Sufis who had healing powers; however, Christians believe it holds two martyrs named Cosmas and Damian.[163] At another pilgrimage site, Sunni Muslims and 'Alawis contest the ownership and history of the place and the 'Alawi position is that their shrine was literally stolen from them by the more powerful Sunnis.[164]

The practice of religious communities visiting shared sites is common. Karbala, an important Islamic site, can be visited by Jews and Christians, as can Mashhad and other shrines in Iran – as long as the inner tomb area is not transgressed. The numerous Sufi shrines in India visited by Muslims and Hindus also are examples of the cohabitation of different religious communities. Jews, Christians, and Muslims share a common ancestor, Abraham, as well as numerous prophetic and religious figures. Historically, these communities have frequently lived together under Islamic rule. Many of the sites visited by Jews, Christians, and Muslims are found in Palestine. In the Middle Ages, these sites were funded and managed by a *waqf* (Islamic charitable foundation) that allowed different pilgrims to visit sites and "perform their ritual practices in their separate as well as their shared heritage spaces."[165]

Medieval Syria also had a rich culture of Jewish–Muslim pilgrimage sites, some of which are active in the contemporary period. Damascus in particular is a city associated with Jews, Christians, and Muslims with a history of adoption, appropriation, and cohabitation of sites going back to ancient times. The Hellenistic temple of the storm god Hadad stood on the site where the Romans erected the Temple of Jupiter, which was later the site of a Christian church and then a congregational mosque.[166] Both Christians and Muslims believe the head of John the Baptist (known in Islam as Yahya b. Zakariya) is buried at the 'Umayyad mosque, along with the heads of several of the martyrs of the Battle of Karbala. In fact, the spot on which John's head was purportedly hung was then appropriated by the Muslims "as the spot where Yazīd b. Mu'āwiya displayed Husayn's head."[167] When Islamic empires moved into a region they often took over sites as a way of establishing power and ownership over a site, sometimes at places held sacred by other religious communities. The Aya Sofya in Istanbul is an example. In this case, Muslims claimed sightings of Khidr that helped to distinguish it as Islamic, and in one story, "Khidr stuck his finger in one of the pillars of the church and turned the building on its own axis until it was aligned with the *qibla*. Then the Muslim conqueror consecrated the building by performing his ritual prayer there."[168]

The cult of Elijah includes numerous shrines in Damascus and Aleppo, as well as in Palestine and Egypt, often associated with places where it is believed the prophet took refuge from Ahab.[169] *Al-Rabwa* (the Hill) in Damascus is associated with many legends and stories, the most important of which is the claim that it is the place where Jesus was born and where he escaped from his prosecutors.[170] The synagogue outside Damascus in Jawbar has survived to the present period and, like many of the sites associated with Elijah, it is also an Islamic pilgrimage site identified with Khidr.[171]

In Turkey, Iran, and Syria, Christians and Muslims have numerous shared sites, places that offer fluid spaces for the expression of different identities and the practice of distinct rituals. In some cases, pilgrimage sites are a matter of geography and the close proximity, or even cohabitation, of different religious communities. In Antalya (Antioch), the shrine of Habib an-Najjar is also the shrine of a Christian martyr from the first century named Agabus (Acts 11.27–28). Cited in Qur'an 36.13–27, the saint is honored with a small mosque (*mescit*) that is built into a mountain that also is graced by Habib an-Najjar's name.

Figure 4.1 Shrine of Habib an-Najjar, Antakya, Turkey (photo courtesy of Scott Alexander).

Accommodation was common in buildings as well as the needs of non-Muslims living under Islamic rule. The Seljuks maintained churches near palaces so that Christians serving the sultan could pray, and myths, legends, and individuals were often adopted by one group or another, such as the Muslim warrior Seyyit Battal Ghazi, whose monument became a pilgrimage destination "for all who considered themselves of frontier heritage."[172] In addition to cultural heroes like Seyyit Battal Ghazi, Muslims and Christians share a number of other religious figures located in religious texts, resulting in both groups visiting places that honor Biblical–Qur'anic individuals, albeit in different ways. As mentioned above, the story of the head of John the Baptist shows how important Christian practices were to Muslims. When al-Walid ibn 'Abd al-Malik had the Byzantine church that became the 'Umayyad mosque torn down, the "relics of John the Baptist were miraculously discovered in a crypt."[173] A rather convenient circumstance, the discovery of John's head allowed the Muslims to take over the site while acknowledging its Christian history. It appears that after seeing John venerated by Damascene Christians, the Muslims decided to follow suit. Like many relics, it had miraculous properties; in this case, according to one report, "the face and hair were still intact."[174] Incorporating John into a newly constructed Islamic space made it possible to create a site at which Christians were included, but Muslims were in control.

Mary, known as Maryam in Islam, has inspired numerous pilgrimage sites that are frequented by Christians and Muslims. One is a chapel in Kevelaer, Germany, built in 1642, where visions of Mary have been reported.[175] While predominantly a Christian pilgrimage, of the 800,000 pilgrims who visit the chapel, some are Muslims.[176] At the central town of Fatima in Portugal, where three shepherd children reported visions of Mary in 1917, five million pilgrims visit the shrine annually, a number that includes some Muslims.[177] Muslim pilgrims often report the personal relationship they have with Maryam, whom they turn to much as Catholics do, as a source of "consolation … for their sufferings."[178] The House of Mary (*Meryem Ana Evi*) near Ephesus in Turkey, a place rich with Christian history, features a Christian minority and many places visited by both Muslims and Christians. It is said that Mary lived out the remainder of her life in a house there, surrounded by a cedar forest atop Mount Koressos near the sea. She went to this place to find peace after the death of her son: "After Jesus was crucified, St. John, fearing for Virgin Mary's life decided to move her to Anatolia."[179] When one enters the shrine, it appears quite Catholic – a small church with candles that pilgrims can light as they pass through. Pilgrims, both Christian and Muslim, also visit the spring outside the shrine, which is believed to have healing water.[180] One focal point of the shrine is a prayer wall, in which thousands of handwritten notes ask for her intercession.

Mary is also popular with Muslims in Egypt. One of the ways this emerges is in the "collective apparitions" of the Virgin – visions of Mary witnessed by both Christians and Muslims – that are popular, local, and often result in pilgrimages.[181] When these visions occur, Christians and Muslims may describe her differently, but the place where the vision takes place, which is often a Christian church, becomes a destination for pilgrimage.[182] It does not matter to Muslim pilgrims that these places are Christian. The case of one Muslim pilgrim who wanted to build two steeples to honor Mary/Maryam suggests that there are a variety of ways to honor her, some involving trans-religious symbols.[183]

In addition to Marian pilgrimages, other sacred places are shared by Christians and Muslims. These include shrines dedicated to St. Anthony of Padua (located in both northern Albania and Istanbul) and the Monastery of St. George in Büyükada.[184] Mixed iconography is sometimes a part of these traditions, such as at the shrine of Seyyid Gazi, which featured a thirteenth-century brass vessel decorated with figures exhibiting Christian and Muslim themes as well as candle stands decorated with images of the Virgin that adorned the sarcophagus of Seyyid Gazi.[185]

In Palestine/Israel, Christians and Muslims share, sometimes quite tensely, a landscape filled with sacred sites.

Figure 4.2 Islamic shrine, Mount Qaimiri, Hebron, Palestine/West Bank (photo courtesy of Alex Shams).

A number of Christian sites host Muslim pilgrims, including those associated with Mary, Elijah, and St. George (identified, as we have seen, as Khidr by Muslims), and within these shrines Muslims pray or gather at specific places.[186] Sites shared by Jews, Christians, and Muslims are less common, but do exist. One example is found atop the Mount of Olives, which functions as a shrine for Muslims, but it is known as the tomb of Pelagia for Christians and the tomb of Hulda for Jews.[187]

When shared pilgrimage sites are contested, the rituals performed by different religious actors may come into conflict, and the rules surrounding where one can pray or perform other duties can be an issue. In Islam, expectations surrounding the proper use of spaces of prayer have often been a contentious issue, played out in numerous opinions and debates on the subject. As Khalek reminds us, "'Umar ibn al-Khattāb's famous refusal to pray in the church of the Holy Sepulcher at the invitation of the Patriarch Sophronius is belied by his reported willingness to do so at the site of Mary's tomb, in spite of his remorse over the act afterward."[188]

In the Chuvash Republic, located in the Middle Volga region of the Russian Federation, Muslim sites are also visited by Chuvash Orthodox Christians. Since the fall of the Soviet Union and the state-sponsored atheism that went along with it, the Mishar Tatars have begun the process of re-sanctifying narratives, customs, and traditions that had long been held in the collective memory of the Muslim community.[189] Chuvash Muslims and Christians have complex ethnic identities and claim to be descendants of the Bolgars. At the Chuvash cemetery of Imenvo, gravestones with epitaphs in Arabic are downplayed by Chuvash scholars who insist true Chuvash remained pagan.[190] This site, like many others, lies at the center of debates about national identity, history, and religion. At the same time, the cult of the saints was shared. As one example, "Many sacred graves (*kiremet*) were named after Bolgar Khans, sheiks and Islamic teachers and located on their supposed burial sites."[191]

In Turkey, Georgian Christians and Muslims have pilgrimage practices, called *ziyara-ba* and *ziyareti*, that often take place concurrently.[192] In some cases, the Muslims are not even aware of the presence of a Christian saint; in other cases, the collective memory upholds a kind of "reconstructed" and collective notion of "ideal cultural artefacts."[193] Pilgrimage spaces function as an example of this interaction between memory and activity, "shaped by their participation in the interactions of which they were previously a part and which they mediate in the present."[194]

The themes and rituals associated with pilgrimage often involve other communities. India's shrine culture is embedded in its various religious traditions, most notably Hinduism. In many instances, Hindu sites were adopted by Muslims, identifying a Sufi with a Hindu individual who was still revered by the local population. India is a landscape full of sacred sites not associated with human bodies. Trees, mountains, rocks, springs, and rivers are just some of the sites co-identified as sacred and in many cases visited by both Hindus and Muslims. The shrine of Zinda Pir stands behind a hot sulfur spring, the Muslim saint Sakhi Sarwar is identified with a Hindu god, and the saint Shams al-Din Daryai is associated with a tree spirit.[195] The Muslim figure Khizr (Khidr), associated with Christian saints, is also identified with former Hindu gods and spirits.[196]

As this survey shows, Muslim pilgrims often perform rituals that have pre-Islamic or non-Islamic origins and influences. Such is the case of the Javanese meditation practiced on Mount Lawu, where pilgrims immerse themselves neck-deep in a sacred pool and perform one of two types of Javanese meditation (*semedi* and *tapa*) in the hopes of gaining esoteric knowledge (*ngelmu*) and seeking unity with Allah.[197] While some would not classify this pilgrimage as Islamic, the Muslims who visit Mount Lawu certainly would. This is perhaps why it is important to take a long view of pilgrimage in Islam, a subject that includes the participation of various traditions, rituals, and, as the next chapter shows, technologies.

5

MODERN MUSLIM PILGRIMS: TOURISM, SPACE, AND TECHNOLOGY

Modernity has opened up the ways in which religious individuals and communities negotiate sacred space, including those involved with pilgrimage. It has also resulted in the mass production of material goods, including pilgrimage souvenirs like ashtrays and T-shirts as well as religious items used ritually like rosaries, prayer carpets, and icons. Famous Muslim personalities like Imam 'Ali and Rumi are found on key chains, posters, magnets, and other items. In some cases, the lines between commercial and religious items are blurred. As Amira El-Zein argues, "Rumi's verse is seen as an enjoyable 'spiritual product' to be consumed in order that one may relax and become more productive after listening to it. It is then used 'efficiently' in stores and boutiques."[1] In Turkey, products featuring Rumi are even more widespread than in North America and Europe, appearing in every imaginable form from CD covers to scarves. The commodification of religious personalities, traditions, and places is not limited to Islam, of course, and in some cases involves a transnational adoption, or colonization, of images that are manufactured and sold in foreign markets. One example is the numerous objects of Native American figures sold in Indonesia, identifying the spiritual energy of Java and Bali with that of indigenous peoples in distant lands.

Although the mass production of religious items, including those related to pilgrimage, is a modern phenomenon, the intersection of commerce and religion is hardly new. In medieval Europe, pilgrims often sought out souvenirs and religious mementos of their travels, including coins, badges, and other items as evidence of their journey. Today, pilgrimage items are more typically produced abroad. For example, the white scarves bought on *hajj* and frequently given as gifts are made in India and China, representing a tenuous relationship to the holy city of Mecca.

Changes in the options pilgrims have for traveling to sacred sites have also affected Islamic pilgrimages. What was once a months-long journey is now a few airplane flights or a bus trip. Mobility involves a number of other developments, including the speedy communication and ever-changing technology that characterizes much of modern life, enabling pilgrims to tweet an image of themselves at the *ka'bah* or use a smartphone app to negotiate the *hajj*. Pilgrims can also use technology to "do" pilgrimage remotely. One can go online and watch a live feed of the *ka'bah* or any number of other religious sites. Individuals can also go to a website, fill out an online form, and request that their prayers be recited at a holy site. Supplications related to saints and other religious figures can be downloaded online and recited in one's home, thus eliminating the need to attend a mosque, community gathering, or pilgrimage. Online pilgrimages are becoming more popular, especially for those who cannot afford travel, or for whom it is not an option due to health, disability, or age, or too dangerous because of political conflict.

This chapter looks at the ways in which capitalism, mobility, and technology help us understand the ways Islamic pilgrimage is changing in the modern world. To this end, the following sections examine the idea of center and decentering, the commodification of pilgrimage sites, tourism and religious souvenirs, virtual pilgrimages, and cyber-pilgrimages. The *ziyarat* examined thus far in this book are largely defined by religious traditions – some local and others transnational – and by physical movement or travel, but the use of technology not only expands the choices available for physical pilgrimage, but opens up possibilities for those who cannot travel. As I have suggested before, pilgrimage is often an active, ongoing practice, creating spaces that signal Soja's idea of Thirdspace, an ineffable entity that is characterized by its "extraordinary simultaneities."[2] As we shall see, some of these spaces are not constructed in the physical world but in the spaces created by the mind (virtual pilgrimages) and the computer (cyber-pilgrimages).

CENTER AND DECENTERING

As the previous chapters have shown, countless places function as important centers of Islamic pilgrimage. These include tombs, cities, graveyards, and natural sites such as springs and mountains. In some cases, pilgrims reconstitute these sites in artwork, in rituals, and through substitutions of the sacred spaces they are removed from, including Mecca, which may be re-imagined as another city (Karbala) or a Javanese mountain (Mount Ciremai). Outside Mecca, sacred sites also function as mnemonic devices, places that symbolize important religious memories in the lives of Muslims. In Senegal, the city of Touba is re-imagined in a myriad of ways. "They reproduce Touba by renaming the neighborhoods and cities where they live and work: Touba Sandaga and Touba Ouakam in Senegal, but also Touba in Turin."[3] These represent extensions of the pilgrimage center that constantly re-identify the local with what is sacred.

Following the work of the Turners, scholars have often referred to these centers as spaces in which inward transformation takes place, a model that is very useful in examining the trajectory of the pilgrim's experience as well as the ways in which sacred sites can serve as loci that offer a transformative nexus of experience. Malcolm X's transformation during *hajj* is perhaps the most famous of these examples. However, the experience of *communitas*, a contemplative or mystical moment, may not take place during the pilgrimage, and in some cases it may occur later (or not at all).

Muslims have numerous traditions that encourage the possibility of constant engagement with the sacred site through items that are used ritually. In Islam, pilgrims often travel to the graves and tombs of the saint or other holy person. Items from these places are often imbued with a religious significance that is permanent – that continues to be in force after the pilgrimage is complete. The earth that surrounds or touches the saint's body, composed of sacred soil like the sand and water from Mecca or the soil of Karbala, or objects connected to these landscapes, provide a way for the pilgrim to connect to a holy person or place. Often, these *pilgrimage mementos* are imbued with the blessing of a saint, through touching a tomb's edges, the corner of a mosque, or a particular place where something miraculous took place. Nigerian pilgrims obtain *kayan Mecca* (Meccan things) and use them after their journey is complete and they have returned home, believing that the water, sand (called *d'ebimu*), or other material is healing and blessed, touched with Allah's *barakah*, which is efficacious even when it is used remotely.[4] Such items do not lose their power once they leave the site, for they are permanently memorialized with the *barakah* of the person and the place from which they came.

Islam is not alone in its production of portable objects that are tied to memory and religious power. Pilgrimage items have been bought and sold on the trails traveled by believers in Europe, Asia, Africa, and elsewhere. Coins, jewelry, badges, and icons are examples of portable religious items that carry meaning beyond the journey, working in a "network of mobilities around which objects, emotions, cultures and people circulate."[5] These items are diverse and range from souvenirs with little religious importance beyond proving that a pilgrim's journey occurred, to objects that are sacred due to their proximity to a saint. In the Christian cult of the saints, much like in Islam, the bodies of the dead generated a whole array of sacred objects and sites based on their sacred power: "The graves of the saints – whether these were the solid rock tombs of the Jewish patriarchs in the Holy Land or, in Christian circles, tombs, fragments of bodies or, even, physical objects that had made contact with these bodies – were privileged places, where the contrasted poles of Heaven and Earth met."[6]

In a similar manner, the importance placed on bodies in Islamic pilgrimage determined the many types of objects that are associated with graves, tombs, shrines, and other places associated with *ziyarat*. In some cases, an object became a source of income because the personality with which it was associated was so great. In sixteenth-century Iran, we find this example: "A Venetian traveler, Michel Membre, writes of followers coming from Anatolia to request a piece of Shāh Tahmāb's turban or handkerchief, which would then be circulated in the countryside so that the poor vendors could earn an income through displaying it and asking for alms."[7] Often the objects associated with a saint's body or sacred site are used ritually, as in the case of the Shi'i prayer stones made from the sand and soil surrounding the graves of the Imams. These items are often used in virtual pilgrimages, which connect the individual to a distant site and the person or people buried there.

Virtual pilgrimages can form a lasting relationship between the pilgrim, the holy person, and the site. Religious items connected to a pilgrimage aid in this linking. One example is the death shroud that is taken to a pilgrimage site where it becomes sacred, and is then used to bury the pilgrim when he or she dies, so that the experience of the pilgrimage remains with the person forever.[8] In other contexts, rituals are performed with or without the aid of an object. Souvenirs connected to a pilgrimage site may be afforded a level of respect that is important but that does not elevate them to the status of a sacred object. This is the case for portraits of Prophet Muhammad and his relatives, which are commonly found for sale at Shi'i sites.

> *Temsal-e Mobarak-e Hazrat-e Peyghambar* [The Noble Likeness of the Holy Prophet] and *Temsal-e Mobarak-e Hazrat-e Amir* [The Noble Likeness of the Holy Prince (of Believers) – the honorific title of Ali ibn Abi Talib] were among the most cherished items purchased as souvenirs as *soghati*. In the Mashhad bazaar we were never allowed to call these transactions 'purchases,' however. We would ask not 'How much does this cost?' but *'Hedyash chand misheh?'* [How much would the 'gist' be for this?][9]

Portable objects constitute a form of visual apportionment, what we might call the currency of pilgrimage. Like the T-shirts and postcards of today, these objects represent the sacred site and serve as a kind of "proof of life" that illustrates that an individual made the journey. In the case of *hajj*, objects from Mecca may be given as gifts. This is the case of *kayan Mecca* (things from Mecca) obtained by Nigerian pilgrims, ranging from Zamzam water to white scarves associated with the *hajj*.[10]

These products of Islamic pilgrimage can be purely touristic and at other times deeply religious. Pilgrimage mementos, which I examine in more detail later in this chapter, point to some of the important ways that tourism, capitalism, and commodification of religion play a role in the life of Muslim pilgrims.

MECCA, INC.

A pilgrim's experience is influenced by numerous factors including the individual's motivations, his or her religious orientation and experience, and the site itself. The commodification of religion also plays an important role in the pilgrim's experience. As the Turners wrote, "A tourist is half a pilgrim, if a pilgrim is half a tourist."[11] Religious pilgrimage is not necessarily a purely sacred experience; rather, it reflects a type of tourism that is both sacred and mundane. The development of Mecca as a pilgrimage site with new hotels, a clock tower that resembles London's Big Ben, and other services for pilgrims is one example of how even the most sacred site can be commodified. Great worth is attached to items bought in Mecca, which are often brought home to relatives, despite the fact that many of them are produced in China.[12] These examples point to the complexities involved in defining pilgrimage as a purely religious experience that is removed from the commercial and material aspects of social life.

Critiques of the Saudi development of Mecca, which include the destruction of sacred sites, are important reminders of this fact. However, it is important to remember that this is not something new. Although the mass production of pilgrimage items is a more recent development, pilgrimage has always involved capital, commodities, and the exchange of goods and services. Mecca served as a center of trade and commerce before the Prophet's lifetime. According to Islamic tradition, his grandfather rediscovered the Zamzam well and distributed the water to pilgrims conducting pagan rites in Mecca.[13] The commodification of Islam's holy sites may be more elaborate than in the past (something that is not restricted to Mecca), in part due to the hyper-materialism associated with modern life and capitalism. Some would argue that the free market has responded to the demands of *hajj*, keeping up with changing populations and emerging technologies. At the end of the nineteenth century, most of those who had an opportunity to make money from pilgrims did so, much like today. These opportunities ranged from small businesses to political and religious authorities.

> Bedouins demanded safe passage; their rapacity and extortion tactics remained the greatest scourge for pilgrims into the twentieth century. Caravan commanders amassed large fortunes from manipulating their control of the budget, and from kickbacks from suppliers or even Bedouin tribes wanting a piece of the action. The populace of Makkah lived largely off the Hajj. At the turn of the century, civil and religious authorities, including the governor and sharif of Makkah, evolved a multitude of schemes to fleece pilgrims.[14]

Today, *hajj* is big business. The two million people a year who make the pilgrimage purchase everything from *hajj* travel packages to items associated with the journey. The variety of products is vast, including "ihram garments, hajj board games and pocket-sized step-by-step guides," holy water, honey from Mecca said to be special due to its origins, and other food products.[15]

Mecca is not alone in its mixture of religion and capitalism. Many Islamic pilgrimage centers function in this way and offer a range of goods, services, and opportunities to make money. Iran, which boasts numerous pilgrimage sites including the shrine of Imam Reza at Mashhad, has numerous companies that run pilgrimage tours. In Lebanon, many small travel agencies (*hamlat*) that specialize in pilgrimage to Shi'a sites in Syria, Iraq, and Iran offer tours to specific shrines or to several of them.[16] These agencies are often named according to the site(s) they specialize in, such as *hamlat al-imam al-rida*, *hamlat al-salam*, and *hamlat al-imam al-'ali*.[17] In Iran and Iraq, one can purchase items associated with popular pilgrimage destinations such as those found in Qom, Mashhad, and Karbala.

Tourism and religious pilgrimage are often recorded through photography and other forms of documentation. Muslim pilgrims are like other religious travelers who want to mark their journey with evidence that they have completed a journey. Photos, tweets, and Facebook posts serve as proof of the pilgrim's journey. These are another example of the ways in which religious pilgrimage functions as a form of tourism. Pilgrimage and travel reflect two different movements – one inward and one outward, something that can be seen in the photos, blogs, and other public expressions of these journeys. As Erik Cohen argues, "pilgrimage, [is] a movement toward the Center, and travel, [is] a movement in the opposite direction, toward the Other."[18] In religious pilgrimage, these two activities often come together, resulting in a complex experience that is unresolved at the end of the journey.

As noted at the beginning of this chapter, the items available for purchase at Islamic pilgrimage sites range from touristic souvenirs like postcards and T-shirts to heavily religious items, such as miniature Qur'ans and Qur'anic verses carved onto wood and metal. In some instances, these items are deeply meaningful, carrying memories, representing past experiences, and serving as the only evidence of a journey from the past. Hamid Dabashi provides us with this recollection of his time in Mashhad as a young man, and the items that were connected to that part of his life:

Among the most popular items to purchase for souvenirs and as *soghati* [gifts for friends and family] from Mashhad were *tasbih* [colorful rosaries], *ja-namaz* [prayer rugs], loads of saffron, clothing items, black or colorful pieces of garment for chador, and, particularly popular, pictures (or *temsal*, 'likenesses,' as we were instructed to call them) of Prophet Muhammad and Imam Ali, printed on pieces of cloth or woven into carpets of various sizes and textures.[19]

Pilgrimage items may function as souvenirs, ritual objects, or both. The portable pilgrim's object is not new: "Historically, pilgrimage has often involved mobility of destinations across space in the form of shrines that echo the architecture of the destination, portable souvenirs that pilgrims take away with them as they return, and examples of forms of liturgical and clerical entrepreneurship in the suppression of as well as the encouragement of shrine construction."[20] People who go on *hajj* often return with a wide array of items, some of which commodify the most religious sites directly, such as Zamzam water.[21] Only some of these items have religious utility, so it is useful to classify them. Objects that represent the pilgrimage site such as magnets or cigarette lighters may serve as "symbolic reminders" of a place or person.[22] Souvenirs serve as proof of the journey and help the pilgrim remember the experience, often through an image. However, objects obtained during pilgrimage or that are otherwise tied to a pilgrimage may also be used ritually. These objects are called "relics" by Ian Reader, which I think is an appropriate term, but may be confused with bodily relics in discussions of pilgrimage.[23] I call these objects *permanent mementos* because they act as permanent or "active" memorial devices for the pilgrim. They play an active role in the life of the individual, often by transporting them to a religious site, such as the grave of an important religious personality like Imam 'Ali, Rumi, or Sayyida Zaynab. In some cases, these objects "serve as metonymic devices to help induce the symbolic presence of the deceased."[24] Painted icons are one example, including the *shama'il* found in some Shi'i communities – portable icons of 'Ali that are used in meditative practices.

Like the souvenir, mementos are material evidence of the pilgrimage journey, a way of saying, "I was *there*." A decal from Memphis's Sun Studio, Zamzam water from Mecca, and the magnets, stickers, carpets, diptychs, and triptychs of Imam Husayn, Imam 'Ali, Hajji Bektash, and Kemal Ataturk for sale in the village of Hacibektas (Karahuyuk) all serve as evidence of the pilgrim's journey. They are, in this sense, "proofs of life," the life of the pilgrim and the places he or she has visited. In some cases, religious mementos are gifted to a donor, as with votive images in the Shi'a tradition. "In that case, the return-gift is the pilgrimage, whereas the image functions as a testimony of the votary's implementation of his or her obligation. The image is brought home and presented as a gift to remind the pilgrim/donor of his or her personal experience."[25] Indeed, souvenirs may be religiously themed, but they are not always religiously functional. Many years ago at the entrance to Bab al-Saghir in Damascus, I purchased a miniature Qur'an and packets of postcards representing famous Damascene sites – sacred and touristic items that were both connected to the cemetery, but in different ways.

Figure 5.0 Souvenirs and mementos, Hacibektas, Turkey (photo courtesy of author).

The religious memento does something in the world that the souvenir does not, serving to continually reenact the pilgrim's religious attachment to the place or person(s) it represents. A cigarette lighter with Imam 'Ali on it might remind one of the day it was purchased, but the devout pilgrim would not use it to perform *salat* (prayers) or to heal a sick relative. The religious memento, on the other hand, has agency. It can aid or even facilitate the performance of ritual obligations and the ongoing mediation of the world. While souvenirs "identify place and delineate a singular experience," permanent mementos identify one's (religious) commitments and recreate or generate experiences long after the journey is over.[26] The focus on these objects and others is part of the material turn that has led to more attention being paid to the "subjective, private, and material."[27] This turn includes the mementos I write about here, as well as all sorts of other things, such as "objects, practices, spaces, bodies, sensations, affects" and more.[28] The examples of permanent mementos that follow help illustrate how powerful these items and the places they are related to are in the religious lives of Muslims.

Portable icons, sometimes called *shama'il*, are often for sale at pilgrimage sites that are frequented by Shi'i, Sufi, and Alevi Muslims. As I argued in the chapter on saints and Sufis, there is seldom a clear delineation between different Muslim sects, or what we might describe as confessional communities. A saint may be identified as Shi'i, but Sufis in a Sunni order may honor him or her in their rituals. Such is the case of the Naqshbandiyya, whose liturgy includes devotional songs (*ilahi*s) about Husayn (and other members of the Prophet's family), often sung on 'Ashura' at the commemoration of his death. Portable icons are also fluid, representing religious figures that are shared between different communities of believers. Here, we look at two examples of these moveable icons that are used to connect the believer to a pilgrimage and a saint.

The visage of Hajji Bektash (*Turk*. Haci Bektas), the founder of the Bektashi Sufi order, is found on a large array of portable objects, some more touristic and others that have ritualistic or religious functions. His story is as follows: "In the thirteenth century, with the Mongols pushing at their backs, Hajji Bektash along with other Islamicized Turkmen peoples came westward from Khorasan across Iran to Anatolia. In central Anatolia, Hajji Bektash drew followers around him, and a Sufi or Islamic mystic order, the Bektashis, was founded in his name."[29] His lineage is discussed below. Alevis, a group discussed in Chapter 3, have not been helped by their classification as a *ghulat* or "extremist" movement, a classification that is associated with political radicalism, rather than the correct reading of the term. *Ghulat*, often translated as "extremist Shi'ites," refers to the "attempt to organize social life outside of or in contrast to the state."[30] Like other minority sub-traditions in Islam, the Alevis have received a fair share of subjective academic treatments.

The town of Hacibektas, the site of Bektash's tomb, is an important pilgrimage site for Alevis. In recent years it has become popular as a tourist site, and a combination of pilgrims and tourists congregate at the shrine.[31] The Alevis, who live in scattered communities around Turkey, including a concentration of Kurds in the east and a group of communities in the south along the border with Syria, are also found in high numbers in Anatolia's center, which is known to some tourists as an area rich in Alevi culture.[32] The Alevis and Bektashis are often referred to as one group, sometimes by the term Alevi-Bektashi, but in fact distinctions exist between the two, the most important of which is that many Alevis believe that Hajji Bektash is a manifestation of 'Ali, which resulted in a distinctly Sufi identity. Bektashis, unlike other Alevis, "formed an organized group" recognized as a Sufi *tariqah*, or order.[33] One can think of it this way – anyone can join the Bektashi order if he or she is found worthy, but you have to be born an Alevi.[34] Another way to think of these two groups is that the Bektashis are but one of the sub-groups that make up the Alevi sect, which constitutes the second-largest group of Muslims in Turkey, after Sunni Islam.[35]

In some portable icons, portraits of one of the Shi'i Imams and Hajji Bektash are accompanied by a portrait of Kemal Ataturk. The combination of two ultra-religious icons with an individual more associated with secularism than any other person in the region may seem curious, but actually represents an attempt to show Bektashi support for the Turkish state, which has had a tenuous relationship with many ethnic and religious communities outside of Sunni Islam. The Alevis are associated with the wider sixteenth-century tensions between the Ottomans and the Safavids, which ultimately resulted in the characterization of Alevis as "collaborators" and "red-heads" (*kizilbas*), a reference to the red turbans that Safavid soldiers wore.[36] More recently, AKP (Justice and Development Party) officials have referred to Alevis and their traditions in less than glowing terms, in statements that often focus on the dances (*ayin-i cem*) that include men and women together.[37] In recent years the identity of Alevis has altered from one of an Othered religious community to a secular Alevism that is a "reflection of the wider transition to becoming part of the modern nation."[38] After the Sivas massacre in 1993, when seventeen Alevis were killed by a group of radical Islamists in a suburb of Istanbul, the political establishment's attitude changed and they began to tone down anti-Alevi rhetoric.[39] In this case, the portable icon functions as both a permanent memento and a political statement.

The Imams 'Ali and Husayn appear with Hajji Bektash in many images, demonstrating the importance members of the Bektashi order place on the Imamate. 'Ali and Husayn play a direct role in their rituals, including the ceremonial dances for which they are known: "The villagers say that they were taught to perform the *cem* by Ali, and a slow-stepping dance in the *cem*, the '*sema* of the forty,' *kurklar semahi*, commemorates the first men and women who gathered around Ali and learnt from him."[40] One of the Bektashi prayers contains these lines:

> O God! Our faces are black, our sins are many ... do not refuse our prayer. In the name of your Godliness, in the name of the great, beautiful Light, in the name of Muhammad Ali Nebi, in the name of the cloaks of the Saints, in the name of Mecca and Medine [Medina], in the name of all the Prophets, in the name of the martyred soul of *Imam Hasan*, in the name of the blood of Huseyin, and in the name of the great Twelve Imams, in the name of the tongues which are saying, "God is Great," in the name of the blood spilt by the martyrs, in the name of the offerings made by the developed ones, in the name of the three, seven, and the forty, in the name of the Saints of Horasan ... accept our prayer.[41]

Like most Sufi orders, the lineage of the *shaykh* is rooted in the Prophet's family. Hajji Bektash is believed to be a descendant of one of the Twelve Imams, and thus is related to Muhammad as a spiritual teacher. "Indeed, there is an unbroken chain of *talibs* and *murshids* through which Bektashis connect themselves to their *Pir*, their 'patron saint,' Haji Bektash Veli. This chain continues from Haji Bektash back to Ali, whose *murshid* was the Prophet Muhammad, whose *murshid* was the Angel Gabriel, and thus to God."[42]

The Bektashis borrow heavily from the Shi'i narrative and the Imamate figures prominently in their belief system, as does the Battle of Karbala. One place this is seen is in the veneration of the Twelve Imams and the Fourteen Innocents (Prophet Muhammad, his daughter Fatima Zahra, and the Twelve Imams), described here in one of the few published academic studies on Bektashi beliefs and rituals: "There is a tradition from *Cafer Sadik* that no one can properly be a *Dede* [shaykh], or a Baba [elder or leader], or a dervish, or even a

Muhip [initiate] unless he knows the Fourteen Innocents, their names and their genealogies, as well as the Twelve Imams."[43]

The Alevi *sama* (ritual dance) serves as an expression of the complicated relationship between Prophet Muhammad, Imam 'Ali, and the Turkic tribes that originated the ritual in the sixteenth century.[44] The narrative expressed in the Dance of the Cranes (*Turnalar Sama*) is a helpful way to understand that the Alevis' identity is both Shi'a and indigenous to Anatolia:

> In the *Turnular Semah* (Dance of the Cranes), the image of the elegant crane (*turna*) preparing for flight symbolizes both the ascending soul of Imam Ali and the metamorphosis of Central Asian miracle-working shamans into birds. In the *Kirklar Semah* [Dance of the Forty Saints], the nocturnal ascent of the Prophet Muhammed (*miraç*) to heaven led him to the gathering of the 40 saints. Basically, in Alevi belief, the gathering of 40 saints refers to the moment after the Prophet's ascension, when he beheld the manifestation of Divine Reality in Ali.[45]

This identity, simultaneously Muslim, Turkic, Shi'i, and Sufi, is played out in numerous images that depict 'Ali, Husayn, and Hajji Bektash either individually or together. Regardless of who is being depicted, this iconography is strongly Shi'i, following the formula found in the many devotional images popular amongst Iranian and other Shi'i communities that function as visual narratives about the history of the *Shi'at 'Ali* (the Party of 'Ali), the role of the Imams in human history, and the qualities these individuals possess.

One way in which icons of the Imams function outside of these qualities is through their representation of Allah's guidance and wisdom, a relationship that begins with *al-Nur* (the Light of Allah), is passed on to Prophet Muhammad (*Nur-i Muhammad*), and then on to 'Ali, Fatima, and various relatives of this line, including the Imamate. Shi'i view the family of the Prophet as representatives of Divine Light, a belief that originates in a Shi'i exegesis of the *Ayat al-Nur* (the Light Verse) and extra-Qur'anic Shi'a traditions. One narrative claims Divine Light was bestowed on the Prophet, his daughter Fatima, and his cousin and son-in-law, 'Ali: "When Allah created paradise, He created it from the light of His face. Then He took the light and dispersed it. One third hit Muhammad, one third hit Fatima, and another third hit 'Ali."[46] Shi'i are not the only Muslims who reflect on *Nur* in their theology and use it symbolically in pilgrimage. The Hadrami Muslims, who come from Tarim and claim to be direct descendants of Prophet Muhammad, also see the Prophetic genealogy as a conduit for this light, in which the saint – through his tomb – is a "vehicle for the transmission of that light."[47]

The Imam's relationship to the Divine also needs to be understood as an expression of the idea that Allah is always watching us; and this is represented in a unique form by a type of Shi'a–Sufi icon in which both Imam 'Ali and Hajji Bektash are present. This particular type of icon would probably be classified as a *shama'il jibi*, or "pocket pious image," even though it lies somewhere between the miniature icons that some Shi'i carry with them as an object of "benediction and protection" and the larger iconic images generally known as *pardeh*, meaning "screen," often found in coffee houses and other businesses.[48]

For some Alevis, Hajji Bektash is believed to be an incarnation of Imam 'Ali. Although some icons feature Imam 'Ali with Hajji Bektash, which makes sense given Alevi ideas about the relationship of these two men, and in particular the latter as an incarnation of the former, portraits of Imam Husayn are also commonly found on paintings, posters, and other representations of the Prophet's grandson, many of which focus on the Battle of Karbala. Devotional imagery serves an important ritual function, while reminding the individual of the dominant Shi'a narrative – the Battle of Karbala. Images of Husayn, the battle, and its aftermath, make:

> fragmented references to the Shia understanding of the role of the Imamate to the continuous survival of the right inter-pretations of Islam, as well as to its eschatological dimen-sion, and frame the battle of Karbala within this worldview. However, to the informed viewer the content does not simply bring Shia dogmas to mind, but calls to mind memories of devotional practices including prayer and pilgrimage, and personal experiences of the mediation of the saints.[49]

In this way, the icon serves as yet another form of *dhikr/ zhikr*, much like the *turbah* and *parche sabz* (green cloths), in which the object brings both the pilgrimage site and the person buried there into the space of the believer. The idea that the Imam, in this case joined by Hajji Bektash, is with the believer is popular among Shi'i Muslims, who often have a painting of Prophet Muhammad or one of the Imams in their home. The act of looking at such an image strengthens the emotional attachment between the believer and the saint.[50] Much like the desire to be near the body of an Imam, as in the case of the large communities of Hazara that have emigrated to Mashhad to be "near" Imam Reza, a similar phenomenon is at work with the icon.[51]

In addition, there is the idea of the "Light of the Imam," an expression of the *Nur-i Muhammad* pointed to earlier, in which the very image of the Imam's face represents the Light of God, described in the *Ayat al-Nur* and in numerous extra-Qur'anic narratives. The Shi'i Sufi order known as the Dhahabiyya even have a secret practice in which the dervishes focus on an image of 'Ali while concentrating on their own heart, all while reciting *dhikr 'Ali* (the recitation of 'Ali's name, which is also one of Allah's names), all of which will bring one to the realization of the "Imam of Light."[52] This realization is, like many Sufi practices, aimed at polishing the heart, contained in the image of the Imam. It trains the eye and then the body on an image that radiates love, which is often understood as the goal of all religious contemplation. The icon functions as a kind of mirror (and in fact, a mirror is often hidden in the icon, behind a portrait) in which the believer sees a reflection of God, through the idea that the "infallible Imam is the Face of God," a Shi'a reflection of the verse, "Everywhere you might turn, there is the face of Allah (2:115)."

Another permanent memento in the Shi'i tradition that serves a ritual function is *parche sabz*, the "green cloths" often seen at the shrines of the *ahl al-bayt* and other Muslim figures.[53] While visiting (*ziyarat*) the tomb (*mazar*) of Sayyida Ruqayya in Damascus in 2010, I made a donation at the shrine's office and was given a large handful of *parche sabz*, which are also called *dakhil*, from the Arabic *dakhl*, which means "inside." The green color is a signifier of both Islam and the Prophet's family – a tradition that was legally sanctioned in the fourteenth century by governmental decree: "In 1371–1372 AD the Mamluk sultan ordered that the descendants of the Prophet should wear some green as an indication of their status, so that proper respect could be paid to them."[54] Islamic iconography commonly uses green as a marker of the Prophet's family, including the Imams, in turbans, flags, and numerous other objects.[55]

Green cloths are tied to the metalwork (*zarih*) of tombs, placed in Qur'ans and prayer books, and also carried home in a series of rituals that involve the memory of a saint as well as the memory of the place where he or she is buried. The cloths are not limited to shrines, and in Iran people tie them to the grillwork of *sagha-kanehs*, ancient water-dispensers, after making a wish.[56] This is very much like what happens at the tombs of the Imams and other holy sites, when pilgrims ask for assistance and tie the green cloth, hoping that their problem will be solved through the intercession of the individual interred there. In both Shi'i and Sufi contexts, *dakhil/parche sabz* are tied to tree trunks, a sign that a wish has been made. This practice is widespread, appearing in Iran, Turkey, and Pakistan, among other places. Around the tomb of Sayyid Abdul Latif at Ezhimala (Kammur, in the district of Kerala), as well as at other shrines in India and Pakistan, one sees small pieces of cloth tied to trees. At shrines and other places, they represent petitions, and often are removed once the wish has been granted.[57]

Before touching the *zarih* or *'alam* (flag), *parche sabz* are simply pieces of green cloth, but once they come into contact with the saint's body – or rather, the metalwork that surrounds the tomb – the cloths become *tabarruk*, or blessed.[58] Indeed, when a believer touches the shrine, he or she receives a blessing. In Muhammad Hasan al-Qazwini's treatise, he explains how through the touching and rubbing of the tomb, the believer seeks intimacy with the saint, and in response receives "the blessing or intercession of the Prophet or the Imams with God."[59] The same process is true for *parche sabz*, when pieces of green cotton or silk cloth change into sacred objects. When a pilgrim ties the cloth to the shrine or rubs it over its surface, he or she hopes to have his or her wishes (*hajat*) fulfilled. It is not uncommon to find a mass of *dakhil/parche sabz* at popular graves, for example at the sprawling cemetery in Damascus known as Bab al-Saghir shown in figure 5.1.

Much like the tomb itself, these green cloths are believed to carry *barakah*. In a sense, they are inanimate objects that "animate" due to their relationship with the tomb complex and their color. The memory of place and its role in ritual is also expressed in the pilgrimage prayers (*ziyarat-nama*) performed at the shrine. In books dedicated to pilgrimage, *kutub al-mazar* or *al-ziyara*, themes, prayers, and rituals related to

Figure 5.1 *Parche sabz/dakhil*, Bab al-Saghir, Damascus, Syria (photo courtesy of author).

these sites are outlined.[60] Books of prayers exist in numerous languages including Arabic, Farsi, and English, and contain the particular supplications that should be performed for a particular saint. At Sufi shrines, a set of rituals exist that appear to be almost identical to the action of rubbing the green cloth on the Shi'i tomb. According to one observer, "People visiting a pīr's tomb or shrine touch it and rub the flat, smooth stones on their persons in order to transfer the *baraka* from the grace to themselves ... In the case of women contact is often made by means of cloth, namely, part of their sārī or dupattā."[61] The process through which this occurs is similar in Sufi and Shi'i traditions, which are arguably mixed up in each other, where the dead changes the quality of an object for the living. For Shi'i, the act of tying a cloth is a way of bringing attention to a request, hence the phrase *dakhil bastan* is invoked, literally meaning "binding the request for help;" in this case, through the binding of green cloth.[62]

Green cloths are also believed to transport the blessings, or *barakat*, that are associated with a shrine or other holy site. In this way, they are similar to the story of the robber who unwittingly picked up dust from Karbala and was allowed into heaven (see p. 171). Pilgrims who rub green cloths on the *mazar* (tomb) may believe that the intercession of the saint who lies inside will be transported into the cloth's fibers, which explains why pilgrims occasionally tie the *dakhil* in their car or wear it on their body. Stories of the bodies of saints being preserved, with light shining from their open eyes, also tells us something about how "alive" these sites are believed to be.[63]

Pilgrims often purchase permanent mementos as a way to be close to Turner's "Center." One case is the prayer stones (*turbah/mohr namaz*) from sites such as Najaf, which are available for purchase at shrines, at bazaars, and on the Internet. The tradition of using prayer stones comes from the teachings of the Imams to pray on the earth, following (Shi'i) *ahadith* of the Prophet. Prayer stones also serve as a physical form of shrines in miniature through the small, pressed pieces of clay that come from this sacred soil.[64] These stones, called *turbah*, *mohr namaz*, or *mohr*, are made from the soil that surrounds the tombs of the Imams, sites very few have the chance to set foot upon.[65] As Hazleton points out, these prayer tablets make it possible to connect to the sacred: "wherever in the world a Shii prostrates himself in prayer, the soil his forehead touches is sacred soil."[66]

A variety of Arabic words and phrases are found on these pieces, as well as images such as pictorial representations of Imam Husayn's tomb in Karbala. These depictions are much like the pilgrims' items from Canterbury, images generated by Christians who hoped to recall and even re-experience their journeys – what some scholars have described as "memory aids."[67] The image of Karbala in Shi'i iconography is the Canterbury of modern Shi'ism and is found on posters, murals, and banners that reflect both a "political and religious battlefield."[68] As we have seen, Karbala is an iconic place; it stands for the battle fought there in 680 and also for all rebellions against tyranny, reflected in the Iranian sociologist Ali Shari'ati's famous call: "Every month of the year is Muharram, every day of the month is Ashura, every piece of land is Karbala."[69] One billboard in Khuzestan reads: "Either Pilgrimage or Martyrdom" (*ya ziyarat ya shahadat*), which means that even if the soldier dies, he will reach the pilgrimage site and be rewarded by sitting in the courtyard in Husayn's shrine (*sahn-i aba 'abd Allah*) at Karbala.[70] It is common to find the name of Imam Husayn etched into the stones. Although 'Ali is an important figure, and Najaf, where he is believed to be buried, is an important pilgrimage destination, Karbala, as the site where Husayn was murdered, is even more popular. In 2012, approximately fifteen million pilgrims visited Karbala.

The touching of images and representations of the Shi'i narrative is a part of both ordered and created traditions, and this includes the prayer stone, which is not used by other Muslims. "The devotional practice of touching the *mohr namaz* is adapted into Shia orthodox ritual practice in connection with the performance of liturgical prayer, *salat*. Devotional practices, such as touching various objects while silently pronouncing a supplication, *du'a*, is not stipulated by orthodox ritual practice but structured through popular sentiments."[71] The use of a prayer stone is a way in which Shi'i can follow the teachings of the Imams to prostrate on earth while forming a connection to Karbala and to the family of the Prophet. The Shi'i requirement for praying on earth is noted in several legal traditions cited by religious authorities, and although it is preferred that one prays on a tablet or stone made from the clay of Karbala, it is not required.[72] Shi'i may use a tissue (which is made from wood pulp) or a product made from cotton, for example, because these come from the earth. There is a quite vociferous debate on the use of cotton and flax as *turbah* (earth) in Shi'a *fiqh* (law), which largely surrounds the issue of dissimulation (disguise, in particular the hiding of Shi'i identity when one's life is under threat); in other words, the use of cotton and flax could reveal someone's Shi'i identity and thus endanger them.[73]

In addition to the miracles associated with Karbala, many tales ascribe a particular olfactory quality to the place, a sweetness that is associated with traditions of the Prophet and his relatives.[74] Al-Shajari's *Kitab al-Amali* (Book of Hope) contains the story of a tribesman from the Banu Asad who picked up soil from Husayn's grave, smelled it, and burst into tears, saying, "I swear by my father and mother, nothing smells sweeter than you and your tomb."[75] Then he composed a verse of poetry, one of the many examples of poems about Husayn: "They intended to hide his grave from his enemies, But the fragrance of the soil of the grave drew people to it."[76] The following story, which remained popular until the mid-twentieth century, expresses how Karbala functioned in the religious lives of Iraqi Shi'i:

> A robber once attacked pilgrims returning from the tomb of Imam Husayn and looted their money. One night the robber had a dream. It was the day of resurrection. People were being judged for their acts, and their destinies were being determined. The robber saw Husayn holding a notebook containing all the names of those who had visited his tomb. When the robber's turn came, Husayn looked at his notebook and found his name, too. The robber was baffled for he had never visited Husayn's tomb. He enquired and was told that the angels wrote down his name because when he robbed the pilgrims, some of the dust from Husayn's tomb that had stuck to their clothes stuck to his too; this in itself was sufficient for the robber to gain access to heaven. The robber then woke up and began chanting:

If it is salvation that you seek, visit Husayn

So that gratified you will encounter God

For the flames [of hell] shall not touch a body

To which some dust from the visitors of Husayn had stuck.[77]

Through such stories, it is apparent that Karbala serves as a locus of religious power that can be manifested through the prayer stones made from its soil. Even when removed from the land and transported for hundreds or thousands of miles, this soil is sacred for Shi'i.

Poets would return with soil from the tomb and throw it at loved ones, who would be blessed and healed.[78] References to the healing power of Karbala's soil are found in religious texts, including *ahadith* from the Twelve Imams, such as this one from Imam Sadiq: "Prostration on the earth of the tomb of Hoseyn illuminates even the seventh heaven."[79] A genre of poems about Husayn and Karbala also references the soil of Karbala and its healing properties, including these lines from the eleventh-century poet Mihyar al-Daylami: "And the visitors brought him my greeting / So that I might see him as my eyes did not see him / Then they returned and strew upon me soil / Which heals me, and drives away fears."[80] Although eating dirt is prohibited in the Shi'i *hadith*, the soil of Karbala, specifically from around the tomb of Husayn (up to seventy cubits from the grave), is the exception to the rule.[81] This tradition states: "He who eats dirt and then dies, then do not pray over him [making him equal to one who has committed suicide] unless he ate of the dirt of the tomb [of Hoseyn – *tīn al-qabr*]. In it is a cure for all ills, though the one who eats it out of greed, will not be cured by it."[82] When people touch their forehead upon the prayer stone, they participate in an act of *dhikr* (remembrance), remembering the martyrdom of

Husayn on the fields of Karbala, a place they may never set foot in during their lives. Karbala is a significant place, and to understand its importance for Shi'i one must recognize that this plain is not only the location of Husayn's martyrdom, it is the site of an almost endless cycle of miracles.

Many tales are found in Karbala literature; many are poems ("Karbalayi poetry") or dramatic enactments of the battle that include references to the soil's sacred qualities.[83] Beginning in the first couple of years after Husayn's death, stories began to emerge about the land where the Prophet's grandson was killed – that when Caliph Mutawakkil sent workers with oxen to plow the soil, the oxen would not walk over Husayn's grave even when beaten; that when a canal was dug so that water would flood the grave, the canal diverted itself.[84]

The production of prayer stones also emerges from another genre of literature related to Husayn that is specifically tied to the soil on which he died. In numerous theological works focused on Karbala, all written in both Arabic and Farsi, "The prostration on the soil of Karbala is highly recommended [as] another effort to externalize the memory of the oppression Imam Husayn endured for safeguarding Islam."[85] Prayer stones, then, not only serve as ritual aids in the performance of daily prayers, they also connect one to the place and time of Husayn's death, serving to mediate the relationship between the believer and the foundational story that guides his or her religious life. They are permanent mementos that form a constant relationship with the past through the act of *salat* (daily prayer), thus referring to two sacred centers – Mecca and Karbala – simultaneously.

VIRTUAL PILGRIMAGES

Pilgrimage mementos play a part in important rituals where an individual interacts with a sacred place or person remotely.

Muslims in South Asia, who live thousands of miles away from cities containing *imamzadeh*, often have sacred objects in their community buildings, used ritually to place the person in close proximity to one of the holy cities of Shi'i Islam, such as Karbala, Mashhad, or Qom. These objects are used to orient the believer to distant locations, creating a virtual pilgrimage. In these cases, sacred objects linked to distant pilgrimage sites and prayers are recited that "are symbolic of actual visitations to the graves of the *ahl al-bayt*."[86]

Virtual pilgrimages allow the pilgrim to connect to a site or ritual while being distant from a holy site. The fact that many pilgrims engage in these journeys from their homes is an often overlooked aspect of modern pilgrimage. As Ian Reader has argued, "Studies of pilgrimage have frequently focused on such themes as movement and on the importance of journeys, of people in transit and of escaping and getting away from the everyday frameworks and constraints."[87] One of the problems with this approach is that it inadvertently excludes large numbers of Muslims who may be too poor, or too distant from a sacred site, to go there physically. Muslims may also be unable to go on *hajj* or other pilgrimages because of poor health. Virtual pilgrimage provides options for these individuals.

Given that the majority of Muslims live in Asia, alternative pilgrimages allow for a performance of religious duties to take place without an actual physical journey that one may not be able to afford or otherwise take. One of the common occasions this occurs is during *hajj*, where Muslims not performing the journey conduct rituals parallel to those taking place in Mecca. The sacrifice of animals at Eid al-Adha is one of these cases. Muslims all over the world commemorate the end of the *hajj* with a large meal, representing the sacrifice of an animal in place of Ishmael. "On the day of *kurban* Muslims everywhere, and Mecca is no exception, sacrifice a sheep or sometimes a cow or camel."[88] The *kurban* (sacrifice) represents Ibrahim's

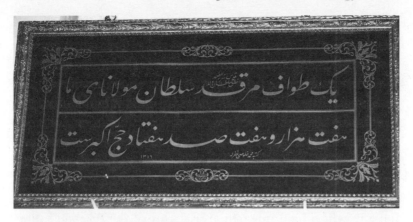

Figure 5.2 Calligraphic tradition from Rumi's tomb, Konya, Turkey (photo courtesy of Omid Safi).

sacrifice, the willingness of the son to obey his father, and the obligation of all Muslims to submit to Allah. In previous chapters, we have also learned about other pilgrimages that mirror the circumambulation of the *ka'bah*, or serve as substitutions altogether, such as the Javanese tradition at Tembayat. Rumi's tomb at Konya is viewed by some as being far more important than the *hajj*. The teaching is even memorialized in a sign that hangs at the shrine that reads (in English translation): "To do one *tawaf* around our sultan is equivalent to doing 7,700 of the great *hajj*."

Shi'i Muslims have a number of virtual pilgrimages that transport them to the sites of the Imams and into the presence of saints and other holy people. Virtual pilgrimage is defined as "non-computer-based pilgrimages such as physically enacting pilgrimage rituals or storytelling from afar."[89] These pilgrimages are not to be confused with cyber-pilgrimages, journeys that use a computer or other device to journey to (and sometimes through) a sacred site. In Shi'ism, numerous virtual rituals exist, connecting disparate communities or, in some cases, supporting an individual believer's relationship with a particular religious figure like 'Ali or Husayn.

At 'Ashura', the Battle of Karbala is narrated and sometimes performed in Shi'i communities. This is an example
of a virtual pilgrimage that uses storytelling to transport the
believer to a sacred site, in this case to the plains on which
Prophet Muhammad's grandson was killed along with many
others. The storyteller, who may be male or female (women
sometimes recite the story to all-female *majlis*), intends to
transport the listeners to Karbala in an intentional re-telling
of the death of Husayn and his companions. Fatimah is often
invoked in these narrations, an individual who is believed to
have mystical qualities – the possessor of the Prophet's *Nur*,
or light, which gives her the power of intercession (*shafa'ah*).
Fatimah is also featured in religious processions that are held
surrounding 'Ashura'. In Shi'i communities in Hyderabad,
processions (*julus*) of mourners march through the Old City,
carrying a battle standard (*'alam*) representing Fatimah that sits
atop an elephant, which is eventually immersed in the waters
of the Musi river, cooling the *'alam* and "reappropriating its
potent power, which sustains and protects Fatimah's devotees
for another year."[90]

Important figures in the Karbala narrative are featured in
these Shi'i processions. These gatherings are often places in
which Fatimah and other individuals appear, in the minds,
hearts, and eyes of Shi'i. Because Fatimah is the intercessory
figure, the key saint, in many of these rituals, for all intents
and purposes she has traveled to the village, mosque, or
Ashurkhana (commemorative building for 'Ashura' rituals)
where the story is being enacted. These magical visitations
are common in Shi'i culture. As one report describes, "Still
vivid in the memory of many Shia, the identity of a woman
unknown to the *majlis* participants was realized only when she
vanished after being offered her share of the food (*tabarruk*),
which is distributed after the mourning assembly."[91] In this
case, the mysterious figure of Fatimah, who had journeyed
to a ritual site that recreates Karbala, comes to the pilgrims,

instead of them traveling to her, in a kind of reverse virtual pilgrimage that represents the powerful nature of the cult of the saints.

Shi'i sometimes construct replicas of shrines in their homes and community centers. Usually called Hussainiyya, these are intentional recreations of Husayn's tomb at Karbala. Replicas of scenes from the battle include those focused on martyrs from the battle, who are believed to intercede on behalf of believers and offer them protection. One example is Ali Ashgar, the infant son of Husayn. Shi'i use replicas of his cradle, as well as his body, in male and female gatherings that honor him, and at Muharram they also dress baby boys in a white jacket and green headband – the costume that represents him.[92] Small replicas of tombs called *rowza* or *ta'ziyeh* (in the case of Husayn) are also used in Shi'i ceremonies. In South Asia, rituals mimic the processions at tombs in Iraq and Iran. In Pakistani Shi'i communities, these replicas are important symbols in the ritual reenactment of distant pilgrimages: "These models are displayed in the visitation house (*ziyaratkhana*), so that people who visit that building can make a surrogate pilgrimage to the martyr's tomb by visiting the miniature of it."[93] Miniature shrines (*tabut*) are often used in Muharram processions in India, where "poor Hindu and Muslim men and women in fulfillment of vows not infrequently throw themselves in the roadway and roll in front of the *tabus*."[94]

Large-scale paintings are also used in virtual pilgrimage. The Iranian move to democratize art – to form a relationship between contemporary art and the Iranian people – is tied to the artistic movement known as "Art of the Revolution" and the founding of the Center of Art and Islamic Thought (*howze-ye honar va andishe-ye eslami*).[95] The democratization of art is seen today in the billboards, monuments, and other expressions of state Shi'ism, something that confronts the public in numerous spaces. Many of these projects connect the viewer to religious figures through an image of a battle, messianic scene, or picture of paradise. Other examples of the democratization of art in Iran constitute a pilgrimage site that is more traditional, as in the case of the mural at the Khoramshahr mosque, located in the city of the same name in the province of Khuzestan. The polyptych (five-part mural) is comprised of various scenes, including one featuring a woman, and the final scene culminates in a martyred soldier rising to heaven and meeting Husayn.[96] The soldier functions as a symbol of the defense of the homeland and the defense of the Muslim faith.[97] The scenes displayed in the mural transport pilgrims to the battlefield, allowing them to imagine themselves in the same struggle, while reminding the pilgrims that they, too, are soldiers in the struggle for justice – the key rhetorical message in Shi'i art. Khoramshahr represents a kind of double pilgrimage. The first pilgrimage takes place during the Persian New Year (which is, like many Iranian cultural traditions, situated in Zoroastrian, not Islamic, rituals) when pilgrims visit the mosque to pray there to the figures in the painting.[98] The second pilgrimage is the one that allows the pilgrim to participate in the battle, the sacrifice, and the redemption. "The human presence on a large scale, of the martyr-soldier, who twice stares at the visitor, encourages the inner meditation of the pilgrim and his identification with the character."[99]

Karbala is the operative narrative in these pilgrimages and includes an arsenal of imagery that is familiar to the public. The popularity of images of Husayn, Zaynab, 'Abbas, and others is used widely in Shi'i communities, allowing individuals to connect to Karbala even when performing the pilgrimage is impossible due to health, finance, or safety. "Recollecting the events at the battle is a cognitive process, and images are used to stimulate it."[100] Objects connected to the pilgrimage such as posters and banners, as well as sacred items like soil, allow one to connect to a place far away, experiencing a kind of inner pilgrimage that may substitute for what is not possible in this life. One can recreate a virtual environment that includes portraits of saints, wall hangings (*parcham*), flags reminiscent of those used at the battle, and black drapes (*siyapoush*) symbolizing the death of Husayn.[101]

In many cases, items from the pilgrimage site are used in these reenactments and parallel rituals. Shi'i often utilize religious objects in their communal gatherings, which range from weekly prayer meetings (Twelver Shi'i perform special prayers on Thursday nights, for example) to commemorations of the Imams. Votive images are especially common, and are believed to carry the *barakah* of the saint or/and the place he or she is buried. Replicas of shrines are frequently used on these occasions, which involve prayer, walking processions, self-flagellation (including by women), and the circling of a model or replica of a site.[102] These represent a small sample of the ways in which pilgrimage involves much more than physical travel. As the remaining sections of this chapter discuss, technology also provides options that expand the boundaries of traditional pilgrimage.

MUSLIMS AND TECHNOLOGY

Muslims are often accused of being anti-modern, refusing to subscribe to institutions like democracy and secularism and being hostile to technology. This thesis has been discredited by scholars who point to the ways in which modernity marks many Muslim-majority states. This includes the use of technology. Daesh is one of the savviest users of the Internet and social media, producing recruitment videos that are distributed to its recruits, videotaping the destruction of ancient monuments deemed *haram* (such as the August 2015 bombing of Palmyra's temple), and creating snuff videos showing the execution of its victims through immolation, drowning, or beheading. In fact, Daesh is all about technology, an example of the violent end of *E-jihad*. As Gary Bunt, a pioneer in the field of Islam and new media, defines it, "E-jihad, or electronic jihad, is a term that can encompass a wide range of meanings."[103]

At the other end of the spectrum, E-jihad has been used to hack websites and engage in other political activities.[104] In a broad sense, electronic jihad applies to those "struggles" that Muslims take on, many of which would be classified as postcolonial or socially conscious. Muslim activists, artists, and intellectuals use E-jihad and new media to protest Daesh, repressive governments, the military industrial establishment, racism, sexism, and Islamophobia. Muslims for Ferguson is an electronic jihad focused on the struggle against insti-tutionalized racism and police brutality. Other online com-munities include the Toronto Unity Mosque, a gender-equal and queer-affirming *masjid*, and the Muslim Anti-Racism Collaborative, both with an active Facebook presence. Bunt has coined the term "Cyber Islamic Environments" for these communities, which range from violent *jihadi* groups to col-lectives of queer Muslims and their supporters.[105]

Muslims are active participants in modernity and its var-ious appendages. Talal Asad, an anthropologist of religion, has emphatically made this point in his work, arguing that we are all conscripted into modernity. As David Scott elu-cidates, "Asad's point is neither that authentic difference is disappearing or surviving, but that difference, such as it is, is increasingly obliged to respond to – and be managed by – the categories brought into play by European modernity."[106] Modernity includes technology and new media – mobile phones, the Internet, Facebook, Twitter, and Tumblr – all of which function in important ways for Muslims. In many cases, Muslims have developed Islamic-specific symbols and technological tools. The development of Islamic emoticons is an example of this trend. These icons populate Muslim online blogs, cell phone texts, and other places, despite vociferous debates about whether they are legally permissible. As Stanton points out, the popularity of Islamic emoticons reflects the "contemporary, decentralized understanding of authority in Islam."[107]

Technology aids in the expression of religious identity, the connection to community, and participation in ritual, including rituals involved in pilgrimage. Technology has radically altered the ways in which Muslims perform pilgrimage and cyberspace creates a wide field of new possibilities for pilgrimage, what we might call cyber-*ziyarat*. Where a physical journey was once the only option, it is now one among many ways that people can connect to sacred people and places, whether or not they are physically traveling to Mecca, Karbala, or Konya. New technologies and media forms have altered these pilgrimages through social media, phone apps, and community chat rooms focused on particular *ziyarat*. Technology has created a wide array of ways in which the pilgrim can interact with a sacred site remotely, ways that were not possible even a few decades ago.

At the same time, scholars of popular culture, new media, and emergent technologies have resisted making sweeping generalizations about how technology functions in these new religious worlds. Just as the use of social media impacts religious authority but does not erase the centers of power, offering different and at times competing sources of power, the same can be said of pilgrimage.[108] New media and its technologies offer additional ways of doing ritual, experiencing sacred sites, and interacting with religious landscapes, but this reflects a movement of texts and technologies that has been present for centuries. The *ziyarat* prayers that were once contained in pilgrim books are now in a cell phone app. The rituals detailed in the previous section, which scholars describe as virtual pilgrimages, can now be performed in numerous ways – with a ritual object such as a portable icon, or with a computer, tablet, or smartphone. The places to which they refer – Mecca, Karbala, Konya – are still part of Islamic history and tradition.

Cyber-pilgrimages are popular with many religious communities. Individuals who live in exile, are part of a diaspora, or simply live far away from a holy site can experience a pilgrimage online. As one example, Virtual Jerusalem (www. virtualjerusalem.com) makes interaction with the Jewish homeland possible. Through the "Send a Prayer" option, individuals can send a prayer by email and then have it physically placed in the Western Wall.[109] Through cyber-*ziyarat*, Muslims can experience Mecca, Karbala, and other sites, often petitioning a saint or leaving a mark on the religious site, in much the same way.

The use of technology in pilgrimage journeys creates options for poor, exiled, or dispersed communities. The Kurds have developed entire online communities ("Cyberkurds") that offer virtual spaces of interactions, allowing for transnational networks that help bring together a huge diaspora.[110] Online Muslim communities include many individuals from war-torn countries like Afghanistan, Syria, and Iraq. Even for those Muslims not affected by political conflicts or living as part of a diaspora, the Internet provides alternative spaces in response to the alienation that is part of modernity, created by the breakdown of traditional familial and local communities, allowing people to reach out to each other at any time, for example as in the context of pilgrimage.[111]

Despite the emergent ways in which Muslim pilgrims can interact with a site, this is, like any religious journey, largely dependent on the economic mobility of the individual. Any serious discussion of Islamic pilgrimage in the twenty-first century should be aware of the fact that Muslim access to technology is, as in much of the world, dependent on social class. The "digital divide" varies among countries and also between social classes.[112] For this reason, any survey of cyber-*hajj*, smartphone apps for *ziyarat*, or other technologies created for Muslim pilgrims should acknowledge that these are only accessible to some in the Muslim community.

Islamic pilgrimage is being shaped by technology and new media, in traditional "physical" pilgrimages as well as in the cyber-pilgrimages that have emerged in recent years. The Internet, which is used in all of the technologies discussed here, is of particular importance when examining religion due to its interactivity, connectivity, labyrinthine form, and status as a liminal space where *communitas* – the very thing that often marks pilgrimage experience – can take place.[113] Scholars of religion and technology argue that spaces created by the Internet offer alternative landscapes that can create important communities of meaning. This idea of landscape is useful, not in the sense of a geographical landscape, but one "composed of sites, nodes, systems, and channels between systems."[114] This perspective is rooted in the work of J.Z. Smith who argues that ritual is situated in communal space, which is constructed by religious actors, sometimes in ways that transcend traditional geography.[115]

Cyberspace contains geographies with landmarks and signposts that are recognizable to those who traverse it. The fact that Muslims take electronic journeys through these landscapes reflects a common practice in religion – symbolic substitution. J.Z. Smith calls these efforts to recreate meaning symbolic "relations of equivalence," seen in the Stations of the Cross and the examples we are examining here.[116] Islam has a long history of symbolic pilgrimage rituals as well, whether in the Sufi writings of the "path" (*tariqah*) that mirror the development of human life or the imitation of *hajj*, as in the case of al-Hallaj whose execution was due in part to his claim that the pilgrimage to Mecca could be performed spiritually without leaving one's home.[117]

Today, scholars point to the "electronic architecture of cyberspace" that houses churches, cathedrals, shrines, mosques, and other sacred sites.[118] There is plentiful scholarship on the electronic architecture of Christianity, but Islam has also created cyber-buildings and spaces, developing a narrative space that may compete with the experiences elicited by the physical sites. One way to understand these sites is through Roland Robertson's idea of *glocalization* – the mediation between the local and the global.[119] Cyberspace offers a space in which the particular is universalized, in part because it is made available to everyone, regardless of their location vis-à-vis the pilgrimage site.

There are many ways in which the Internet alters and enriches the pilgrim's experiences. Scholars have made an important distinction between "religion online" – information one gains from the Internet – and "online religion," which reflects religious practices and experiences through the Internet.[120] In some ways, modern pilgrimage, which is so often aided by the Internet, reflects both of these fields, for individuals often learn about their journey through websites and other platforms as well as experience journeys to sacred sites through their computer, tablet, or cell phone. Religious apps for mobile phones include a number of categories: lifestyle, reference, education, books, utilities, entertainment, games, and music.[121] The majority of apps are scripturally oriented, focused on Arabic, the Qur'an, *ahadith*, and other textual sources.[122]

Considerable debate surrounds the use of technologies in learning verses from the Qur'an, doing prayers, and other religious tasks. Muslim scholars have considered the appropriateness of sacred texts and cell phones, with one Egyptian scholar arguing that Qur'anic recitation should not be used as a tone on mobile devices and a Saudi scholar seeking to ban cameras on cell phones due to their potential for immoral uses.[123] Other concerns have been voiced over the presence of sacred content on cell phones due to the mobility of such devices, for, like the Qur'an, the computerized sacred word should not be near impure places such as bathrooms. As a possible solution, one scholar recommends leaving cell phones outside such areas, which avoids the danger of ritual contamination.[124] Under this reasoning, the sacred status of the Qur'an, as well as certain words like Allah, can exist on cellular devices as long as certain rules are followed. This suggests that the cell phone can function as a sacred enclosure – housing a holy text. At one Shi'i site (moharram.ir) the visitor is asked to enter the site in a state of religious purity, representing the importance of *niyyat* (intention) in Shi'i theology and practice.[125]

Religious apps, much like other types of material consumption, are part of what Nabil Echchaibi calls the *halal marketplace*, an industry worth over 2.3 billion dollars that includes everything from Islamic banking to Fulla (the Islamic version of Barbie).[126] Mobile apps for pilgrimage include many for *hajj* that focus on everything from the rules and rituals associated with the journey to devices that help orient pilgrims, aid in their navigation of sites, and identify the location of their specific tour group. Some apps are informational, providing cues on the sequence of rituals that help to reiterate important religious beliefs about Islamic history and in particular the life of Prophet Ibrahim, around whom so much of the *hajj* is focused. One example is the website of the Saudi Ministry of Hajj, which retraces the steps of both Muhammad and Abraham.[127] IslamiCity is a website that serves a similar purpose, offering a *"hajj* information center" that provides helpful links to Saudi government sites as well as Shi'i sites and texts, including Shari'ati's text on *hajj*.[128]

Hajj guide systems help orient pilgrims before, during, and after their journey. AlHajj is one such app that according to one review is "an interactive guide to Hajj, allowing users to walk through the process of the Hajj to develop a better understanding of the obligations, locations, dates, and sequence they need to perform."[129] Another application called Hajjdoc aids pilgrims in the documentation of their pilgrimage, including a feature that allows users to see reports from other pilgrims using the app.[130] Instructional content is offered for other pilgrims, including those who perform *ziyarat* to Shi'i tombs, with instructions on prayer, photo galleries, and advice on how to perform ritual practices that are distinct to each shrine.[131]

As briefly discussed earlier, documenting the journey through social media represents another way in which technology is used in Islamic pilgrimages even when there are religious sanctions against cameras and other devices in sacred spaces. One pilgrim who completed the *hajj* in 2007 reported that cameras were not allowed in the *haram* (the Grand Mosque, the *ka'bah*, and its environs) but she snuck one in anyway.[132] Five years later, countless pilgrims were taking photos inside the courtyard that surrounds the *ka'bah* and were uploading them to social media platforms like Facebook, Twitter, and Instagram.[133] Now, self-documenting one's *hajj* is very common.

Technology has changed the nature of *hajj*, which brings us back to the questions posed by the previous chapter surrounding the intersection of sacred travel and tourism. Even for deeply religious people undertaking sacred journeys, technology has a seductive quality:

> The Saudi development of the *hajj* has created pilgrimage 2.0 in which Muslims can tweet their *tawaf* and all the rituals they perform throughout the pilgrimage. In fact, pilgrims can be guided through the hajj rites via iPhone apps and keep friends and family updated with their progress with photos and blog updates. The struggles of *hajj* have been transformed, the rites remain the same but the rhythm of the pilgrimage has altered.[134]

Hajj is just one of the pilgrimages featured on a website, smartphone app, or other technological interface. Shi'i have numerous portals that provide instructions on holy people, sacred sites, and other topics related to *ziyarat*. The Al-Imam portal (www.al-islam.org) includes a component on Imam Husayn, featuring iconography related to his martyrdom and recordings of the rituals of Muharram; a feature on Fatima that asks where her grave is; and another area of the website on the destruction of holy sites including those of the Imams and other relatives of Prophet Muhammad.[135]

Cyber-pilgrimages use computers or another interface to experience a sacred site online. In these cases, the pilgrim's body is not physically present at the sacred site. Cyber-pilgrimage offers a wide range of environments, from simple renderings of a site to live camera feeds. Critics of this type of pilgrimage argue that such journeys are inauthentic, for they involve no travel and no experience of sensing the site (except visually), and fail to satisfy the religious requirement to conduct particular rituals, such as making an offering or touching an object such as a stone or altar. Others have countered these arguments by stating that cyber-pilgrimage offers something else – the opportunity to be part of a social community (often called a "virtual community") that would not be possible with a physical pilgrimage, due to the physical risk, crowds, and exhaustion entailed by the latter.[136]

It is perhaps important to remember when thinking about cyber-*ziyarat* that pilgrimage is an "intensely visual experience."[137] Islamic pilgrimage often involves the "seeing" of a building, tomb, or other object. Take *hajj*, for example, a journey that includes the sighting of the *ka'bah*, the hill on which Prophet Muhammad gave his farewell sermon, and other places and objects imbued with religious meaning. Cyber-*hajj* is a modern way of experiencing these sightings using a live feed and, in other cases, providing rich images of the *ka'bah* and the *haram*. In addition to the visual sighting of the *ka'bah* and other important places on *hajj*, cyber-pilgrimage offers alternative ways of seeing.

Pilgrimage can also be very involved with community. One way online pilgrims construct community is through guest books, a way to create a sense of community through technology. Another way that community is formed is through the use of avatars. At least one cyber-*hajj* offers this option: "In *Second Life*'s *hajj*, cyberpilgrims can 'journey' *together* in pilgrimage garb via their avatars, an undertaking that can attract large numbers during real-life *hajj*. Using chat-windows, pilgrims can discuss personal experiences, motivations, thoughts and problems, with other pilgrims, who form visible 'presences' onscreen."[138] Second Life's *hajj* offers a three-dimensional cyber-environment and functions as a kind of role-playing religious game.[139] The recreations of the Grand Mosque, the *ka'bah*, and other major religious sites, combined with the use of role-playing avatars, offer a kind of computerized pilgrimage experience that is both faith-driven and entertaining.

Computer-based Islamic pilgrimages are growing in number and variety. One website offers the opportunity to send prayers through cyberspace as a replacement for the small papers that are often left at Shi'i shrines and another site offers an online pilgrimage under the link "Pilgrimage from distance" that reads:

> The Holy Shrine of Imam Ridha (A.S.) is in fact the venerable object of the eager hearts of his lovers throughout the world. The enthusiasts for Imam with many troubles go toward holy Shrine, and sometimes when they are broken-hearted longing for pilgrimage causes them to be so impatient that, although impossible, they wished they would reside at the threshold of the Holy Shrine. It order to provide facilities for the lovers of this Ziyarat from distant places, the software of 'cosmoplayer' is here suggested for the visitors of the official website of the Holy Shrine of Imam Ridha (A.S.).[140]

The Al-Imam website features numerous ways for Shi'i to experience a pilgrimage online. They enable individuals who live far away from Iraq, Iran, and other countries with Shi'i shrines to be part of a vibrant transnational community. The options for engagement include recordings of the *adhan* (the call to prayer) given at shrines, *nashids* (vocal chants), and *azaas* (ritual recitations associated with the dead).[141] In addition to these examples, pilgrims can go to the sites that have live feeds, such as the Jamkaran Mosque in Qom (www.jamkaran.ir).

Muslims have numerous options for interacting with religious personalities and holy places outside of the pilgrimages like *hajj* and the *ziyarat* documented in previous chapters. Pilgrimage is not just a physical movement where an individual places his or her body in a sacred space, moving from the mundane to the sacred. Rather, it is a wide range of active, ongoing, and dynamic rituals, traditions, and performances that involve the material, religious, and imaginative formulation of space, what Soja calls the "collectively created spatiality" that is such an important part of the human experience.[142]

AFTERWORD

PRESUPPOSITIONS AND POSSIBILITIES IN THE STUDY OF ISLAMIC PILGRIMAGE

REFLECTIONS

My favorite professor in graduate school liked to say, "You will forever, as an academic, feel overwhelmed and inadequate." I kept his words in mind while writing this book, mining through nearly three hundred sources, deliberating about geographical, sectarian, and ethnic equity, and creating a foundational text on Islamic pilgrimage. Pilgrimage in Islam is not a subject that can be covered fully in one volume, and while I do not claim this book is the authoritative or final study on the topic, I have tried to produce a new option for our framing of Islamic pilgrimage – the myriad religious journeys that Muslims undertake, and have undertaken, for over 1,400 years. Great effort was made to paint a portrait of the great diversity within Islam, reflecting Shahab Ahmed's call for the "inclusion of difference" that marks Muslim belief and tradition.[1] Nevertheless, there are undoubtedly shortcomings – places, people, and pilgrimages I missed – due to the immense number of Muslims in the world, and for this I apologize.

As I have argued, Islamic pilgrimage is a large topic that benefits from many perspectives, which is why this book includes the work of anthropologists, historians, cultural critics, and art historians, and why I did not limit myself solely to the field of religious studies. The chapters contained within this volume do not make a grand statement about which theory or methodology is best, a point I shall get to in the latter part of this chapter. Instead, what I have done here is to suggest some of the ways we might understand this thing we call Islamic pilgrimage and be more careful about the assumptions we make as scholars. In this sense, the two aims of this project – the presentation of Islamic pilgrimage as a grand subject and the attention we need to give to the problems in our field – are embedded in each other.

First, Islamic pilgrimage is not restricted to *hajj*, nor is it something in which a tiered model of sacred importance – with Mecca at the center – is always in force. The negotiation of sacred space in Islam is, like in many traditions, an ongoing project. In the case of American Shi'i, the construction of local religious sites "serve to evoke Karbala and to publicly claim space," through a process of tying *imambargah*s to Karbala through decorative symbols.[2] This enactment of a localized sacred space in relation to a holy city is common in the context of Islamic pilgrimages. One scholar, following Henri Lefebvre, describes these spaces as "beyond what is lived and conceived, real and imagined."[3] Due to the ephemeral quality of sacred space, there is no one religious center around which all others necessarily revolve.

A second point this book makes is that Islamic pilgrimages are rarely isolated from each other. They often function within large local, regional, or transnational networks. This is certainly true of Shi'i pilgrimage, which includes sites in Iraq, Iran, Syria, Lebanon, Saudi Arabia, and elsewhere. In Iran and Iraq alone, there are numerous shrines visited by pilgrims including those in the Iraqi cities of Najaf, Karbala,

Kazimayn, and Samarra (known as *'atabat*).[4] However, other sites are visited in conjunction with these, including those that are not restricted to only Shi'i. Even in the early centuries of Islam, Muslim pilgrims rarely visited one site and excluded others. The story of early Islam is one of a nexus of traditions of which Mecca was visited along with numerous other places in Jerusalem, Medina, and elsewhere. In some cases, Muslims, Jews, Christians, and Zoroastrians even visited the same places together.[5] Pilgrimage sites did not exist in isolation, but in a nexus of people, dreams, visions, and sites, which often referred to each other in vernacular literature and other texts. Illustrated pilgrimage manuals often included numerous images of these sacred places, including "stylized plans of the Prophet's mosque in Medina, where his tomb is located, and of the Dome of the Rock in Jerusalem, the goal of Muhammad's Night Journey and the place from which tradition said he ascended to heaven."[6] Muslims often visited the graves of local saints, or long-dead ancestors, alongside major sites like the *ka'bah*, as they do today.

Another issue this book raises is that scholars often present an idealized vision of pilgrimage. In particular, *communitas*, or the communal experience of pilgrims, is too often the focus of scholarship. Despite the popularity of this concept – the mystical moment the pilgrim experiences in community with his or her co-religionists – the claim that a majority of pilgrims have these experiences is unsubstantiated. The reliance on *communitas* suggests that pilgrimage is necessarily an internal, deep, mystical experience, when in fact it may include no mystical moment. Pilgrimage can include such an experience, but it may be disappointing. In recent years, scholars have been more willing to look at these cases. In one case, a *hajji* came away with an attitude that inoculated him to "ideology in general," after experiencing an even more profound "distaste for the literalism of much religious practice" during his time in Mecca.[7] Another Muslim complained of being harassed by fellow female pilgrims, being accosted for having her hair peek out from under her veil.[8] Such cases, which are not rare, illustrate that pilgrimage is an activity that entails numerous experiences and outcomes.

One of the ways in which the study of pilgrimage can be expanded beyond the focus on *communitas* is by focusing on other aspects of pilgrimage, such as the material, and in particular the body's relationship to sacred sites. I have included many examples of these aspects of Muslim journeys – the trees and springs that mark pilgrimage sites, the importance of the bodies of saints, the use of objects in rituals connected to pilgrimage sites – all of which point to a richer understanding of this subject. While I do not think that focusing solely on the material provides a complete picture of Islamic pilgrimage, some of the most interesting studies being done today include those focused "in the material word, including the human body and its sensorium."[9] One way of thinking creatively about the Muslim individual's corporeal interaction with the sacred, which extends beyond the journey alone, is the concept of the permanent memento, an object that negotiates space beyond the religious center and into the world of the pilgrim's home and local community.

This book also argues that technology is an important aspect of contemporary Muslim pilgrimages that is impossible to ignore. Modernity has transformed Islamic pilgrimage in numerous ways. Muslims have more options for travel, engaging in community, and aiding their religious journeys – whether they involve physical travel or an alternative type of mobility, such as the cyber-pilgrimage offers. The more attentive scholars are to the negotiations of religion and technology, the better the ways in which pilgrimage as a changing and active phenomenon can be understood. As one scholar notes, "The hyper-textual structure of the World Wide Web is conducive to seeking, with links that can take you on spiritual quests that condense both time and space."[10]

The theoretical challenges I have tried to illuminate in this study are ones to which scholars need to be attentive. It is an unfortunate condition of academia that scholars often rely on theories that are deeply embedded in the histories and ideologies of political power, colonialism, and racism. In particular, some of the scholarship still exhibits a reliance on post-Enlightenment models of religious life, ignores or downplays the impact that Orientalism has on the field, and is unconscious of the cohabitation of religion and race in academia, all of which affect the way we understand Islam and Muslim practice, including pilgrimage. It to these concerns I now turn.

NEGOTIATING A DIFFICULT TERRAIN: PROBLEMATIC VOICES IN THE STUDY OF RELIGION

Theory is an indispensable but problematic academic tool. Those who study religious communities outside of Protestant Christianity often find themselves fenced in by problematic theoretical frameworks. The effort to distinguish human practice, including pilgrimage, from the textual and authoritative systems in force within religions is one such problem – an effort that largely ignores the interactions between texts, religious authorities, movements of communities, rituals, and social capital. In many of these cases, the relationship between colonialism and scholarship is evident. As one study on Morocco concludes, "In both colonial discourse and contemporary religious scholarship, 'popular Islam' refers to heterodox and heteroprax forms particularly associated with Berber peoples."[11] This is but one of the many instances in which religious scholarship has a hand in politics, ethnonationalism, and colonialism; evidence of the biases enforced by scholars. This is often the case for Islamic subjects, for this is a subject area with a colonial history and a neocolonial present.

"[P]erpetuation [of outdated scholarship about Islam] serves a number of interests – religious, economic, and colonial – that are socially instituted and maintained."[12]

In fact, the regions where non-Christians were studied were often colonial territories. In the case of India, British Orientalists developed broad categories of knowledge that shaped academic discourse. In the study of Buddhism, texts were viewed as representative of the tradition, so much so that doctrine might not even be recognized outside of texts.[13] The notion of *true religion* was based on the standards set forth by the Reformation, including the idea that pilgrimage was something that other people did – people who were less modern than those who had the benefit of the Reformation. It is no surprise that this bias often found its way into scholarship on Hindus, Buddhists, Muslims, and others, whose rituals and traditions were explained in terms of their measuring up to the standards established by scholars – in a sense, a test that required religion "only exists in texts."[14] This is why Native Americans were viewed as having no religion at all.

Islam, like other religions outside of Christianity, is an academic category created by Western scholars and, as such, includes assumptions and projections that are embedded in modern Christian thought. This is a part of the reason why the *hajj* has received more attention than other pilgrimage traditions, because it is based on the textual canon – in this case, the Qur'an and *hadith* – considered as authoritative by scholars. Pilgrimage outside of *hajj* has often been seen as a popular practice less based on texts and more on local traditions, vernacular literature, and other influences. Scholars have often been resistant to take traditions that live outside the text seriously. As Schopen has argued, the idea of "true religion" is shaped by "the assigning of primacy to literary materials in the study of religion" and this "looks very much like a more recent manifestation of the sixteenth-century

Protestant distrust and devaluation of actual religious and historical human behavior."[15]

Part of this text-based religious test, which often describes Islam in terms of authoritative (Qur'an, *hadith*) versus popular (what is actually practiced, never mind what the canon says), is related to Orientalism. Edward Said's seminal work provides an anthropology of the field of Orientalism and its dissemination in academia, which is extensive. As Said wrote, "There are grants and other rewards, there are organizations, there are hierarchies, there are institutes, centers, faculties, departments, all devoted to legitimizing and maintaining the authority of a handful of basic, basically unchanging ideas about Islam, the Orient, and the Arabs."[16] Today, Orientalism is alive and well, evident in area studies programs (which often focus on language and texts and less on theory and methods), the production of scholars whose casting of Islam is narrow and outdated, and the popularity of topics like "political Islam" and "terrorism." As Carl Ernst and Richard Martin point out:

> One consequence of continuing to define vacant and new positions in Islamic studies in terms of the structure of the field in the heyday of Orientalism is that many among the current generation of graduate students (and their mentors) seem ready to believe that the study of Arabic legal and exegetical texts from the eighth to the twelfth centuries is sufficient to define Islamic civilization in a normative sense, without feeling the need to refer to the questions of contemporary scholarship and methodology.[17]

One of the ways this affects our reading of pilgrimage is that it limits the texts, theories, and frameworks through which it is studied.

This is not to say that the field of Islamic Studies is hopelessly mired in the past. Much of the scholarship today speaks to current theories and perspectives, including Scott Kugle's use of queer theory, Hamid Dabashi's attentiveness to post-colonial theory, and Amina Wadud's deployment of wom-anist and liberationist thought. However, the presentation of Islamic pilgrimage as consisting of a singular tradition in Islam – or even one that supersedes and then silences other traditions – reflects the Orientalist tendency to essentialize what is complex. There is also a racist edge to ignoring the complexities in Islam that must be acknowledged. Islam is too often seen as the religion of the Arabs, who are stereotyped or typecast as super-religious automatons, all praying the same and doing the same pilgrimage. The binary of orthodox and popular Islam comes into play here as well. Framing Sufism as "mysticism" contrasts the rationalism of modern Christianity to that of the "denial of rationality" of the religious Other, whose traditions are always subordinated.[18] This is certainly the case in pilgrimage, where "Sufi" traditions are contrasted with the grand pilgrimage to Mecca.

Orientalism is embedded in the language of modernity and its view of race. However, the cohabitation of the academic study of religion and modern racial theory is a story that has been, until now, left largely untold. Theodore Vial's book *Modern Religion, Modern Race* (2016) provides an anthropol-ogy of the ways in which the concept of race was mapped onto religious peoples, including Muslims. As he argues, religion is a racialized category that is such an integral part of modern discourse that scholars of religion are generally "not aware that we are talking about race."[19] According to Vial, this is a legacy that we cannot easily disentangle ourselves from. This is why it is so present in our academic discourse. Vial gives us the example of Daesh, a group that has often been described as necessarily Islamic because they take the Qur'an literally (as if non-violent Muslims have no appreciation of the text). Here we have an example of a case in which Daesh is cast as "more Islamic than other groups who read the Koran's texts on crucifixion and slavery less literally."[20] Here, not only is

Daesh quintessentially Islamic, but also they are so because
they are text-centered, representing the "true religion" of
Islam that Other people – Christian (white) people – would
reject on rational, modern principles. This is a problematic
way to talk about Muslims, but it is one based in our modern
racial and religious ideologies. The ways in which this affects
our academic reading of Islam are also profound. In terms of
pilgrimage, we see this view expressed in the presentation of
hajj as "true religion" and the exclusion of other traditions
and communities that reflect the diverse humanity of Muslims
around the world. Instead, what we often have is a picture of
Islamic pilgrimage that is situated in the racial taxonomies
that early scholars used to talk about non-Christians.

The issues raised here are not an argument that modern
academia should be rejected; however, white scholars in
particular need to be aware of the history of which we are a
part. Being a responsible scholar requires that we recognize
the reality of what we do when we construct knowledge, and
when we make history while the Other "undergoes history."[21]
One approach that can aid in this work is to adopt a mul-
ti-sighted model. Scholars that work with materiality argue
that this approach – one that focuses on the body, objects,
commodities, ritual, and other material matter – can help to
remedy the academic fixation on belief, texts, and authority.
As argued by Birgit Meyer and Dick Houtman, "the study of
religion itself has inherited the Enlightenment project of the
evolution of religion toward interiority, transcendence, and
reason, indeed toward religion's evaporation."[22]

Texts are also important and they often function in important relationships with bodies, places, and rituals. When studying pilgrimage, it is especially important to be attentive to
experiences and faculties, but they are often so fixated upon
texts that nothing else seems to matter. As I have tried to
show in this discussion, the ghost of the Enlightenment and of
Protestant methodology looms large in religious studies. This

is the point Robert Orsi argues in his work, in which he asks that scholars be aware of "the discipline's implicit Western and Christian biases, of the hidden, normative Christianity within the basic methodologies and philosophical orientations of religious studies."[23]

Religion is not an easy academic subject to define. As J.Z. Smith puts it, "What we study when we study religion is the variety of attempts to map, construct and inhabit such positions of power through the use of myths, rituals and experiences of transformation."[24] The reason why scholars have no universal definition of religion is a beautiful mess – of texts, beliefs, rituals, bodies, objects, relationships, maps, personalities, and emotions. Islamic pilgrimage is all of these things. This is why focusing solely on texts does not work, unless it engages the material, the commercial, the technological, and the human. It is my hope that this book has resulted in driving this point home by creating a study that utilizes the different approaches scholars have taken in the past and will hopefully take in the future. As this book comes to a close, it is my hope that scholars will continue to engage these various perspectives in conversation with each other, toward a richer, more accurate, and complex picture of Islamic pilgrimage, one that does justice to the lives Muslims lived in the past and live today.

ACKNOWLEDGMENTS

I began researching Islamic pilgrimage in 2009, when the Society for Arts in Theological Studies awarded me a fellowship to travel to Syria to study *aineh kari*, the mirror mosaics that cover the inside of many Shi'i shrines. Over the past seven years, I have spent considerable time contemplating pilgrimage – why people embark on religious journeys, how pilgrimage is studied, and what it tells scholars about the religious worlds people create for themselves and for others. As part of a long conversation I had with fellow scholar Dr. Omid Safi, he suggested that I write this book, in part to produce a text for the classroom that would more fairly represent the traditions of the world's nearly two billion Muslims. To Omid I am forever grateful for encouraging me to write this book. There are a number of other individuals I would like to acknowledge here. The editors I worked with at Oneworld, Jonathan Bentley-Smith and Novin Doostdar, offered feedback, encouragement, and patience, all of which I deeply appreciate. The number of individuals who served as conversation partners along the way are too numerous to list here, but include my loyal writing partner Blayne Harcey, my personal editor Jean Charney, and those many people who provided articles, photographs, and other resources, including Alex Shams, Beeta Baghoolizadeh, Brian Spivey, Kristian Petersen, Kawa Aahangar, Edith Szanto, Gary Bunt, and Jens Kreinath. Lastly, I would like to thank my family, my husband Bayu and our two children, who brought me countless iced lattes, provided a quiet place to work, and gave me so much support and encouragement during this entire project. It is to them that I dedicate this book.

GLOSSARY

Note: All words are Arabic unless otherwise specified.

ahl al-bayt: the Prophet's family; house of the Prophet.

ahl al-sunnah: the people of tradition.

Ahmadiyyah (Ahmadis): a twentieth-century proselytizing Islamic reform movement.

aineh kari **(Persian)**: mirror work; the mirrored mosaic work that often decorates the inside of Shi'i shrines.

akhlaq: correct Muslim behavior.

'Alawiyyah ('Alawis): descendants or followers of 'Ali; name used for Islamic sects that emerge from Shi'ism; the Shi'i sect of Islam that regards 'Ali as divine.

'Ali b. Abi Talib: the Prophet's cousin and son-in-law who serves as the fourth caliph in Islam; the first Shi'i Imam.

Allah: the Arabic word for God.

alwah: tablet gravestones.

ansab: upright tombs.

arbaeen: the pilgrimage to Karbala on 'Ashura'.

asar **(Persian)**: Relics.

'**Ashura**': the tenth day of the Islamic month of Muharram when the death of Husayn is mourned.

'*atabat*: the sacred cities of Najaf, Karbala, Kazimayn, and Samarra.

ayatollah: Shi'a religious leader; "sign of God".

azaas: ritual recitations that are often associated with Shi'i holy sites.

Baha'i: the religious community established by Baha'u'llah, whose members believe in prophecy after Muhammad.

*barakah (*pl. *barakat)*: blessing; the spiritual power associated with the bodies of Islamic saints and Imams; a communicable power that can bring good or bad tidings.

batin: hidden.

bid'ah: innovation.

cem: Alevi ceremony involving singing, dancing, and music.

communitas: the feeling of belonging that occurs at the pilgrimage site, according to some Western scholars.

dargah **(Urdu)**: Sufi shrine or tomb.

darih: the encasing around a tomb, very common in Persian/ Iranian shrines; a cenotaph.

darwish **(dervish)**: a Sufi; someone who is devoted to God.

dhikr/zikr: remembrance of Allah; recollection of the presence of God.

Dhu-l-Hijja: the twelfth month of the Islamic lunar calendar when *hajj* takes place.

didar: to see; to encounter; to visit; the act of seeing the Living Imam in Isma'ili Shi'ism.

doviste **(Bosniak)**: sacred nature pilgrimage sites.

Fatima: the Prophet's daughter who marries 'Ali.

fiqh: Islamic jurisprudence; "understanding".

ghusl: ritual washing; ablution.

gunbadh: dome.

hadith: an account of something Muhammad said or did during his lifetime.

hafiz: an individual who has recited the entire Qur'an.

hajj: the great pilgrimage to Mecca.

hajji/hajjah: an individual who has performed the *hajj*.

hammam: public bath.

haram: sacred; forbidden; a holy place or territory.

hatim: the wall that marks where Hajar and Ishmael are buried.

hawl/haul: The death anniversary of a saint or revered scholar.

al-Hujra: the chamber; the Prophet's tomb.

al Nuqta: the place where Husayn's blood dropped near Aleppo after his death; "the drop".

ihram: the state of ritual purity entered for *hajj*; the two seamless white cloths worn by men for *hajj*.

ijlal: reverence.

ilahis: Turkish devotional songs often performed as part of pilgrimage.

Imam: a person who leads prayer; for Shi'i, Imam refers to 'Ali and his descendants from his marriage to Fatima.

Imam al-Rida: alternate name for Imam Reza, the eighth Shi'ite Imam.

Imamzadeh (**Persian**): places where the Imams in Shi'a Islam are entombed.

Isa: Jesus.

isra: Prophet Muhammad's Night Journey.

jamarat: the stoning of Shaytan; the part of *hajj* where pilgrims throw stones at pillars representing the devil; "place of pebbles".

ka'bah: the cube-shaped construction in Mecca toward which all Muslims pray; "cube".

kafir: unbelievers.

karamah (pl. *kamarat*): miracles; God's favors bestowed on his followers; "generosity".

kayan Mecca (**Nigerian**): objects from Mecca; "Meccan things".

kejawén (**Bahasa**): the religious beliefs and traditions of the people of Java; Javanese spiritual traditions, which includes Islam and other influences.

khalwa/khilwah: Sufi retreat; a Sufi lodge.

khanaqah: a Sufi lodge.

Khidr: the mysterious figure who instructs Musa (Moses) in mystical knowledge.

khutbah: sermon.

kraton (**Bahasa**): the area where the sultan is buried; the sacred part of a Javanese city that contains tombs of dead leaders.

madhhab: Islamic legal school.

Madinah (Madinah al-Nabi): the city of the Prophet.

madrasah: a religious school.

Mahdi: the individual who appears at the End of Days; for Shi'i, the Twelfth Imam.

majlis/majalis **(Persian)**: Shi'i religious gatherings.

maqam: a place that a holy person visited, sometimes marked by a footprint.

maqathil: hagiographic literature that praises Imam Husayn.

marbat: tomb of a Sufi saint.

Maryam: Mary; the mother of Prophet Isa (Jesus).

mashhad: a place of witnessing or martyrdom; shrine; Mashhad is the city where Imam Reza is entombed.

masjid: mosque; the place where Muslims worship.

Masjid an-Nabawi: the Prophet's mosque in Medina.

mawlid: a celebration of a saint's death; birthday of the Prophet (*mawlid an-nabi*).

mazar: a tomb or grave.

meydan **(Persian)**: the Persian center square often found in Iranian cities.

mi'raj: Prophet Muhammad's journey to heaven; the ascension (also called *isra*).

mohr: the clay of Karbala; Shi'a prayer stone (also called *turbah*).

mojizih **(Persian)**: miracles.

mortoba: (spiritual) power.

mubarak: sacred or blessed.

muraqaba: Sufi meditative practice.

murid: a Sufi disciple.

namaz **(Persian)**: prayer.

namaz-khana **(Persian)**: prayer-room.

nashid: vocal chanting; devotional songs about Prophet Muhammad or another holy individual.

Nur: God's Divine Light.

*qabr (*pl. *qubur)*: a tomb.

qadam: footprint of Prophet Muhammad or another holy figure.

qadosh **(Hebrew)**: holy or sacred.

qalandar: wandering Sufi.

qibla: the direction of prayer.

*qubbah (*pl. *qibab)*: a domed structure that often housed a tomb.

Qubbat al-Sakhra: the Dome of the Rock.

al-Quds: the Arabic name for Jerusalem.

rawzeh khwani (**Persian**): Recitations of the narrative surrounding the Battle of Karbala.

sa'ee/sa'y: the running between the two hills of Safa and Marwa that commemorates Hajar's frantic search for water.

sakhra: a boulder placed at the head of a grave.

salat/salah: the daily prayers.

sama/sema: devotional Sufi music; audition for Allah through music.

sannyasi: Hindu ascetic.

sawm: fasting during Ramadan.

sayyid: descendant of Prophet Muhammad.

shafa'ah: Intercession with God through saints, common in Sufi and Shi'a pilgrimage rituals.

shahadah: the Islamic profession of faith.

shaykh: a Sufi teacher; the founder or leader of a Sufi order.

Shi'i: Muslims who believe that 'Ali, the Prophet's son-in-law, should have led the community after Muhammad's death (from Shi'i 'Ali, the "followers of Ali").

shirk: the association with something else besides God.

silsilah: the line of transmission in a Sufi order.

Sufiyyun: the Sufis.

suhbah: companionship; the companionship between a student and a teacher in a Sufi order.

*tabbaruk (*pl. *tabarrukat)*: sacred relic.

tahlil: the recitation of "La Ilaha Illa-lla" (There is no god but God).

takbir: the phrase "Allahu 'Akbar" (God is great).

talbiyah: the Muslim prayer that expresses the intention to perform *hajj*.

talqin: instruction to the dead on the basics of Islam.

*tariqah (*pl. *turuq)*: path or way; a Sufi order.

tasawwuf: Sufism; the practices associated with contemplative and devotional Islam.

tasbih: Muslim rosary; the act of saying "Praise be to God!".

tasfir: Qur'anic exegesis.

tawaf: the circumambulation of the *ka'bah*.

taswiyat al-qubur: the leveling of graves.

tawassul: saintly intercession.

tawhid: the unicity of God.

ta'ziyeh: dramatic re-enactments of the Battle of Karbala; a replica of Husayn's tomb.

tekke (**Turkish**): a Sufi lodge, meeting place, or site of worship.

tevhid (**Bosniak**): Turkish or Bosnian martyrs.

turba: Shi'a prayer stone; "earth"; mausoleum.

'ummah: the world's Muslims; community.

'urs: an annual festival at a Sufi shrine that commemorates the death anniversary of an important individual; wedding.

*wali (*pl. *awliya)*: a friend of Allah; a companion; a helper.

waqf: an Islamic charitable foundation that often funded the care of pilgrimage sites; endowments used to support Muslims, including Islamic pilgrimage.

wuquf: the act of standing or stopping during *hajj*.

zahir: manifest; what is seen or evident.

zakat: charitable giving.

Zamzam: the well near Mecca associated with Hajar's search for water.

zanjir-zani: the self-flagellation practiced by some Shi'i during Muharram.

zawiyah: a small mosque or shrine associated with a Sufi saint; a place of retreat; a space where Muslims do *dhikr.*

zaynabiyyah: a place at which Shi'i gather for communal prayers.

ziyarat (ziarat, ziyarah): to visit; pilgrimage.

BIBLIOGRAPHY

Abrahamian, Ervand. *Khomeinism: Essays on the Islamic Republic.* Berkeley: University of California Press, 1993.

Abramson, David M. and Elyor E. Karimov. "Sacred Sites, Profane Ideologies: Religious Pilgrimage and the Uzbek State." In *Everyday Life in Central Asia: Past and Present*, edited by Jeff Shahadeo and Russell Zanca, 319–338. Bloomington: Indiana University Press, 2007.

Afsaruddin, Asma. *The First Muslims: History and Memory.* Oxford: Oneworld, 2008.

Aghaie, Kamran Scott. *The Martyrs of Karbala: Sh'i Symbols and Rituals in Modern Iran.* Seattle: University of Washington Press, 2004.

Ahmadi, Nader and Fereshteh Ahmadi. *Iranian Islam: The Concept of the Individual.* New York: St. Martin's Press, 1998.

Ahmed, Shahab. *What Is Islam? The Importance of Being Islamic.* Princeton: Princeton University Press, 2016.

Ahmed-Ghosh, Huma. "Portraits of Believers: Ahmadi Women Performing Faith in the Diaspora." *Journal of International Women's Studies* 6, no. 1 (2004): 73–92.

Akçapar, Sebnam Koser and Smita Tewari Jassal. "Sites of Power and Resistance or Melting Pots? A Gendered Understanding of Islam through Sufi Shrines in Turkey." *Contemporary Review of the Middle East* 1, no. 1 (2014): 95–110.

Akkach, Samer. *Cosmology and Architecture in Premodern Islam: An Architectural Reading of Mystical Ideas.* Albany: State University of New York Press, 2005.

Aksland, Markus. *The Sacred Footprint*. Oslo: Yeti Consult, 1990.

Alatas, Ismail Fajrie. "Pilgrimage and Network Formation in Two Contemporary Bā 'Alawi Hawl in Central Asia." *Journal of Islamic Studies* 25, no. 3 (2014): 298–324.

Amir-Moezzi, Mohammad Ali. "Icon and Meditation: Between Popular Art and Sufism in Imami Shi'ism." In *The Art and Material Culture of Iranian Shi'ism: Iconography and Religious Devotion in Shi'i Islam*, edited by Pedram Khosronejad, 25–45. New York: I.B. Tauris, 2012.

Anabsi, Ghalib. "Popular Beliefs as Reflected in 'Merits of Palestine and Syria' (*Fadā'il al Shām*) Literature: Pilgrimage Ceremonies and Customs in the Mamluk and Ottoman Periods." *Journal of Islamic Studies* 19, no. 1 (2008): 59–70.

Anjum, Tanvir. *Chistī Sufis in the Sultanate of Delhi 1190–1400: From Restrained Indifference to Calculated Defiance*. New York: Oxford University Press, 2011.

Ardalan, Nader and Laleh Bakhtiar. *The Sense of Unity: The Sufi Tradition in Persian Architecture*. Chicago: University of Chicago Press, 1973.

Armstrong, Karen. "Jerusalem: The Problems and Responsibilities of Sacred Space." *Islam and Christian–Muslim Relations* 13, no. 2 (2002): 189–196.

Asher, Catherine B. "Pilgrimage to the Shrines in Ajmer." In *Islam in South Asia in Practice*, edited by Barbara D. Metcalf, 77–92. Princeton: Princeton University Press, 2009.

Aslan, Reza. "General Introduction." In *One Thousand Roads to Mecca: Ten Centuries of Travelers Writing about the Muslim Pilgrimage*, edited by Michael Wolfe, xiii–xxxi. New York: Grove Press, 1998.

Azra, Azyumardi. *The Origins of Islamic Reformism in Southeast Asia: Networks of Malay-Indonesian and Middle Eastern 'Ulamā in the Seventeenth and Eighteenth Centuries*. Honolulu: University of Hawai'i Press, 2004.

Babayan, Kathryn. "'In Spirit We Ate Each Other's Sorrow': Female Companionship in Seventeenth-Century Safavi Iran." In *Islamicate Sexualities: Translations across Temporal Geographies of Desire*, edited by Kathryn Babayan and Afsaneh Najmabadi, 239–274. Cambridge: Harvard Middle Eastern Monographs, 2008.

Bajc, Vida, Simon Coleman, and John Eade. "Introduction: Mobility and Centering in Pilgrimage." *Mobilities* 2, no. 3 (2007): 321–329.

Bakhtiar, Laleh. *Sufi: Expressions of the Mystic Quest*. London: Thames and Hudson, 1976.

Bang, Anne K. "My Generation: Umar b. Ahmad b. Sumayt (1886–1973): Inter-generational Network Transmission in a Trans-Oceanic Hadramī 'Alawī Family, ca. 1925–1973." In *Diasporas within and without Africa: Dynamism, Heterogeneity, Variation*, edited by Leif Manger and Munzoul A.M. Assoul, 87–103. Stockholm: Nordiska Afrikainstitutet, 2006.

Barkey, Karen. "Religious Pluralism, Shared Sacred Sites, and the Ottoman Empire." In *Choreographies of Shared Sacred Sites: Religion and Conflict Resolution*, edited by Elazar Barkan and Karen Barkey, 33–65. New York: Columbia University Press, 2015.

Bashear, Suliman. "Qur'an 2:114 and Jerusalem." *Bulletin of the School of Oriental and African Studies* 52, no. 2 (1989): 215–238.

Bashear, Suliman. "Jesus in an Early Muslim Shahada and Related Issues: A New Perspective." *Studies in Early Islamic Tradition* xv (2004): 1–18.

Bashir, Shahzad. *Sufi Bodies: Religion and Society in Medieval Islam*. New York: Columbia University Press, 2011.

Bazzano, Elliott. "Sufism." In *The Encyclopedia of Global Religions*, edited by Wade Clark Room and Mark Jurgensmeyer, 1228–1232. Thousand Oaks: Sage Publications, 2011.

Beranek, Ondrej and Pavel Tupek. "From Visiting Graves to their Destruction: The Question of Ziyara through the Eyes of Salafis." Brandeis University Crown Center for Middle East Studies, Crown Paper 2 (2009): 1–36.

Berriane, Johara. "Ahmad al-Tijani and His Neighbors: The Inhabitants of Fez and Their Perceptions of the Zawiya." In *Prayer in the City: The Making of Muslim Sacred Places and Urban Life*, edited by Patrick A. Desplat and Dorothea E. Schulz, 57–75. Piscataway, NJ: Transaction Publishers, 2012.

Betteridge, Anne H. "Muslim Women and Shrines in Shiraz." In *Everyday Life in the Muslim Middle East*, edited by Donna Lee Bowen and Evelyn A. Early, 276–289. Bloomington: Indiana University Press, 2002.

Bhardwaj, Surinder. "Non-Hajj Pilgrimage in Islam: A Neglected Dimension of Religion Circulation." *Journal of Cultural Geography* 17, no. 2 (1988): 69–87.

Bhattacharya, Ananda. "Understanding Madariya *Silsila*." *Journal of Muslim Minority Affairs* 32, no. 3 (2012): 384–399.

Bianchi, Robert R. *Guests of God: Pilgrimage and Politics in the Islamic World*. New York: Oxford University Press, 2004.

Birge, John Kingsley. *The Bektashi Order of Dervishes*. Hartford: Hartford Seminary Press, 1937.

Boivin, Michel. "Representations and Symbols in Muharram and Other Rituals: Fragments of Shiite Worlds from Bombay to Karachi." In *The Other Shiites: From the Mediterranean to Central Asia*, edited by Alessandro Monsutti, Silvia Naff, and Farian Sabahi, 149–172. New York: Peter Lang, 2007.

Bombardier, Alice. "War Painting and Pilgrimage in Iran." *Visual Anthropology* 25, no. 1–2 (2012): 148–166.

Bowman, Glenn. "Popular Palestinian Practices around Holy Places and Those Who Oppose Them: A Historical Perspective." *Religion Compass* 7, no. 3 (2013): 69–78.

Brown, Peter. *The Cult of the Saints: Its Rise and Function in Latin Christianity*. Chicago: University of Chicago Press, 1981.

Bunt, Gary R. *Islam in the Digital Age: E-Jihad, Online Fatwas and Cyber Islamic Environments*. London: Pluto Press, 2003.

Bunt, Gary R. "'Rip. Burn. Pray.': Islamic Expression Online." In *Religion Online: Finding Faith on the Internet*, edited by Lorne L. Dawson and Douglas E. Cowan, 123–134. New York: Routledge, 2004.

Bunt, Gary R. *I-Muslims: Rewiring the House of Islam*. Chapel Hill: University of North Carolina Press, 2009.

Bunt, Gary R. "Surfing the App Souq: Islamic Applications for Mobile Devices." *Online Journal of the Virtual Middle East* 4, no. 1 (2010). www.cyberorient.net/article.do?articleId=3817

Callan, Alyson. "Female Saints and the Practice of Islam in Sylhet, Bangladesh." *American Ethnologist* 35, no. 3 (2008): 396–412.

Campbell, Heidi. *Exploring Religious Community Online: We Are One in the Network*. New York: Peter Lang, 2005.

Campbell, Heidi, Brian Altenhofen, Wendi Bellar, and Kyong James Cho. "There's a Religious App for That! A Framework for Studying Religious Mobile Applications." *Mobile Media & Communication* 2, no. 2 (2014): 154–172.

Chittick, William C. *A Shi'ite Anthology*. Albany: State University of New York Press, 1981.

Clarke, Lynda. "Sainthood." *Oxford Encyclopedia of the Modern Islamic World*, edited by John Esposito. New York: Oxford University Press, 1995.

Cohen, Erik. "Pilgrimage and Tourism: Convergence and Divergence." In *Sacred Journeys: The Anthropology of Pilgrimage*, edited by Alan Morinis, 47–64. Westport: Greenwood Press, 1992.

Collins-Kreiner, Noga and Jay D. Gatrell. "Tourism, Heritage, and Pilgrimage: The Case of Haifa's Bahá'i Gardens." *Journal of Heritage Tourism* 1, no. 1 (2006): 32–50.

Cone, James. *Martin & Malcolm & America: A Dream or a Nightmare*. Maryknoll, NY: Orbis Books, 1992.

Cornell, Rkia Elaroui. "Rabi'a from Narrative to Myth: The Tropics of Identity of a Muslim Woman Saint." PhD diss., University of Amsterdam, 2013.

Couldry, Nick. "Pilgrimage in Mediaspace: Continuities and Transformations." *Etnofoor* 20, no. 1 (2007): 63–74.

Currie, P.M. *The Shrine and Cult of Mu'īn Al-Dīn Chishtī of Ajmer*. New York: Oxford University Press, 1989.

Curtis, Edward E. "Islamizing the Black Body: Ritual and Power in Elijah Muhammad's Nation of Islam." *Religion and American Culture: A Journal of Interpretation* 12, no. 2 (2002): 167–196.

Curtis, Edward E. *Black Muslim Religion and the Nation of Islam, 1960–1975*. Chapel Hill: University of North Carolina Press, 2006.

Dabashi, Hamid. *Islamic Liberation Theology: Resisting the Empire*. New York: Routledge, 2008.

Dabashi, Hamid. *Shi'ism: A Religion of Protest*. Cambridge: Harvard University Press, 2012.

Daftary, Farhad. *The Ismā'īlīs: Their History and Doctrines*. New York: Cambridge University Press, 2007.

Danesh, Roshan. "The Journey Motif in the Baha'i Faith: From Doubt to Certitude." *Journal of Baha'i Studies* 22, no. 1–4 (2012): 1–23.

Dangor, Suleman. "The Expression of Islam in South Africa." *Journal of Muslim Minority Affairs* 17, no. 1 (1997): 141–151.

Darwish, Linda. "Defining the Boundaries of Sacred Space: Unbelievers, Purity, and the Masjid al-Haram in Shi'a Exegesis of Qur'an 9:28." *Journal of Shi'a Islamic Studies* 7, no. 3 (2014): 283–319.

Dawson, Lorne L. "Religion and the Quest for Virtual Community." In *Religion Online: Finding Faith on the Internet*, edited by Lorne L. Dawson and Douglas E. Cowan, 75–89. Routledge: New York, 2004.

de Bellaigue, Christopher. *In the Rose Garden of the Martyrs: A Memoir of Iran*. New York: HarperCollins, 2005.

Delaney, Carol. "The *Hajj*; Sacred and Secular." *American Ethnologist* 17, no. 3 (1990): 513–530.

DeWeese, Devin. "Sacred Places and 'Public' Narratives: The Shrine of Ahmad Yasavī in Hagiographical Traditions of the Yasavī Sūfī

Order, 16th–17th Centuries." *Muslim World* 90, no. 3–4 (2000): 353–376.

Diouf, Mamadou. "The Senegalese Murid Trade Diaspora and the Making of a Vernacular Cosmopolitanism." [Translated by Steven Rendall] *Public Culture* 12, no. 3 (2000): 679–702.

Drijvers, Jan Willem. "Transformation of a City: The Christianization of Jerusalem in the Fourth Century." In *Cults, Creeds and Identities in the Greek City after the Classical Age*, edited by Richard Alston, Onno M. van Nijf, and Christina Williamson, 309–329. Walpole, MA: Peeters, 2013.

Echchaibi, Nabil. "Mecca Cola and Burqinis: Muslim Consumption and Religious Identities." In *Religion, Media and Culture: A Reader*, edited by Gordon Lynch and Jolyon Mitchell, 31–39. New York: Routledge, 2011.

Egresi, Istvan, Büsra Bayram, Fatih Kara, and Ozan Arif Kesik. "Unlocking the Potential of Religious Tourism in Turkey." *GeoJournal of Tourism and Geosites* 9, no. 1 (2012): 63–80.

Eisenlohr, Patrick. "Mediality and Materiality in Religious Performance: Religion as Heritage in Mauritius." *Material Religion* 9, no. 3 (2013): 328–348.

Elad, Amikam. *Medieval Jerusalem and Islamic Worship: Holy Places, Ceremonies, Pilgrimage*. New York: E.J. Brill, 1995.

Ephrat, Daphna. *Spiritual Wayfarers, Leaders in Piety: Sufis and the Dissemination of Islam in Medieval Palestine*. Cambridge: Harvard University Press, 2008.

Ernst, Carl W. and Richard C. Martin. "Introduction: Toward a Post-Orientalist Approach to Islamic Religious Studies." In *Rethinking Islamic Studies: From Orientalism to Cosmopolitanism*, edited by Carl W. Ernst and Richard W. Martin, 1–19. Columbia: University of South Carolina Press, 2010.

Erol, Ayhan. "Reimagining Identity: The Transformation of the Alevi Semah." *Middle Eastern Studies* 6, no. 3 (2010): 375–387.

Esposito, John. *Islam: The Straight Path*. New York: Oxford, 2011.

Fadiman, James and Robert Frager, eds. *Essential Sufism*. New York: HarperCollins, 1997.

El Fadl, Khaled Abou. "The Ugly Modern and the Modern Ugly: Reclaiming the Beautiful in Islam." In *Progressive Muslims: On Justice, Gender, and Pluralism*, edited by Omid Safi, 33–77. Oxford: Oneworld, 2003.

Fakhr-Rohani, Muhammad-Reza. "Reflections on Ashura-oriented Literature." *Message of Thaqalayn* 12, no. 3 (2011): 95–101.

Finster, Barbara. "An Outline of the History of Islamic Religious Architecture in Yemen." *Muqarnas* 9 (1992): 124–147.

Flaskerud, Ingvild. *Visualizing Belief and Piety in Iranian Shiism*. New York: Continuum, 2010.

Flaskerud, Ingvild. "Redemptive Memories: Portraiture in the Cult of Commemoration." *Visual Anthropology* 25, no. 1 (2012): 22–46.

Foley, Kathy. "The *Ronggeng*, the *Wayang*, the *Wali*, and Islam: Female or Transvestite Male Dancers-Singers-Performers and Evolving Islam in West Java." *Asian Theatre Journal* 32, no. 2 (2015): 356–386.

Ford, Heidi A. "Hierarchical Inversions, Divine Subversions: The Miracles of Râbi'a al-'Adawîya." *Journal of Feminist Studies in Religion* 15, no. 2 (1999): 5–24.

Frank, Allen J. "Some Political Features of Finno-Ugrian and Muslim Hagiolatry in the Volga-Ural Region." In *Central Asian Pilgrims: Hajj Routes and Pious Visits between Central Asia and the Hijaz*, edited by Alexandre Papas, Thomas Welsford, and Thierry Zarcone, 295–311. Berlin: Klaus Schwarz Verlag, 2012.

Franke, Patrick. "Khidr in Istanbul: Observations on the Symbolic Construction of Sacred Spaces in Traditional Islam." In *On Archaeology of Sainthood and Local Spirituality in Islam: Past and Present Crossroads of Events and Ideas (Yearbook of the Sociology of Islam, Book 5)*, edited by Georg Stauth, 36–56. New York: Transcript Verlag and Columbia University Press, 2003.

Frembgen, Jürgen Wasim. *The Friends of God: Sufi Saints in Islam, Popular Poster Art in Pakistan*. New York: Oxford University Press, 2006.

Gardner, Katy. "Global Migrants and Local Shrines: The Shifting Geography of Islam in Sylhet, Bangladesh." In *Muslim Diversity: Local Islam in Global Contexts*, edited by Leif Mager, 37–57. Richmond: Curzon, 1999.

Geijbels, Mathieu. "Aspects of the Veneration of Saints in Islam, with Special Reference to Pakistan." *Muslim World* 68, no. 3 (1978): 176–186.

Ghadially, Rehana. "Devotional Empowerment: Women Pilgrims, Saints, and Shrines in a South Asian Muslim Sect." *Asian Journal of Women's Studies* 11, no. 4 (2005): 79–101.

Glazebrook, Diana and Mohammad Jalal Abbasi-Shavazi. "Being Neighbours to Imam Reza: Pilgrimage Practices and Return Intentions of Hazara Afghans Living in Mashhad, Iran." *Iranian Studies* 40, no. 2 (2007): 187–201.

Gleave, Robert. "Prayer and Prostration: Imāmī Shiʻi Discussions of al-sujūd ʻalā al-turba al-Husayniyya." In *The Art and Material Culture of Iranian Shiʻism: Iconography and Religious Devotion in Shiʻi Islam*, edited by Pedram Khosronejad, 233–253. New York: I.B. Tauris, 2012.

Grabar, Oleg. "The Earliest Islamic Commemorative Structures, Notes and Documents." *Ars Orientals* 6 (1996): 7–46.

Green, Nile. *Indian Sufism Since the Seventeenth Century: Saints, Books and Empires in the Muslim Deccan*. New York: Routledge, 2006.

Green, Nile. *Making Space: Sufis and Settlers in Early Modern India*. New York: Routledge, 2012.

Gruber, Christiane. "The Martyrs' Museum in Tehran: Visualizing Memory in Post-Revolutionary Iran." *Visual Anthropology* 25, no. 1–2 (2012): 68–97.

Hackett, Rosalind I.J. "Religion and the Internet." *Diogenes* 211 (2006): 67–76.

Haider, Najam. *The Origins of the Shiʻa: Identity, Ritual, and Sacred Space in Eighth-Century Kufah*. New York: Cambridge University Press, 2011.

Haleem, M.A.S. Abdel, translator. *The Qurʼan: English Translation and Parallel Arabic Text*. New York: Oxford University Press, 2010.

Halevi, Leor. *Muhammad's Grave: Death Rites and the Making of an Islamic Society*. New York: Columbia University Press, 2007.

Hallam, Elizabeth and Jenny Hockey. *Death, Memory and Material Culture*. Oxford: Berg Publishers, 2001.

Hasan, Perween. "The Footprint of the Prophet." *Muqarnas* 10, Essays in Honor of Oleg Grabar (1993): 335–343.

Hasson, Isaac. "Muslim Literature in Praise of Jerusalem: Fadāʼil Bayt al-Maqdis." *The Jerusalem Cathedra: Studies in the History, Archaeology, Geography and Ethnography of the Land of Israel* 1 (1981): 168–184.

Hasson, Izhak. "The Muslim View of Jerusalem: The Qurʼan and Hadith." In *The History of Jerusalem: The Early Muslim Period*, edited by Joshua Prawer and Haggai Ben-Shammai, 349–385. New York: NYU Press, 1996.

Hazard, Sonia. "The Material Turn in the Study of Religion." *Religion and Society: Advances in Research* 4 (2013): 58–78.

Hazleton, Lesley. *After the Prophet: The Epic Story of the Shia–Sunni Split in Islam*. New York: Anchor Books, 2009.

Heern, Zachary M. *The Emergence of Modern Shiʻism: Islamic Reform in Iraq and Iran*. London: Oneworld, 2015.

Henig, David. "'This Is Our Little Hajj': Muslim Holy Sites and Reappropriation of the Sacred Landscape in Contemporary Bosnia." *American Ethnologist* 39, no. 4 (2012): 751–765.

Heo, Angie. "The Virgin between Christianity and Islam: Sainthood, Media, and Modernity in Egypt." *Journal of the American Academy of Religion* 81, no. 4 (2013): 1117–1138.

Hill-Smith, Connie. "Cyberpilgrimage: The (Virtual) Reality of Online Pilgrimage Experience." *Religion Compass* 5/6 (2011): 236–246.

Ho, Engseng. *The Graves of Tarim: Genealogy and Mobility across the Indian Ocean.* Berkeley: University of California Press, 2006.

Ho, Engseng. "The Two Arms of Cambay: Diasporic Texts of Ecumenical Islam in the Indian Ocean." *Journal of the Economic and Social History of the Orient* 50, no. 2/3 (2007): 347–361.

Hodgson, Marshall. *The Venture of Islam: Conscience and History in a World Civilization, Volume 1: The Classical Age of Islam.* Chicago: University of Chicago Press, 1961.

Hoffman, Valerie. *Sufism, Mystics, and Saints in Modern Egypt.* Columbia: University of South Carolina Press, 1995.

Hofheinz, Albrecht. "Nextopia? Beyond Revolution 2.0." *Oriente Moderno* 91. no. 1 (2011): 23–39.

Holland, Dorothy and Michael Cole. "Between Discourse and Schema: Reformulating a Cultural-Historical Approach to Culture and Mind." *Anthropology & Education Quarterly* 26, no. 4 (1995): 475–490.

Honarpisheh, Donna. "Women in Pilgrimage: Senses, Places, Embodiment, and Agency: Experiencing *Ziyarat* in Shiraz." *Journal of Shi'a Islamic Studies* 6, no. 4 (2013): 383–410.

Al-Houdalieh, Salah Hussein. "Visitation and Making Vows at the Shrine of Shaykh Shihāb al-Dīn." *Journal of Islamic Studies* 21, no. 3 (2010): 377–390.

Hussain, Ali J. "The Mourning of History and the History of Mourning: The Evolution of Ritual Commemoration of the Battle of Karbala." *Comparative Studies of South Asia, Africa and the Middle East* 25, no. 1 (2005): 78–88.

Iloliev, Abdulmamad. "Popular Culture and Religious Metaphor: Saints and Shrines in Wakhan Region and Tajikistan." *Central Asian Survey* 27, no. 1 (2008): 59–73.

Jansen, Willy and Meike Kühl. "Shared Symbols: Muslims, Marian Pilgrimages and Gender." *European Journal of Women's Studies* 15, no. 3 (2008): 295–311.

Kalinock, Sabine. "Touching a Sensitive Topic: Research on Shiite Rituals of Women in Tehran." *Iranian Studies* 37, no. 4 (2004): 665–674.

Kalinock, Sabine. "Going on Pilgrimage Online: The Representation of the Twelver-Shia in the Internet." *Online: Heidelberg Journal of Religions on the Internet* 2, no. 1 (2006): 6–23.

Kamalkhani, Zahra. *Women's Islam: Religious Practice among Women in Today's Iran*. New York: Kegan Paul International, 1998.

Kaptein, N.J.G. *Muhammad's Birthday Festival: Early History in the Central Muslim Lands and Development in the Muslim West until the 10th/16th Century*. New York: E.J. Brill, 1993.

Karamustafa, Ahmet T. *Sufism: The Formative Period*. Edinburgh: Edinburgh University Press, 2007.

Karim, Jamillah. "Between Immigrant Islam and Black Liberation: Young Muslims Inherit Global Muslim and African Legacies." *Muslim World* 95, no. 4 (2005): 497–513.

Keddie, Nikki R. *Modern Iran: Roots and Results of Revolution*. New Haven: Yale University Press, 2003.

Kennedy, John G. and Hussein Fahim. "Nubian Dhikr Rituals and Cultural Change." *Muslim World* 63, no. 3 (1974): 205–219.

Kenny, Erin. "Gifting Mecca: Importing Spiritual Capital to West Africa." *Mobilities* 2, no. 3 (2007): 363–381.

Keshavjee, Rafique. *Mysticism and the Plurality of Meaning: The Case of the Ismailis of Rural Iran*. New York: I.B. Tauris, 1998.

Khalek, Nancy. *Damascus after the Muslim Conquest: Text and Image in Early Islam*. New York: Oxford University Press, 2011.

Khalvashi, Tamta. "Ziyareti: Imagined Sacred Places and Cultural Transmission among Georgians in Turkey." *Anthropology of the Middle East* 4, no. 2 (2009): 84–96.

Khan, Adil Hussain. *From Sufism to Ahmadiyya: A Muslim Minority Movement in South Asia*. Bloomington: Indiana University Press, 2015.

Khan, Hasan-Uddin. "Architectural Conservation as a Tool for Cultural Continuity: A Focus on the Built Environment of Islam." *International Journal of Architectural Research* 9, no. 1 (2015): 1–18.

El-Khatib, Abdallah. "Jerusalem in the Qur'an." *British Journal of Middle Eastern Studies* 28, no. 1 (2001): 25–53.

Khosronejad, Pedram. "Anthropology, Islam and Sainthood." In *Saints and Their Pilgrims in Iran and Neighbouring Countries*, edited by Pedram Khosronejad, 1–20. Wantage: Sean Kingston Publishing, 2012.

Khosronejad, Pedram. "Lions' Representation in Bakhtiari Oral Tradition and Funerary Material Culture." In *The Art and Material Culture of Iranian Shi'ism: Iconography and Religious Devotion in Shi'i Islam*, edited by Pedram Khosronejad, 195–214. New York: I.B. Tauris, 2012.

King, Richard. *Orientalism and Religion: Postcolonial Theory, India and "The Mythic East."* New York: Routledge, 1999.

Kister, Meir J. "'You Shall Only Set Out for Three Mosques': A Study of an Early Tradition." *Le Muséon* 82 (1969): 173–196.

Knappert, Jan. "Some Notes on the Pilgrimage of the Ithna-Ashari Branch of the Shia." *Orientalia Lovaniensia Periodica* 20 (1989): 241–252.

Knysh, Alexander. "The *Tariqa* on a Landcruiser: The Resurgence of Sufism in Yemen." *Middle East Journal* 55, no. 3 (2001): 399–414.

Köchümkulova, Elmira. "Introduction." In *Cities of the Dead: The Ancestral Cemeteries of Kyrgyzstan*, 3–10. Seattle: University of Washington Press, 2014.

Kreinath, Jens. "Virtual Encounters with Hizir and Other Muslim Saints: Dreaming and Healing at Local Pilgrimage Sites in Hatay, Turkey." *Anthropology of the Contemporary Middle East and Central Eurasia* 2, no. 1 (2014): 25–66.

Kucuk, Hulya. "Dervishes Make a City: The Sufi Culture in Konya." *Critique: Critical Middle Eastern Studies* 16, no. 3 (2007): 241–253.

Kugle, Scott. *Sufis and Saints' Bodies: Mysticism, Corporeality, and Sacred Power in Islam*. Chapel Hill: University of North Carolina Press, 2007.

Lake, Rose. "The Making of a Mouride Mahdi: Serigne Abdoulaye Yakhine Diop of Thies." In *African Islam and Islam in Africa*, edited by Eva Evers Rosander, 216–253. Athens, OH: Ohio University Press, 1997.

Laksana, Albertus Bagus. *Muslim and Catholic Pilgrimage Practices: Explorations through Java*. New York: Ashgate, 2014.

Langer, Robert. "From Private Shrine to Pilgrim-Center: The Spectrum of Zoroastrian Shrines of Iran." In *Zoroastrian Rituals in Context*, edited by Michael Stausberg, 563–592. Boston: Brill, 2004.

Laremont, Ricardo René. "Race, Islam, and Politics: Differing Visions among Black American Muslims." *Journal of Islamic Studies* 10, no. 1 (1999): 33–49.

Lee, Jennifer. "Beyond the Locus Sanctus: The Independent Iconography of Pilgrims' Souvenirs." *Visual Resources: An International Journal of Documentation* 21, no. 4 (2005): 363–381.

Livne-Kafri, Ofer. "Jerusalem: The Navel of the Earth in Muslim Tradition." *Der Islam* 84, no. 1 (2007): 46–72.

Lux, Abdullah. "Yemen's Last Zaydī Imām: The Shabāb al-Mu/min, the Malāzim, and 'Hizb Allāh' in the Thought of Husayn Badr al-Dīn al-Hūthī." *Contemporary Arab Affairs* 2, no. 3 (2009): 369–434.

MacWilliams, Mark W. "Virtual Pilgrimages on the Internet." *Religion* 32, no. 4 (2002): 315–335.

Marable, Manning. *Malcolm X: A Life of Reinvention*. New York: Viking, 2011.

Masterson, Rebecca. "A Comparative Exploration of the Spiritual Authority of the *Awliyā* in Shi'i and Sufi Traditions." *American Journal of Islamic Social Sciences* 32, no. 1 (2015): 49–74.

McHugh, Neil. *Holymen of the Nile: The Making of an Arab-Islamic Community in the Nilotic Sudan, 1500–1850*. Evanston: Northwestern University Press, 1994.

Meri, Josef W. *The Cult of Saints among Muslims and Jews in Medieval Syria*. New York: Oxford, 2002.

Metcalf, Barbara D. *Islamic Contestations: Essays on Muslims in India and Pakistan*. New York: Oxford University Press, 2004.

Meyer, Birgit and Dick Houtman. "Introduction: Material Religion: How Things Matter." In *Things: Religion and the Question of Materiality*, edited by Dick Houtman and Birgit Mayer, 1–26. New York: Fordham University Press, 2012.

Miller, Michael Barry. "Pilgrims' Progress: The Business of the Hajj." *Past & Present* 1919 (2006): 189–228.

Miura, Toru. "The Sālihiyya Quarter in the Suburbs of Damascus: Its Formation, Structure, and Transformation in the Ayyūbid and Mamlūk Periods." *Bulletin d'études Orientales* 47 (1995): 129–181.

Momen, Moojan. *An Introduction to Shi'i Islam*. New Haven: Yale University Press, 1987.

Moors, Annelies. "Popularizing Islam: Muslims and Materiality – An Introduction." *Material Religion* 8, no. 3 (2012): 272–279.

Morikawa, Tomoko. "Pilgrimages to the Iraqi 'Atabat from Qajar Era Iran." In *Saints and Their Pilgrims in Iran and Neighbouring Countries*, edited by Pedram Khosronejad, 41–59. Wantage: Sean Kingston Publishing, 2012.

Mostowlansky, Till. "Making Kyrgyz Spaces: Local History as Spatial Practice in Murghab (Tajikistan)." *Central Asian Survey* 31, no. 3 (2012): 251–264.

Moussavi, Ahmad Kazemi. "Shi'ite Culture." *Iranian Studies* 31, no. 3–4 (1998): 639–659.

Mukul, Sharif Ahmed, A.Z.M. Manzoor Rashid, and Mohammad Belal Uddin. "The Role of Spiritual Beliefs in Conserving Wildlife Species in Religious Shrines of Bangladesh." *Biodiversity* 12, no. 2 (2012): 108–114.

Al-Muqaddasī, Shams al-Dīn Abū 'Abdallāh Muhammad ibn Ahmad. *Descriptio Imperii Moslemici*, edited by M. J. De Geoje. Leiden: Brill, 1906.

Murrani, Sana. "Baghdad's Thirdspace: Between Liminality, Anti-Structures and Territorial Mappings." *Cultural Dynamics* 28, no. 2 (2016): 189–210.

Nabieva, Olima. "Pilgrimage to the Cemeteries of Chor Bakr (Bukhara) and Shahi Zinda (Samarkand)." In *Cities of Pilgrimage*, edited by Soheila Shahshahani, 79–84. New Brunswick: Transaction Publishers, 2009.

Nakash, Yitzhak. "The Visitation of the Shrines of the Imams and Shi'i Mujtahids in the Early Twentieth Century." *Studia Islamica* 8 (1995): 153–164.

Nasr, Seyyed Hossein. "Shiism: Ithna 'Ashariya." In *The Encyclopedia of Religion*, edited by Mircea Eliade, 8337–8346. New York: MacMillan, 1987.

Nasr, Vali. *The Shia Revival: How Conflicts within Islam Will Shape the Future*. New York: W.W. Norton & Company, 2006.

Nimitz, August H. *Islam and Politics in East Africa: The Sufi Order in Tanzania*. Minneapolis: University of Minnesota Press, 1980.

Norton, Augustus Richard. "Al-Najaf: Its Resurgence as a Religious and University Center." *Middle East Policy* 18, no. 2 (2011): 132–145.

O'Connor, Paul. "Hong Kong Muslims on Hajj: Rhythms of the Pilgrimage 2.0 and Experience of Spirituality among Twenty-First Century Global Cities." *Journal of Muslim Minority Affairs* 34, no. 3 (2014): 315–329.

Öktem, Kerem. "Being Muslim at the Margins: Alevis and the AKP." *Middle East Report* 246 (2008): 5–7.

O'Leary, Stephen D. "Cyberspace as Sacred Space: Communicating Religion on Computer Networks." In *Religion Online: Finding Faith on the Internet*, edited by Lorne L. Dawson and Douglas E. Cowan, 37–58. New York: Routledge, 2004.

Orsi, Robert. *Between Heaven and Earth: The Religious Worlds People Make and the Scholars Who Study Them*. Princeton: Princeton University Press, 2005.

Osman, Malak and Adnan Shaout. "Hajj Guide Systems – Past, Present, and Future." *International Journal of Emerging Technology and Advanced Engineering* 4, no. 8 (2014): 25–31.

Papas, Alexandre. "Pilgrimages to Muslim Shrines in Western China." In
Living Shrines of Uyghur China: Photographs by Lisa Ross, 11–17.
New York: Monacelli Press, 2013.

Papas, Alexandre and Lisa Ross. "On Ancient Central Asian Tracks."
Steppe 4 (2008): 50–79.

Pemberton, Kelly. "Women *Pirs*, Saintly Succession, and Spiritual Guidance
in South Asian Sufism." *Muslim World* 96, no. 1 (2006): 61–87.

Perret, Daniel. "Some Reflections on Ancient Islamic Tombstones Known
as Batu Aceh in the Malay World." *Indonesia and the Malay World*
35, no. 103 (2007): 313–340.

Peters, F.E. *The Hajj: The Muslim Pilgrimage to Mecca and the Holy
Places.* Princeton: Princeton University Press, 1994.

Petersen, Kristian. "The Multiple Meanings of Pilgrimage in Sino-Islamic
Thought." In *Islamic Thought in China: Sino-Muslim Intellectual
Evolution from the 17th to the 21st Century*, edited by Jonathan Lipman,
81–104. Edinburgh: Edinburgh University Press, 2016.

Philippon, Alix. "Bridging Sufism and Islamism." *ISIM Review* 17 (2006):
16–17.

Phillips, Shailoh. "Cyberkurds and Cyberkinetics." *Etnofoor* 20, no. 1
(2007): 7–29.

Pinault, David. "Zaynab Bint 'Ali and the Place of the Women of the
Households of the First Imams in Shi'ite Devotional Literature." In
Women in the Medieval Islamic World, edited by Gavin G. Hambly,
69–98. New York: St. Martin's Press, 1998.

Poyraz, Bedriye. "The Turkish State and Alevis: Changing Parameters
of an Uneasy Relationship." *Middle Eastern Studies* 4, no. 4 (2005):
503–516.

Prager, Laila. "Alawi Ziyāra Tradition and Its Interreligious Dimensions:
Sacred Places and Their Contested Meanings among Christians, Alawi
and Sunni Muslims in Contemporary Hatay (Turkey)." *Muslim World*
103, no. 1 (2013): 41–61.

Quinn, Charlotte A. and Frederick Quinn. *Pride, Faith, and Fear: Islam
in Sub-Saharan Africa.* New York: Oxford University Press, 2003.

Rahnema, Ali. *An Islamic Utopian: A Political Biography of Ali Shari'ati.*
New York: I.B. Tauris, 2000.

Reader, Ian. *Pilgrimage in the Marketplace.* New York: Routledge,
2014.

Renard, John. *Seven Doors to Islam: Spirituality and the Religious Life of
Muslims.* Berkeley: University of California Press, 1996.

Renne, Elisha P. "Photography, Hajj Things, and Spatial Connections between Mecca and Northern Nigeria." *Photography and Culture* 8 (2015): 1–27.

Rippin, Andrew and Jan Knappert. *Textual Sources for the Study of Islam.* Chicago: University of Chicago Press, 1986.

Rizvi, Kishwar. "'It's Mortar Mixed with the Sweetness of Life:' Architecture and Ceremonial at the Shrine of Safī al-dīn Ishāq Ardabīlī during the Reign of Shāh Tahmāsb I." *Muslim World* 90, no. 3/4 (2000): 323–352.

Rizvi, Kishwar. "Religious Icon and National Symbol: The Tomb of Ayatollah Khomeini in Iran." *Muqarnas* 20 (2003): 209–224.

Robertson, Roland. *Globalization: Social Theory and Global Culture.* London: Sage, 1992.

Robinson, Neal. *Islam: A Concise Introduction.* Washington: Georgetown University Press, 1999.

Roff, William R. *Studies on Islam and Society in Southeast Asia.* Singapore: NUS Press, 2009.

Rosiny, Stephan. "The Twelver Shi'a Online: Challenges for Its Religious Authorities." In *The Other Shiites: From the Mediterranean to Central Asia*, edited by Alessandro Monsutti, Silvia Naef, and Farian Sabahi, 245–262. New York: Peter Lang, 2007.

Ross, Eric. "Touba: A Spiritual Metropolis in the Modern World." *Canadian Journal of African Studies* 29, no. 2 (1995): 222–259.

Rubin, Uri. "Pre-existence and Light: Aspects of the Concept of Nur Muhammad." *Israel Oriental Studies* 5 (1975): 62–119.

Rubin, Uri. "Between Arabia and the Holy Land: A Mecca–Jerusalem Axis of Sanctity." *Jerusalem Studies in Arabic and Islam* 34 (2008): 345–362.

Ruffle, Karen G. "May Fatimah Gather Our Tears: The Mystical and Intercessory Powers of Fatimah al-Zahra in Indo-Persian, Shi'i Devotional Literature and Performance." *Comparative Studies of South Asia, Africa and the Middle East* 30 no. 3 (2010): 186–197.

Rustomji, Nerina. *The Garden and the Fire: Heaven and Hell in Islamic Culture.* New York: Columbia University Press, 2009.

Safi, Omid. "Bargaining with *Baraka*: Persian Sufism, 'Mysticism,' and Pre-Modern Politics." *Muslim World* 90 (2000): 259–288.

Safi, Omid. *Memories of Muhammad: Why the Prophet Matters.* New York: HarperOne, 2009.

Said, Edward W. *Orientalism.* New York: Vintage, 1979.

Saniotis, Arthur. "Contesting the Sacred at Muslim Shrines in India: Conflict and Retrieval in the 'Spiritual' Arena." *Journal of Muslim Minority Affairs* 33, no. 1 (2013): 139–151.

Sawada, Minoru. "Pilgrimage to Sacred Places in the Taklamakan Desert: Shrines of Imams in Khotan Prefecture." In *Central Asian Pilgrims: Hajj Routes and Pious Visits between Central Asia and the Hijaz*, edited by Alexandre Papas, Thomas Welsford, and Thierry Zarcone, 278–294. Berlin: Klaus Schwarz Verlag, 2012.

Sayyid, Ayman Fu'ād, Paul E. Walker, and Maurice A. Pomeranz. *The Fatimids and Their Successors in Yaman: The History of an Islamic Community. Arabic Edition and English Summary of Idrīs 'Imād al-Dīn's 'Uyān al-akhbār, vol. 7.* New York: I.B. Tauris, 2002.

Scheifinger, Heinz. "The Jagannath Temple and Online Darshan." *Journal of Contemporary Religion* 24, no. 3 (2009): 277–290.

Scheele, Judith. "A Pilgrimage to Arawan: Religious Legitimacy, Status, and Ownership in Timbuktu." *American Ethnologist* 40, no. 1 (2013): 165–181.

Schimmel, Annemarie. *Deciphering the Signs of God: A Phenomenological Approach to Islam.* Albany: State University of New York Press, 1994.

Schlosser, Dominik. "Digital Hajj: The Pilgrimage to Mecca in Muslim Cyberspace and the Issue of Religious Online Authority." In *Digital Religion*, edited by Tore Ahlback, 35–49. Turku: Donner Institute for Research and Religious History, 2014.

Schopen, Gregory. "Archaeology and Protestant Presuppositions in the Study of Indian Buddhism." *History of Religions* 31, no. 1 (1991): 1–23.

Schubel, Vernon James. *Religious Performance in Contemporary Islam: Shi'i Devotional Rituals in South Asia.* Columbia: University of South Carolina Press, 1993.

Schubel, Vernon James. "Karbala as Sacred Space among North American Shi'a: 'Every Day Is Ashura, Everywhere Is Karbala.'" In *Making Muslim Space in North America and Europe*, edited by Barbara Daly Metcalf, 186–203. Berkeley: University of California Press, 1996.

Scott, David. *Conscripts of Modernity: The Tragedy of Colonial Enlightenment.* Durham: Duke University Press, 2004.

Shaery-Eisenlohr, Roschanack. "Imagining Shi'ite Iran: Transnationalism and Religious Authenticity in the Muslim World." *Iranian Studies* 40, no. 1 (2007): 17–35.

Shafi, Sophia Rose. "Light Upon Light: Aineh-Kari in Shi'a Pilgrimage Architecture." *ARTS* 22, no. 3 (2011): 44–52.

Shafi, Sophia Rose. "Glass Palaces: The Role of Aineh-Kari in Shi'a Pilgrimage." *Shi'a Studies* 2 (2011): 6–9.

Shahshahani, Soheila. "Introduction and Cities of Pilgrimage in Iran." In *Cities of Pilgrimage*, edited by Soheila Shahshahani, 11–32. New Brunswick: Transaction Publishers, 2009.

Shankland, David. *The Alevis in Turkey: The Emergence of a Secular Islamic Tradition*. New York: Routledge Curzon, 2003.

Shankland, David. "Maps and the Alevis: On the Ethnography of Heterodox Islamic Groups." *British Journal of Middle Eastern Studies* 37, no. 3 (2010): 230–258.

Shannahan, Dervla Zaynab. "'I Love You More': An Account of Performing Ziyarat in Iraq." *Performing Islam* 4, no. 1 (2015): 61–92.

Sharafuddin, Mohammed. *Islam and Romantic Orientalism: Literary Encounters with the Orient*. New York: I.B Tauris, 1994.

Shoemaker, Stephen J. *The Death of a Prophet: The End of Muhammad's Life and the Beginnings of Islam*. Philadelphia: University of Pennsylvania Press, 2012.

Shokoohy, Mehrdad. "The Shrine of Imām-i Kalān in Sar-i Pul, Afghanistan." *Bulletin of the School of Oriental and African Studies* 52, no. 2 (1989): 306–314.

Shomali, Mohammad A. *Shi'i Islam: Origins, Faith & Practices*. London: ICAS, 2003.

Silverstein, Paul A. "In the Name of Culture: Berber Activism and the Material Politics of 'Popular Islam' in Southeastern Morocco." *Material Religion* 8, no. 3 (2012): 330–353.

Sindawi, Khalid. "Visit to the Tomb of Al-Husayn b. Alī in Shiite Poetry: First to Fifth Centuries AH (8th–11th Centuries CE)." *Journal of Arabic Literature* 37, no. 2 (2006): 230–258.

Sindawi, Khalid. "The Role of the Lion in Miracles Associated with Shī'ite Imāms." *Der Islam* 84, no. 2 (2007): 356–390.

Sindawi, Khalid. "The Zaynabiyya *Hawza* in Damascus and Its Role in Shi'ite Religious Instruction." *Middle Eastern Studies* 45, no. 6 (2009): 859–879.

Sindawi, Khalid. "The Sanctity of Karbala in Shiite Thought." In *Saints and Their Pilgrims in Iran and Neighbouring Countries*, edited by Pedram Khosronejad, 21–40. Wantage: Sean Kingston Publishing, 2012.

Sirriya, Elizabeth. "'Ziyarat' of Syria in 'Rihla' of 'Abd al-Ghanī al-Nābulusī (1050/1641–1143/1731)." *Journal of the Royal Asiatic Society of Great Britain and Ireland* 2 (1979): 109–122.

Smith, Jane. *Islam in America*. New York: Columbia University Press, 1999.

Smith, Jonathon Z. *To Take Place: Toward Theory in Ritual*. Chicago: University of Chicago Press, 1992.

Smith, Jonathon Z. *Map Is Not Territory*. Chicago: University of Chicago Press, 1993.

Smith, Jonathon Z. "Differential Equations." In *Relating Religion: Essays in the Study of Religion*, edited by Jonathon Z. Smith, 230–250. Chicago: University of Chicago Press, 2004.

Smith, Jonathon Z. "Religion, Religions, Religious." In *Relating Religion: Essays in the Study of Religion*, edited by Jonathon Z. Smith, 179–196. Chicago: University of Chicago Press, 2004.

Soja, Edward. *Thirdspace: Journeys to Los Angeles and Other Real-and-Imagined Places*. Cambridge: Blackwell, 1996.

Spiegelman, J. Marvin. "Divine Among in Islam: The Hajj or Pilgrimage to Mecca." *Psychological Perspectives: A Quarterly Journal of Jungian Thought* 49, no. 1 (2005): 136–142.

Stanton, Andrea L. "Islamic Emoticons: Pious Sociability and Community Building in Online Muslim Communities." In *Internet and Emotions*, edited by Tova Benski and Eran Fisher, 80–98. New York: Routledge, 2014.

Subhāni, Ayatullāh Shaykh Ja'far. *Ziyāratu 'Ashūrā': An Analytical Study of the Reports of the Pilgrimage to Imām al-Husayn (a.s.) on the Day of 'Ashūra*, translated by Afzal Sumar. Birmingham: The Sun Behind the Clouds Publications, 2002.

Swanson, Kristen K. and Dallen J. Timothy. "Souvenirs: Icons of Meaning, Commercialization and Commodification." *Tourism Management* 33 (2012): 489–499.

Szanto, Edith. "Sayyida Zaynab in the State of Exception: Shi'i Sainthood as 'Qualified Life' in Contemporary Syria." *International Journal of Middle East Studies* 44 (2012): 285–299.

Szanto, Edith. "Contesting Fragile Saintly Traditions: Miraculous Healing among Twelver Shi'is in Contemporary Syria." In *Politics of Worship in the Contemporary Middle East: Sainthood in Fragile States*, edited by Andreas Bandak and Mikkel Bille, 33–52. Boston: Brill, 2013.

Tabbaa, Yasser. "Invented Pieties: The Rediscovery and Rebuilding of the Shrine of Sayyida Ruqayya in Damascus, 1975–2006." *Artibus Asiae* 67, no. 1 (2007): 95–112.

Takim, Liyakatali (translator). *Pilgrims' Guide: Selected Supplications*. Toronto: Hyderi Press, 1998.

Takim, Liyakatali (translator). *Guide to Ziyarat: Selected Supplications*. Toronto: Mebs Printing Pluss, 2000.

Takim, Liyakatali. "Charismatic Appeal or Communitas? Visitation to the Shrines of the Imams." In *Contesting Rituals: Islam and Practices of Identity-Making*, edited by Pamela J. Stewart and Andrew Strathern, 181–203. Durham: Carolina Academic Press, 2005.

Takim, Liyakatali. "Offering Complete or Shortened Prayers? The Traveler's *Salat* at the 'Holy Places.'" *Muslim World* 96, no. 3 (2006): 401–422.

Talmon-Heller, Daniella. *Islamic Piety in Medieval Syria: Mosques, Cemeteries and Sermons under the Zangids and Ayyūbids (1146–1260)*. Boston: Brill, 2007.

Tambar, Kabir. "Iterations of Lament: Anachronism and Affect in a Shi'i Islamic Revival in Turkey." *American Ethnologist* 38, no. 3 (2011): 484–500.

Tapper, Nancy. "*Ziyaret*: Gender, Movement, and Exchange in a Turkish Community." In *Muslim Travellers: Pilgrimage, Migration, and the Religious Imagination*, edited by Dale E. Eickelman and James Piscatori, 236–255. Berkeley: University of California Press, 1990.

Taylor, Christopher. *In the Vicinity of the Righteous: Ziyara and the Veneration of Muslim Saints in Late Medieval Egypt*. Leiden: Brill, 1998.

Thum, Rian. *The Sacred Routes of Uyghur History*. Cambridge: Harvard University Press, 2014.

Timothy, Dallen J. and Thomas Iverson. "Tourism and Islam: Considerations of Culture and Duty." In *Tourism, Religion and Spiritual Journeys*, edited by Dallen J. Timothy and Daniel H. Olsen, 186–205. New York: Routledge, 2006.

Tolmacheva, Marina. "Female Piety and Patronage in the Medieval 'Hajj.'" In *Women in the Medieval Islamic World*, edited by Gavin G. Hambly, 161–179. New York: St. Martin's Press, 1998.

Toorawa, Shawkat M. "Performing the Pilgrimage." In *The Hajj: Pilgrimage in Islam*, edited by Eric Tagliacozzo and Shawkat M. Toorawa, 215–230. New York: Cambridge University Press, 2016.

Trix, Frances. *Spiritual Discourse: Learning with an Islamic Master*. Philadelphia: University of Pennsylvania Press, 1993.

Türk, Hüseyin. "Alawi Syncretism: Beliefs and Traditions in the Shrine of Hüseyin Gazi." *Journal of Religious Culture* 69 (2004): 1–15.

Turner, Bryan S. *Weber and Islam*. London: Routledge, 1975.

Turner, Victor. "Pilgrimage and Communitas." *Studia Missionalia* 23 (1974): 305–327.

Turner, Victor and Edith Turner. *Image and Pilgrimage in Christian Culture: Anthropological Perspectives*. New York: Columbia University Press, 1978.

Um, Nancy. "Eighteenth-Century Patronage in San'ā: Building for the New Capital during the Second Century of the Qāsimī Imamate." *Proceedings of the Seminar for Arabian Studies* 34 (2004): 361–375.

Vahed, Goolam H. "A Sufi Saint's Day in South Africa: The Legend of Badsha Peer." *South African Historical Journal* 49, no. 1 (2003): 96–122.

van Doorn-Harder, Nelly and Kees de Jong. "The Pilgrimage to Tembayat: Tradition and Revival in Indonesian Islam." *Muslim World* 91, no. 3–4 (2001): 325–353.

Vial, Theodore. *Modern Religion, Modern Race*. New York: Oxford University Press, 2016.

Vikør, Knut S. "Sufi Brotherhoods in Africa." In *The History of Islam in Africa*, edited by Nehemia Levtzion and Randall L. Pouwels, 441–476. Athens, OH: Ohio University Press, 2000.

Vovina, Olessia. "Islam and the Creation of Sacred Space: The Mishar Tatars in Chuvashia." *Religion, State and Society* 34, no. 3 (2006): 255–269.

Walker, Paul E. "Purloined Symbols of the Past: The Theft of Souvenirs and Sacred Relics in the Rivalry between the Abbasids and Fatimids." In *Culture and Memory in Medieval Islam: Essays in Honor of Wilferd Mandelung*, edited by Farhad Daftary and Josef W. Meri, 364–387. New York: I.B. Tauris, 2003.

Werbner, Pnina. *Pilgrims of Love: The Anthropology of a Global Sufi Cult*. Bloomington: Indiana University Press, 2003.

Wheeler, Brannon. *Mecca and Eden: Ritual, Relics, and Territory in Islam*. Chicago: University of Chicago Press, 2006.

Williams, Alison M. "Surfing Therapeutic Landscapes: Exploring Cyberpilgrimage." *Culture and Religion: An Interdisciplinary Journal* 14, no. 1 (2013): 78–93.

Williams, Caroline. "The Cult of 'Alid Saints in the Fatimid Monuments of Cairo Part II: The Mausolea." *Muqarnas* 3 (1985): 39–60.

Wolf, Richard K. "The Poetics of 'Sufi' Practice: Drumming. Dancing, and Complex Agency at Madho Lal Husain (and Beyond)." *American Ethnologist* 33, no. 2 (2006): 246–268.

Wolfe, Michael. "The Pilgrim's Complaint: Recent Accounts of the Hajj." In *The Hajj: Pilgrimage in Islam*, edited by Eric Tagliacozzo and Shawkat M. Toorawa, 250–268. New York: Cambridge University Press, 2016.

Wolper, Ethel Sara. "Khidr, Elwan Celebi and the Conversion of Sacred Sanctuaries in Anatolia." *Muslim World* 90, no. 3–4 (2000): 309–322.

Woodward, Mark R. *Islam in Java: Normative Piety and Mysticism in the Sultanate of Yogyakarta*. Tucson: University of Arizona Press, 1989.

Yagmur, Huseyin. *Pilgrimage in Islam: A Comprehensive Guide to the Hajj*. Somerset, NJ: The Light, 2007.

Yeler, Abdülkadir. "Shi'ism in Turkey: A Comparison of the Alevis and Ja'faris." *Journal of Shi'i Islamic Studies* 3, no. 3 (2010): 331–340.

Yürekli, Zeynep. *Architecture and Hagiography in the Ottoman Empire: The Politics of Bektashi Shrines in the Classical Age*. Burlington, VT: Ashgate, 2012.

El-Zein, Amira. "Spiritual Consumption in the United States: The Rumi Phenomenon." *Islam and Christian–Muslim Relations* 11, no. 1 (2000): 71–85.

Zilberman, Ifrah. "The Renewal of the Pilgrimage to Nabi Musa." In *Sacred Space in Israel and Palestine: Religion and Politics*, edited by Marshall J. Breger, Yitzhak Reiter, and Leonard Hammer, 103–115. New York: Routledge, 2012.

NOTES

INTRODUCTION: BEYOND *HAJJ*

1   Momen, *An Introduction to Shi'i Islam*, pp. 181–182.
2   Nasr, *The Shia Revival*, p. 50.
3   Shomali, *Shi'i Islam*, p. 147.
4   Tabbaa, "Invented Pieties," p. 100.
5   Williams, "The Cult of 'Alid Saints," pp. 39–40.
6   Wheeler, *Mecca and Eden*, p. 101.
7   Laksana, *Muslim and Catholic Pilgrimage Practices*, p. 41.
8   Meri, *The Cult of Saints*, p. 24.
9   Masterson, "A Comparative Exploration," p. 51.
10 Shoemaker, *The Death of a Prophet*, p. 229.
11 Schimmel, *Deciphering the Signs of God*.
12 Shannahan, "'I Love You More,'" p. 67.
13 Thum, *The Sacred Routes of Uyghur History*, p. 113.
14 J.Z. Smith, *Map Is Not Territory*, p. 309.
15 Szanto, "Contesting Fragile Saintly Traditions," p. 33.
16 Sirriya, "'Ziyarat' of Syria," p. 109.
17 Hallam and Hockey, *Death, Memory and Material Culture*, p. 18.
18 Nabieva, "Pilgrimage to the Cemeteries," pp. 81–82.
19 Walker, "Purloined Symbols of the Past," p. 381.

20   Kreinath, "Virtual Encounters," p. 26.
21   Mukul, Rashid, and Uddin, "The Role of Spiritual Beliefs," p. 110.
22   Sawada, "Pilgrimage to Sacred Places," p. 278.

1. RECONSIDERING ISLAMIC PILGRIMAGE: THEORETICAL AND SECTARIAN DEBATES

1   Ho, *The Graves of Tarim*, p. 7.
2   Moors, "Popularizing Islam," p. 276.
3   Vovina, "Islam and the Creation of Sacred Space," p. 256.
4   Soja, *Thirdspace*, pp. 56–57.
5   Ibid., p. 1.
6   Talmon-Heller, *Islamic Piety in Medieval Syria*, p. 157.
7   Khalvashi, "Ziyareti," p. 89.
8   The Afghan scholar Kawa Aahanger related these stories to me.
9   Green is the color associated with Islam, and in particular, the Prophet's family.
10   The Afghan scholar Kawa Aahanger related these stories to me.
11   Green, *Making Space*, p. 71.
12   Meri, *The Cult of Saints*, pp. 263–271.
13   Papas and Ross, "On Ancient Central Asian Tracks," pp. 53–54.
14   McHugh, *Holymen of the Nile*, p. 86.
15   Ibid., p. 86.
16   Ahmed, *What Is Islam?*, p. 78.
17   Khosronejad, "Anthropology, Islam and Sainthood," p. 3.
18   Takim, "Offering Complete or Shortened Prayers?," p. 418.
19   Pemberton, "Women *Pirs*," p. 71.
20   Renard, *Seven Doors to Islam*, p. 60.
21   Schubel, *Religious Performance in Contemporary Islam*, p. 73.
22   Alatas, "Pilgrimage and Network Formation," p. 317.
23   Meri, *The Cult of Saints*, p. 145.
24   Norton, "Al-Najaf," p. 133.
25   Köchümkulova, "Introduction," p. 3.
26   Al-Houdalieh, "Visitation and Making Vows," pp. 379–380.

27   Eisenlohr, "Mediality and Materiality in Religious Performance," p. 341.

28   Thum, *The Sacred Routes of Uyghur History*, p. 127.

29   Nimitz, *Islam and Politics in East Africa*, p. 56.

30   Renard, *Seven Doors to Islam*, p. 60.

31   Meri, *The Cult of Saints*, p. 141.

32   Williams, "The Cult of 'Alid Saints," p. 40.

33   Lake, "The Making of a Mouride Mahdi," p. 216.

34   Frank, "Some Political Features," p. 300.

35   Silverstein, "In the Name of Culture," p. 333.

36   Woodward, *Islam in Java*, p. 69.

37   Petersen, "The Multiple Meanings of Pilgrimage," p. 83.

38   Silverstein, "In the Name of Culture," p. 333.

39   Gardner, "Global Migrants and Local Shrines," pp. 40–41.

40   Rizvi, "'It's Mortar Mixed with the Sweetness of Life,'" p. 333.

41   King, *Orientalism and Religion*, p. 40.

42   J.Z. Smith, *To Take Place*, p. 102.

43   Williams, "Surfing Therapeutic Landscapes," p. 82.

44   Takim, "Offering Complete or Shortened Prayers?," p. 416.

45   Ibid.

46   *Hajji* and *hajjah* are the Arabic used for males and females who complete the *hajj*.

47   Khalek, *Damascus after the Muslim Conquest*, p. 116.

48   Hasan, "The Footprint of the Prophet," p. 335.

49   Haider, *The Origins of the Shi'a*, p. 242.

50   Standing on Arafat is a tradition connected to the Prophet's farewell sermon.

51   Grabar, "The Earliest Islamic Commemorative Structures," p. 7.

52   Ibid.

53   Vahed, "A Sufi Saint's Day in South Africa," p. 99.

54   van Doorn-Harder and de Jong, "The Pilgrimage to Tembayat," p. 325.

55   Miura, "The Sālihiyya Quarter," p. 150.

56   Halevi, *Muhammad's Grave*, p. 231.

57   Ibid., p. 209.

58   Ibid., p. 211.

59   Grabar, "The Earliest Islamic Commemorative Structures," pp. 14–15.

60   Beranek and Tupek, "From Visiting Graves to Their Destruction,"
      p. 6.

61   Grabar, "The Earliest Islamic Commemorative Structures," p. 12.

62   Shokoohy, "The Shrine of Imām-i Kalān," pp. 311–312.

63   Ahmed, *What Is Islam?*, p. 92.

64   Beranek and Tupek, "From Visiting Graves to Their Destruction,"
      p. 6.

65   Hoffman, *Sufism, Mystics, and Saints*, p. 120.

66   Beranek and Tupek, "From Visiting Graves to Their Destruction,"
      p. 7.

67   Shoemaker, *The Death of a Prophet*, p. 260.

68   Miura, "The Sālihiyya Quarter," p. 134.

69   Frank, "Some Political Features," p. 299.

70   Beranek and Tupek, "From Visiting Graves to Their Destruction,"
      p. 18.

71   El Fadl, "The Ugly Modern," p. 53.

72   Metcalf, *Islamic Contestations*, p. 59.

73   Hoffman, *Sufism, Mystics, and Saints*, p. 120.

74   Laksana, *Muslim and Catholic Pilgrimage Practices*, p. 11. See also
      Taylor, *In the Vicinity of the Righteous*, p. 188.

75   Knysh, "The *Tariqa* on a Landcruiser," p. 404.

76   Diouf, "The Senegalese Murid Trade Diaspora," p. 686.

77   Kugle, *Sufis and Saints' Bodies*, p. 7.

78   Khosronejad, "Anthropology, Islam and Sainthood," p. 5.

79   Wolf, "The Poetics of 'Sufi' Practice," pp. 251–2.

80   Foley, "The *Ronggeng*, the *Wayang*, the *Wali*, and Islam," pp. 359–61.

81   Babayan, "'In Spirit We Ate Each Other's Sorrow,'" pp. 261–2.

82   Beranek and Tupek, "From Visiting Graves to Their Destruction,"
      p. 2.

83   Philippon, "Bridging Sufism and Islamism," p. 17.

84   Vikør, "Sufi Brotherhoods in Africa," p. 459.

85   Described in Collins-Kreiner and Gatrell, "Tourism, Heritage, and
      Pilgrimage," p. 34.

86 Turner, "Pilgrimage and Communitas," p. 305.

87 MacWilliams, "Virtual Pilgrimages on the Internet," p. 325.

88 Hill-Smith, "Cyberpilgrimage," p. 237.

89 Delaney, "The *Hajj*," p. 521.

90 Couldry, "Pilgrimage," p. 63.

91 Turner and Turner, *Image and Pilgrimage*, p. 241.

92 Diouf, "The Senegalese Murid Trade Diaspora," p. 688.

93 Ross, "Touba," p. 227.

94 Petersen, "The Multiple Meanings of Pilgrimage," p. 92.

95 Thum, *The Sacred Routes of Ughyur History*, p.104.

96 van Doorn-Harder and de Jong, "The Pilgrimage to Tembayat," p. 326.

97 Reader, *Pilgrimage in the Marketplace*, pp. 13–14.

98 Woodward, *Islam in Java*, p. 137.

99 Peters, *The Hajj*, p. 46.

100 Rustomji, *The Garden and the Fire*, p. 139.

101 Beranek and Tupek, "From Visiting Graves to Their Destruction," p. 1.

102 J.Z. Smith, "Religion, Religions, Religious," p. 179.

103 King, *Orientalism and Religion*, p. 7.

104 Safi, "Bargaining with *Baraka*," p. 263.

105 J.Z. Smith, "Differential Equations," p. 241.

106 Sharafuddin, *Islam and Romantic Orientalism*, p. 87.

107 Rippin and Knappert, *Textual Sources for the Study of Islam*, p. 89.

108 Men on *hajj* are required to wear the *ihram*, a special white cloth, but women are permitted to wear a wide assortment of garments while on *hajj*.

109 Marable, *Malcolm X*, p. 311.

110 Laremont, "Race, Islam, and Politics," p. 42.

111 Aslan, "General Introduction," p. xiii.

112 Safi, *Memories of Muhammad*, p. 162.

113 Ahmed-Ghosh, "Portraits of Believers," p. 74.

114 Esposito, *Islam*, p. 147.

115 Ahmed-Ghosh, "Portraits of Believers," p. 78.

116 Khan, *From Sufism to Ahmadiyya*, p. 79.

117   Marable, *Malcolm X*, pp. 83–84.

118   Karim, "Between Immigrant Islam and Black Liberation," p. 499.

119   Cone, *Martin & Malcolm & America*, p. 14.

120   Curtis, "Islamizing the Black Body," pp. 183–184.

121   Curtis, *Black Muslim Religion*, p. 164.

122   Danesh, "The Journey Motif," p. 8.

123   Collins-Kreiner and Gatrell, "Tourism, Heritage and Pilgrimage," p. 45.

124   Armstrong, "Jerusalem," p. 193.

125   Meri, *The Cult of Saints*, p. 13.

126   Fadiman and Frager, *Essential Sufism*, p. 92.

127   Akkach, *Cosmology and Architecture*, p. 151.

128   Bakhtiar, *Sufi*, p. 107.

129   Kugle, *Sufis and Saints' Bodies*, p. 76.

130   Wheeler, *Mecca and Eden*, p. 12.

131   Walker, "Purloined Symbols of the Past," p. 368.

132   Ardalan and Bakhtiar, *The Sense of Unity*, p. 11.

2. NASCENT PILGRIMAGE CENTERS: JERUSALEM, MECCA, AND MEDINA

1   Rustomji, *The Garden and the Fire*, p. 129.

2   Shoemaker, *The Death of a Prophet*, p. 252.

3   Livne-Kafri, "Jerusalem," p. 46.

4   Shoemaker, *The Death of a Prophet*, p. 255.

5   Ephrat, *Spiritual Wayfarers*, p. 18.

6   Ibid., p. 19.

7   Livne-Kafri, "Jerusalem," p. 51.

8   Ibid., p. 57.

9   Ibid., p. 60.

10   Ibid.

11   Hasson, "Muslim Literature in Praise of Jerusalem," p. 177.

12   Livne-Kafri, "Jerusalem," p. 46.

13   Meri, *The Cult of Saints*, p. 13.

14 Shoemaker, *The Death of a Prophet*, p. 223.

15 Bashear, "Jesus in an Early Muslim Shahada," p. 4.

16 Hasson, "Muslim Literature in Praise of Jerusalem," p. 169.

17 Shoemaker, *The Death of a Prophet*, p. 227.

18 Halevi, *Muhammad's Grave*, p. 191.

19 Livne-Kafri, "Jerusalem," pp. 48, 62.

20 Kister, "'You Shall Only Set Out for Three Mosques,'" p. 173.

21 Shoemaker, *The Death of a Prophet*, p. 218.

22 Hasson, "Muslim Literature in Praise of Jerusalem," p. 170.

23 Shoemaker, *The Death of a Prophet*, p. 223.

24 Hasson, "Muslim Literature in Praise of Jerusalem," p. 171.

25 Ibid.

26 Akkach, *Cosmology and Architecture*, p. 167.

27 El-Khatib, "Jerusalem in the Qur'an," p. 32.

28 Rubin, "Between Arabia and the Holy Land," p. 345.

29 Bashear, "Qur'an 2:114 and Jerusalem," p. 238.

30 El-Khatib, "Jerusalem in the Qur'an," p. 28.

31 Hasson, "Muslim Literature in Praise of Jerusalem," pp. 169–170.

32 Kister, "'You Shall Only Set Out for Three Mosques,'" p. 185.

33 Akkach, *Cosmology and Architecture*, p. 167.

34 Hasson, "The Muslim View of Jerusalem," p. 363.

35 Rubin, "Between Arabia and the Holy Land," p. 348.

36 Armstrong, "Jerusalem," p. 194.

37 Hasson, "The Muslim View of Jerusalem," p. 359.

38 Drijvers, "Transformation of a City," p. 323.

39 Elad, *Medieval Jerusalem and Islamic Worship*, p. xix.

40 Ibid., pp. 87, 99, 131.

41 Ibid., p. 171.

42 Zilberman, "The Renewal of the Pilgrimage to Nabi Musa," pp. 104–105.

43 Ibid., p. 111.

44 Timothy and Iverson, "Tourism and Islam," p. 198.

45 Anabsi, "Popular Beliefs," p. 69.

46 Peters, *The Hajj*, p. 10.

47 Wheeler, *Mecca and Eden*, p. 101.

48   Peters, *The Hajj*, p. 31.
49   Ibid., p. 31.
50   Kaptein, *Muhammad's Birthday Festival*, p. 39.
51   Ibid., p. 40.
52   Peters, *The Hajj*, p. 11.
53   Robinson, *Islam*, p. 127.
54   Twelver Shi'i comprise the largest group of Shi'i in the world.
55   Takim, "Offering Complete or Shortened Prayers?," p. 414. Takim cites Murtada al-Burujardi, the notes of lectures by al-Khu'i in Najaf, for this tradition.
56   Ibid., p. 412.
57   Robinson, *Islam*, pp. 129–30.
58   Ibid., p. 131. See also verses 9.3, 18, and 28.
59   Peters, *The Hajj*, p. 12.
60   Khan, "Architectural Conservation," pp. 4–5.
61   Timothy and Iverson, "Tourism and Islam," p. 192.
62   Peters, *The Hajj*, p.14.
63   Ibid., pp. 15–16.
64   Timothy and Iverson, "Tourism and Islam," p. 193.
65   Peters, *The Hajj*, p.16.
66   Haleem (translator), *The Qur'an*, p. 336.
67   Ibid., p. 63.
68   Schlosser, "Digital Hajj," p. 35.
69   Bianchi, *Guests of God*, p. 9.
70   Toorawa, "Performing the Pilgrimage," p. 219.
71   Tolmacheva, "Female Piety and Patronage," p. 167.
72   Roff, *Studies on Islam and Society*, p. 276.
73   Ibid., p. 276.
74   Wheeler, *Mecca and Eden*, p. 65.
75   Toorawa, "Performing the Pilgrimage," p. 222.
76   Tolmacheva, "Female Piety and Patronage," p. 167.
77   Darwish, 'Defining the Boundaries of Sacred Space," p. 305.
78   Smith, *Islam in America*, p. 20.
79   Tolmacheva, "Female Piety and Patronage," p. 167.
80   Roff, *Studies on Islam and Society*, p. 277.

81   Bianchi, *Guests of God*, p. 8.

82   O'Connor, "Hong Kong Muslims on Hajj," p. 322.

83   Bianchi, *Guests of God*, p. 8.

84   Roff, *Studies on Islam and Society*, p. 278.

85   Smith, *Islam in America,* 20.

86   Chittick, *A Shi'ite Anthology*, p. 98.

87   Roff, *Studies on Islam and Society*, p. 278.

88   Toorawa, "Performing the Pilgrimage," p. 227.

89   Timothy and Iverson, "Tourism and Islam," p. 197.

90   The materials on these traditions were given to me by a Saudi citizen who must remain anonymous for his safety and that of his family.

91   Kaptein, *Muhammad's Birthday Festival*, p. 87.

92   Ibid., p. 87.

93   Shoemaker, *The Death of a Prophet*, p. 257.

94   Ibid., p. 257.

95   Ibid., p. 257.

96   Akkach, *Cosmology and Architecture*, p. 194.

97   Khan, "Architectural Conservation," p. 6.

98   Armstrong, "Jerusalem," p. 194.

99   Timothy and Iverson, "Tourism and Islam," p. 198.

100 Yagmur, *Pilgrimage in Islam*, p. 178.

101 Ibid., p. 178.

102 Shomali, *Shi'i Islam*, p. 160.

103 Takim, *Pilgrims' Guide*, p. 120.

104 Peters, *The Hajj*, p. 138.

105 Ibid., p. 138.

106 Khalek, *Damascus after the Muslim Conquest*, p. 124.

107 Ibid., p. 125.

108 Wheeler, *Mecca and Eden*, p. 72.

3. SHI'I PILGRIMAGE: THE PROPHET'S HOUSEHOLD

1   Ibid., p. 87.

2   Sindawi, "The Sanctity of Karbala in Shiite Thought," p. 24.

3   Ibid., p. 25.

4   Dabashi, *Islamic Liberation Theology*, p. 214.

5   Hussain, "The Mourning of History," p. 80.

6   Ibid., p. 81.

7   Norton, "Al-Najaf," p. 133.

8   Shahshahani, "Introduction," p. 16.

9   Shannahan, "'I Love You More,'" p. 74.

10   Subhāni, *Ziyāratu 'Ashūrā'*, p. 12.

11   Hussain, "The Mourning of History," p. 83.

12   *Majlis* also refers to the gatherings of Shi'i in communal prayer.

13   Moussavi, "Shi'ite Culture," p. 644.

14   Ibid., p. 646.

15   Shaery-Eisenlohr, "Imagining Shi'ite Iran," p. 19.

16   Kugle, *Sufis and Saints' Bodies*, p. 60.

17   Takim, "Offering Complete or Shortened Prayers?," p. 418.

18   Betteridge, "Muslim Women and Shrines in Shiraz," p. 286.

19   Szanto, "Sayyida Zaynab in the State of Exception," p. 286.

20   Nakash, "The Visitation of the Shrines," p. 155.

21   Ibid., p. 157. Nakash quotes Ibn Qulawayh's *Kamil al-ziyarat*.

22   Bhardwaj, "Non-Hajj Pilgrimage in Islam," p. 73.

23   Nasr, "Ithna 'Ashariyah," p. 8345.

24   Szanto, "Sayyida Zaynab in the State of Exception," p. 286.

25   Honarpisheh, "Women in Pilgrimage," p. 384.

26   Flaskerud, "Redemptive Memories," p. 23.

27   Ibid., p. 24.

28   Pinault, "Zaynab Bint 'Ali," p. 75.

29   Ibid., p. 75.

30   Ruffle, "May Fatimah Gather Our Tears," p. 187.

31   Bang, "'My Generation," p. 88.

32   Pinault, "Zaynab Bint 'Ali," p. 72.

33   Ibid., p. 71.

34   Hazleton, *After the Prophet*, p. 194.

35   Szanto, "Sayyida Zaynab in the State of Exception," p. 287.

36   Ibid., p. 287.

37   Bashir, *Sufi Bodies*, p. 27.

38 Sawada, "Pilgrimage to Sacred Places in the Taklamakan Desert: Shrines of Imams in Khotan Prefecture," p. 288.

39 Meri, *The Cult of Saints*, p. 140.

40 Flaskerud, *Visualizing Belief*, p. 181.

41 Takim, "Charismatic Appeal or Communitas?," p. 183.

42 Tabbaa, "Invented Pieties," p. 97.

43 Ibid.

44 Williams, "The Cult of 'Alid Saints," p. 44.

45 Ibid.

46 Szanto, "Contesting Fragile Saintly Traditions," p. 45.

47 Shokoohy, "The Shrine of Imām-i Kalān," p. 306.

48 Williams, "The Cult of 'Alid Saints," pp. 53–54.

49 Keddie, *Modern Iran*, p. 7.

50 Glazebrook and Abbasi-Shavazi, "Being Neighbors to Imam Reza," p. 197.

51 Esposito, *Islam*, p. 49.

52 Lux, "Yemen's Last Zaydī Imām," p. 378.

53 Ibid., p. 378.

54 Williams, "The Cult of 'Alid Saints," p. 53.

55 Esposito, *Islam*, p. 49.

56 Ibid., p. 49.

57 Lux, "Yemen's Last Zaydī Imām," p. 397.

58 Halevi, *Muhammad's Grave*, p. 39.

59 Um, "Eighteenth-Century Patronage in San'ā," p. 362.

60 Ibid., p. 368.

61 Finster, "An Outline," p. 141.

62 Ibid., p. 140.

63 Sayyid, Walker, and Pomeranz. *The Fatimids*, p. 67.

64 Ahmed, *What Is Islam?*, p. 5.

65 Iloliev, "Popular Culture and Religious Metaphor," p. 62.

66 Ibid., p. 62.

67 Williams, "The Cult of 'Alid Saints," p. 44.

68 Daftary, *The Ismā'īlīs*, p. 294.

69 Ibid., p. 492.

70 Ibid., p. 492.

71   Ghadially, "Devotional Empowerment," p. 80.

72   Ibid., pp. 82–3.

73   Ibid., p. 85.

74   Iloliev, "Popular Culture and Religious Metaphor," p. 59.

75   Ibid., pp. 60, 65.

76   Ibid., p. 62.

77   Ibid., p. 64.

78   Ibid., p. 65.

79   Ibid., p. 67.

80   Keshavjee, *Mysticism and the Plurality of Meaning*, pp. 13–14.

81   Ibid., p. 15.

82   Abrahamian, *Khomeinism*, p. 18.

83   Heern, *The Emergence of Modern Shi'ism*, p. 44.

84   Ibid., p. 44.

85   Kalinock, "Touching a Sensitive Topic," p. 670.

86   Grabar, "The Earliest Islamic Commemorative Structures," p. 7.

87   Honarpisheh, "Women in Pilgrimage," p. 386.

88   Masterson, "A Comparative Exploration," p. 52.

89   Ibid., p. 53.

90   Dabashi, *Shi'ism*, p. 138.

91   Takim, "Offering Complete or Shortened Prayers?," p. 416.

92   Haider, *The Origins of the Shi'a*, p. 239.

93   Ibid., p. 237.

94   Ibid., p. 239.

95   Ibid., p. 236.

96   Takim, "Offering Complete or Shortened Prayers?," p. 416.

97   Renard, *Seven Doors to Islam*, p. 62.

98   Takim, "Offering Complete or Shortened Prayers?," p. 417.

99   Norton, "Al-Najaf," pp. 133–134.

100 Takim, "Offering Complete or Shortened Prayers?," p. 416.

101 Norton, "Al-Najaf," p. 133.

102 Glazebrook and Abbasi-Shavazi, "Being Neighbors to Imam Reza," p. 197.

103 Shomali, *Shi'i Islam*, p. 163.

104 Glazebrook and Abbasi-Shavazi, "Being Neighbors to Imam Reza," p. 198.

105　de Bellaigue, *In the Rose Garden*, p. 89.

106　Honarpisheh, "Women in Pilgrimage," p. 387.

107　Szanto, "Contesting Fragile Saintly Traditions," p. 43.

108　Gruber, "The Martyrs' Museum in Tehran," p. 71.

109　Aghaie, *The Martyrs of Karbala*, p. 138.

110　Gruber, "The Martyrs' Museum in Tehran," p. 74.

111　Momen, *An Introduction to Shi'i Islam*, p. 182.

112　Shafi, "Glass Palaces," p. 9.

113　Shafi, "Light Upon Light," p. 51.

114　Alatas, "Pilgrimage and Network Formation," p. 307.

115　Kamalkhani, *Women's Islam*, p. 102.

116　Takim, *Guide to Ziyarat*, p. 16.

117　Ibid., p. 18.

118　Kamalkhani, *Women's Islam*, p. 102.

119　Ibid., p. 103.

120　Flaskerud, *Visualizing Belief*, p. 201.

121　Kamalkhani, *Women's Islam*, p. 103.

122　Ibid., p. 103.

123　Flaskerud, *Visualizing Belief*, p. 181.

124　Sindawi, "The Zaynabiyya *Hawza* in Damascus," p. 863.

125　Flaskerud, "Redemptive Memories," p. 23.

126　Aghaie, *The Martyrs of Karbala*, pp. 138–139.

127　Flaskerud, "Redemptive Memories," p. 37.

128　Khosronejad, "Lions' Representation," pp. 206–207.

129　Sindawi, "The Role of the Lion," p. 380.

130　Hodgson, *The Venture of Islam*, 265.

131　Prager, "Alawi Ziyāra Tradition," p. 45.

132　Ibid., p. 45.

133　Ibid., p. 46.

134　Ibid., p. 48.

135　Ibid., p. 48.

136　Türk, "Alawi Syncretism," pp. 6, 9.

137　Kreinath, "Virtual Encounters," p. 38.

138　Prager, "Alawi Ziyāra Tradition," pp. 49–50.

139　Kreinath, "Virtual Encounters," p. 34.

140　Ibid., p. 38.

141 Ibid., p. 46.

142 Al-Houdalieh, "Visitation and Making Vows," p. 379.

143 Tambar, "Iterations of Lament," p. 486.

144 Yeler, "Shi'ism in Turkey," p. 332.

145 Ibid., pp. 332–333.

146 Shankland, *The Alevis in Turkey*, p. 78.

147 Ibid., p. 79.

148 Yeler, "Shi'ism in Turkey," pp. 332–334.

149 Franke, "Khidr in Istanbul," p. 47.

150 Yeler, "Shi'ism in Turkey," pp. 332–336.

151 Yürekli, *Architecture and Hagiography*, p. 42.

152 Yeler, "Shi'ism in Turkey," pp. 332–336.

153 Bashir, *Sufi Bodies*, p. 95.

154 Akçapar and Jassal, "Sites of Power and Resistance or Melting Pots?,"
      p. 100.

4. SUFI AND SHARED PILGRIMAGES: CONTESTATIONS OF IDENTITY

1   Bazzano, "Sufism," p. 1228.

2   Masterson, "A Comparative Exploration," p. 54.

3   Kucuk, "Dervishes Make a City," p. 241.

4   Sirriya, "'Ziyarat' of Syria," pp. 110–112.

5   Karamustafa, *Sufism*, p. 136.

6   Bazzano, "Sufism," pp. 1230, 1232.

7   Ahmadi and Ahmadi, *Iranian Islam*, pp. 44–45.

8   Knysh, "The *Tariqa* on a Landcruiser," p. 408.

9   Alatas, "Pilgrimage and Network Formation," p. 302.

10 Williams, "The Cult of 'Alid Saints," p. 56.

11 Quinn and Quinn, *Pride, Faith, and Fear*, p. 96.

12 Ibid., p. 97.

13 Ho, *The Graves of Tarim*, p. 200.

14 Karamustafa, *Sufism: The Formative Period*, vii.

15 Afsaruddin, *The First Muslims*, p. 143.

16 Bashir, *Sufi Bodies*, pp. 8, 9.

17 Clarke, "Sainthood," p. 461.

18 Iloliev, "Popular Culture and Religious Metaphor," p. 61.

19 Meri, *The Cult of Saints*, p. 17.

20 Rizvi, "'It's Mortar Mixed with the Sweetness of Life,'" p. 332.

21 Anjum, *Chistī Sufis in the Sultanate of Delhi*, p. 60.

22 Vahed, "A Sufi Saint's Day in South Africa," p. 103.

23 Green, *Indian Sufism Since the Seventeenth Century*, p. 59.

24 Ross, "Touba," p. 230.

25 Ibid.

26 Anjum, *Chistī Sufis in the Sultanate of Delhi*, p. 61.

27 Knysh, "The *Tariqa* on a Landcruiser," p. 401.

28 Scheele, "A Pilgrimage to Arawan," pp. 166–167.

29 Vahed, "A Sufi Saint's Day in South Africa," pp. 99–100.

30 Alatas, "Pilgrimage and Network Formation," p.308.

31 Ibid., 310.

32 Tapper, "*Ziyaret*," p. 244.

33 Armstrong, "Jerusalem," p. 194.

34 See Chapter 1 for a more extensive discussion of *baraka* and its role in *ziyarat*.

35 Khalek, *Damascus after the Muslim Conquest*, p. 121.

36 This is the old term for the Syrian region, which was larger than the modern Arab state.

37 Meri, *The Cult of Saints*, p. 15.

38 Ibid., p. 74.

39 van Doorn-Harder and de Jong, "The Pilgrimage to Tembayat," p. 335.

40 Vahed, "A Sufi Saint's Day in South Africa," p. 101.

41 DeWeese, "Sacred Places and 'Public' Narratives," p. 361.

42 Green, *Indian Sufism Since the Seventeenth Century*, p. 35.

43 Meri, *The Cult of Saints*, p. 76.

44 According to one *hadith*, dreams are 1/46 of prophecy.

45 Ruffle, "May Fatimah Gather Our Tears," p. 393.

46 Hasson, "Muslim Literature in Praise of Jerusalem," pp. 171–172.

47 van Doorn-Harder and de Jong, "The Pilgrimage to Tembayat," p. 340.

48 Ibid., p. 346.

49   Azra, *The Origins of Islamic Reformism*, p. 2.

50   Turner, *Weber and Islam*, p. 1.

51   Callan, "Female Saints," p. 399.

52   Ford, "Hierarchical Inversions, Divine Subversions," p. 11.

53   Frembgen, *The Friends of God*, p. 1.

54   Foley, "The *Ronggeng*, the *Wayang*, the *Wali*, and Islam," pp. 362–64.

55   Woodward, *Islam in Java*, pp. 170–171.

56   Safi, "Bargaining with *Baraka*," p. 270.

57   Ibid., p. 266.

58   Green, *Indian Sufism Since the Seventeenth Century*, p. 37.

59   Frembgen, *The Friends of God*, p. 13.

60   Kreinath, "Virtual Encounters," p. 33.

61   Franke, "Khidr in Istanbul," pp. 47–48.

62   Kreinath, "Virtual Encounters," p. 27.

63   Laksana, *Muslim and Catholic Pilgrimage Practices*, p. 33.

64   Ford, "Hierarchical Inversions, Divine Subversions," p. 17.

65   al-Muqaddasī, *Descriptio Imperii Moslemici*, p. 130.

66   Cornell, "Rabi'a from Narrative to Myth," p. 192.

67   Callan, "Female Saints," pp. 396, 404.

68   Kucuk, "Dervishes Make a City," p. 251.

69   Rizvi, "'It's Mortar Mixed with the Sweetness of Life,'" p. 324.

70   Szanto, "Contesting Fragile Saintly Traditions," pp. 46–47.

71   Alatas, "Pilgrimage and Network Formation," p. 300.

72   Woodward, *Islam in Java*, p. 175.

73   Wheeler, *Mecca and Eden*, p. 99.

74   Hoffman, *Sufism, Mystics, and Saints*, p. 332.

75   Rizvi, "'It's Mortar Mixed with the Sweetness of Life,'" p. 334.

76   Wheeler, *Mecca and Eden*, pp. 79–80.

77   Hoffman, *Sufism, Mystics, and Saints*, p. 332.

78   Mukul, Rashid, and Uddin, "The Role of Spiritual Beliefs," p. 110.

79   Khalek, *Damascus after the Muslim Conquest*, p. 121.

80   Miura, "The Sālihiyya Quarter," p. 145.

81   Ibid., p. 145.

82   Ibid., p. 151.

83   Wheeler, *Mecca and Eden*, p. 89.

84   Berriane, "Ahmad al-Tijani and His Neighbors," pp. 60–61.

85   Perret, "Some Reflections," p. 318.

86   Ibid., pp. 315–316.

87   Ibid., p. 335.

88   Werbner, *Pilgrims of Love*, p. 265.

89   Hasan, "The Footprint of the Prophet," p. 335.

90   Green, *Indian Sufism Since the Seventeenth Century*, p. 121.

91   Ibid., p. 121.

92   Meri, *The Cult of Saints*, p. 17.

93   Wheeler, *Mecca and Eden*, p. 79.

94   Hasan, "The Footprint of the Prophet," p. 341.

95   Ibid., p. 342.

96   Betteridge, "Muslim Women and Shrines in Shiraz," p. 278.

97   Callan, "Female Saints," p. 404.

98   Ibid., p. 404.

99   Papas, "Pilgrimages to Western Shrines," p. 14.

100 Thum, *The Sacred Routes of Uyghur History*, p. 5.

101 Frembgen, *The Friends of God*, p. 85.

102 Henig, "'This Is Our Little Hajj,'" p. 754.

103 Ibid., p. 756.

104 Ibid., p. 760.

105 van Doorn-Harder and de Jong, "The Pilgrimage to Tembayat," pp. 339–40.

106 Bang, "'My Generation," p. 90.

107 Kucuk, "Dervishes Make a City," p. 246.

108 Rizvi, "'It's Mortar Mixed with the Sweetness of Life,'" p. 330.

109 Wolf, "The Poetics of 'Sufi' Practice," p. 252.

110 Kennedy and Fahim, "Nubian Dhikr Rituals," p. 212.

111 Spiegelman, "Divine Among in Islam," 139.

112 El Fadl, "The Ugly Modern," p. 53.

113 Alatas, "Pilgrimage and Network Formation," p. 299.

114 Abramson and Karimov, "Sacred Sites, Profane Ideologies," pp. 324–326.

115 Currie, *The Shrine and Cult of Mu'īn Al-Dīn Chishtī of Ajmer*, pp. 119–120.

116   Wolf, "The Poetics of 'Sufi' Practice," p. 248.

117   Ibid., p. 255.

118   Currie, *The Shrine and Cult of Mu'īn Al-Dīn Chishtī of Ajmer*, p. 9.

119   Henig, "'This Is Our Little Hajj,'" p. 754.

120   Ibid., p. 754.

121   Mostowlansky, "Making Kyrgyz Spaces," p. 259.

122   Ibid., p. 259.

123   Woodward, *Islam in Java*, p. 121.

124   Ibid., pp. 121–122.

125   Kucuk, "Dervishes Make a City," p. 250.

126   Henig, "'This Is Our Little Hajj,'" p. 755.

127   Green, *Indian Sufism Since the Seventeenth Century*, p. 90.

128   Asher, "Pilgrimage to the Shrines of Ajmer," p. 79.

129   Ibid., p. 79.

130   Currie, *The Shrine and Cult of Mu'īn Al-Dīn Chishtī of Ajmer*, p. 119.

131   Ibid., p. 120.

132   Papas, "Pilgrimages to Western Shrines," p. 14.

133   Frank, "Some Political Features," p. 303.

134   Woodward, *Islam in Java*, p. 153.

135   van Doorn-Harder and de Jong, "The Pilgrimage to Tembayat," p. 330.

136   Woodward, *Islam in Java*, pp. 199–200.

137   Ibid., p. 153.

138   Ibid., p. 153.

139   van Doorn-Harder and de Jong, "The Pilgrimage to Tembayat," p. 327.

140   Ibid., p. 327.

141   Ibid., p. 327.

142   Ibid., p. 331.

143   Vahed, "A Sufi Saint's Day in South Africa," p. 113.

144   Ibid., pp. 114–15.

145   Dangor, "The Expression of Islam in South Africa," pp. 143–144.

146   Bhattacharya, "Understanding Madariya *Silsila*," p. 395.

147 Abramson and Karimov, "Sacred Sites, Profane Ideologies," p. 321.

148 Akçapar and Jassal, "Sites of Power and Resistance or Melting Pots?," p. 96.

149 Kreinath, "Virtual Encounters," p. 27.

150 Meri, *The Cult of Saints*, p. 52.

151 Khalek, *Damascus after the Muslim Conquest*, p. 97.

152 Ibid., pp. 97–98.

153 Langer, "From Private Shrine to Pilgrim-Center," p. 566.

154 Wolper, "Khidr," p. 310.

155 Bowman, "Popular Palestinian Practices," p. 71.

156 van Doorn-Harder and de Jong, "The Pilgrimage to Tembayat," pp. 339–42.

157 Wolper, "Khidr," p. 314.

158 Ibid., p. 315.

159 Ibid., p. 315.

160 Abramson and Karimov, "Sacred Sites, Profane Ideologies," p. 325.

161 Saniotis, "Contesting the Sacred," p. 144.

162 Aksland, *The Sacred Footprint*, pp. 109–110.

163 Prager, "Alawi Ziyāra Tradition," p. 52.

164 Ibid., p. 56.

165 Al-Houdalieh, "Visitation and Making Vows," p. 380.

166 Meri, *The Cult of Saints*, p. 38.

167 Ibid., p. 44.

168 Franke, "Khidr in Istanbul," pp. 43–44.

169 Meri, *The Cult of Saints*, p. 33.

170 Ibid., p. 55.

171 Ibid., p. 225.

172 Barkey, "Religious Pluralism," p. 49.

173 Khalek, *Damascus after the Muslim Conquest*, p. 92.

174 Ibid., p. 115.

175 Jansen and Kühl, "Shared Symbols," p. 298.

176 Ibid., p. 298.

177 Ibid., p. 300.

178 Ibid., p. 299.

179   Egresi, Bayram, Kara, and Kesik, "Unlocking the Potential," p. 72.

180   Jansen and Kühl, "Shared Symbols," p. 302.

181   Heo, "The Virgin Between Christianity and Islam," pp. 1117–1119.

182   Ibid., p. 1129.

183   Ibid., p. 1129.

184   Barkey, "Religious Pluralism," p. 57.

185   Yürekli, *Architecture and Hagiography*, p. 80.

186   Bowman, "Popular Palestinian Practices," p. 75.

187   Ibid., p. 75.

188   Khalek, *Damascus after the Muslim Conquest*, p. 96.

189   Vovina, "Islam and the Creation of Sacred Space," p. 256.

190   Ibid., p. 260.

191   Ibid., p. 261.

192   Khalvashi, "Ziyareti," p. 86.

193   Ibid., p. 86.

194   Holland and Cole, "Between Discourse and Schema," p. 476.

195   Currie, *The Shrine and Cult of Mu'īn Al-Dīn Chishtī of Ajmer*, p. 9.

196   Ibid., p. 9.

197   van Doorn-Harder and de Jong, "The Pilgrimage to Tembayat," p. 326.

5. MODERN MUSLIM PILGRIMS: TOURISM, SPACE, AND TECHNOLOGY

1   El-Zein, "Spiritual Consumption in the United States," p. 83.

2   Soja, *Thirdspace*, p. 57.

3   Diouf, "The Senegalese Murid Trade Diaspora," p. 694.

4   Renne, "Photography," p. 20.

5   Bajc, Coleman, and Eade, "Mobility and Centring in Pilgrimage," p. 321.

6   Brown, *The Cult of the Saints*, p. 3.

7   Rizvi, "'It's Mortar Mixed with the Sweetness of Life,'" p. 334.

8   Shahshahani, "Introduction," p. 16.

9   Dabashi, *Shi'ism*, pp. 29–30.

10 Renne, "Photography," p. 20.

11 Turner and Turner, *Image and Pilgrimage*, p. 20.

12 Kenny, "Gifting Mecca," p. 372.

13 O'Connor, "Hong Kong Muslims on Hajj," p. 326.

14 Miller, "Pilgrims' Progress," p. 198.

15 Schlosser, "Digital Hajj," p. 43.

16 Shaery-Eisenlohr, "Imagining Shi'ite Iran," p. 24.

17 Ibid., p. 24.

18 Cohen, "Pilgrimage and Tourism," p. 50.

19 Dabashi, *Shi'ism*, p. 29.

20 Bajc, Coleman, and Eade, "Mobility and Centring in Pilgrimage," pp. 325–326.

21 Delaney, "The *Hajj*," p. 515.

22 Swanson and Timothy, "Souvenirs," p. 490.

23 Reader, *Pilgrimage in the Marketplace*, p. 149.

24 Gruber, "The Martyrs' Museum in Tehran," p. 77.

25 Flaskerud, *Visualizing Belief*, p. 181.

26 Swanson and Timothy, "Souvenirs," p. 491.

27 Hazard, "The Material Turn", p. 58.

28 Ibid., p. 58.

29 Trix, *Spiritual Discourse*, p. 6.

30 Shankland, *The Alevis in Turkey*, p. 231.

31 In recent years, the *tekke* (Sufi lodge), which includes a memorial to Bektash, has been transformed more and more into a museum, so that rooms that once felt sacred are full of dioramas and vitrines.

32 Shankland, *The Alevis in Turkey*, p. 231.

33 Erol, "Reimagining Identity," p. 376.

34 Ibid., p. 376.

35 Shankland, "Maps and the Alevis," p. 232.

36 Erol, "Reimagining Identity," p. 375.

37 Öktem, "Being Muslim at the Margins," p. 6. *Sama* is the word most often used for the Alevi ritual dances. *Sama* is often translated as "listening," but in other contexts it means "audition," suggesting a ritual that allows humans to demonstrate their loyalty and love for Allah.

38   Poyraz, "The Turkish State and Alevis," p. 505.

39   Öktem, "Being Muslim at the Margins," p. 6.

40   Shankland, *The Alevis in Turkey*, p. 79.

41   Ibid., p. 115.

42   Trix, *Spiritual Discourse*, p. 9.

43   Birge, *The Bektashi Order of Dervishes*, p. 147.

44   Erol, "Reimagining Identity," p. 379.

45   Ibid., p. 379.

46   Rubin, "Pre-existence and Light," p. 65.

47   Ho, "The Two Arms of Cambay," p. 358.

48   Amir-Moezzi, "Icon and Meditation," p. 25.

49   Flaskerud, *Visualizing Belief*, p. 219.

50   Ibid., p. 65.

51   Glazebrook and Abbasi-Shavazi, "Being Neighbors to Imam Reza," pp. 187–201.

52   Amir-Moezzi, "Icon and Meditation," p. 28.

53   For example, at Bab al-Saghir, many *parche sabz* are tied to the metalwork of tombs, including those of Bilal and some of the Prophet's companions.

54   Flaskerud, *Visualizing Belief*, p. 44.

55   The origin of green as the color of Islam is a matter of debate. Some scholars believe that the tradition has its origins in the *mi'raj*, the story of the Prophet's ascension to heaven when he sees a tree at the edge of heaven. Surahs 55 and 76 also refer to green as a color associated with heaven in the cushions and clothing worn by the inhabitants of Paradise. Al-Khidr, the "green man" that is such a popular figure in Sufi narratives and other genres of Islamic literature, is believed to have traveled with *Musa* (Moses) and for some Sufis is believed to be eternally alive, possibly present but invisible (like Elijah).

56   A candle is also lit at some *sagha-khanehs*.

57   Geijbels, "Aspects," p. 183.

58   *Tabarruk* means "blessing" and usually refers to a blessing from the saint, but it is also used as a verb, "to be blessed," and means "blessed portion."

59   Nakash, "The Visitation of the Shrines," p. 161. Also, see Nakash's discussion of Muhammad Mahdi al-Kazimi's discussion of shrine

visitation, where he argues that the visitation of the Imams is like the visitation of the Prophet, and is equal to visiting the *ka'bah* (p. 162).

60   Khalid Sindawi, "Visit to the Tomb of Al-Husayn b. Alī," p. 231. *Kutub al-mazar* ("books for the tomb") and *al-ziyara* ("the visitations") point to the same thing.

61   Geijbels, "Aspects," p. 185.

62   Flaskerud, *Visualizing Belief*, p. 187. Flaskerud characterizes this as "enhancing the calling."

63   According to one story of the condition of saint's bodies after being dug up from the grave, "God protects the bodies of the holy men against decomposition in their graves. The saints are apparently alive even though they died more than twelve centuries ago. They have their eyes open so that it seems they can see and think but they do not speak." Knappert, "Some Notes," p. 245.

64   Shi'as around the globe can also connect to Karbala on the website www.karbala.tv.net, which features links to five different foundations focused on Imam Husayn.

65   Prayer stones are made from the soil of holy sites. *Turbah* is a word that means both "earth" and "tomb," while *mohr* means "stamp" and refers to the appearance of the prayer stone.

66   Hazleton, *After the Prophet*, p. 70.

67   Lee, "Beyond the Locus Sanctus," p. 364.

68   Rizvi, "Religious Icon and National Symbol," p. 212.

69   Rahnema, *An Islamic Utopian*, p. 315. As Rahnema points out, Shari'ati's rallying cry was uttered at a speech he gave in 1972 at a *masjid*, a clear sign that SAVAK's efforts to pacify the charismatic intellectual were not working.

70   Rizvi, "Religious Icon and National Symbol," p. 212.

71   Flaskerud, *Visualizing Belief*, p. 196.

72   See the foldable pamphlet on Shi'a use of the *turbah* at www.al-islam. org/nutshell/files/turbah.pdf

73   Gleave, "Prayer and Prostration," pp. 234–6.

74   At Rumi's tomb in Konya, the small museum includes a case in which a relic is displayed – a hair from the Prophet. A person can lean down, place his or her nose next to the small hole, and breathe in the scent of the Prophet, which is said to resemble sandalwood.

75 Sindawi, "Visit to the Tomb of Al-Husayn b. Alī," p. 237.

76 Ibid., p. 237. Quoted from Al-Shajari's Kitab al-Amali, 1:163.

77 Quoted in Nakash, "The Visitation of the Shrines," p. 157, from Ibn Quiwayh's *Kamil al-ziyarat*, 147–9.

78 Sindawi, "Visit to the Tomb of Al-Husayn b. Alī," p. 249.

79 Gleave, "Prayer and Prostration," p. 242.

80 Sindawi, "Visit to the Tomb of Al-Husayn b. Alī," p. 250.

81 Gleave, "Prayer and Prostration," p. 242.

82 Ibid., p. 241.

83 Fakhr-Rohani, "Reflections on Ashura-oriented Literature," p. 98.

84 Knappert, "Some Notes," p. 247.

85 Ibid., p. 247.

86 Schubel, *Religious Performance in Contemporary Islam*, p. 73.

87 Reader, *Pilgrimage in the Marketplace*, p. 144.

88 Delaney, "The *Hajj*," p. 519.

89 Williams, "Surfing Therapeutic Landscapes," p. 79.

90 Ruffle, "May Fatimah Gather Our Tears," pp. 391–2.

91 Ibid., p. 393.

92 Flaskerud, *Visualizing Belief*, pp. 138–139.

93 Renard, *Seven Doors to Islam*, pp. 69–70.

94 Boivin, "Representations and Symbols," p. 163.

95 Bombardier, "War Painting and Pilgrimage in Iran," p. 149.

96 Ibid., p. 158.

97 Ibid., p. 159.

98 Ibid., p. 163.

99 Ibid., p. 164.

100 Flaskerud, "Redemptive Memories," p. 39.

101 Ibid., p. 39.

102 Flaskerud, *Visualizing Belief*, p. 186.

103 Bunt, *I-Muslims: Rewiring the House of Islam*, p. 183.

104 Ibid., p. 215.

105 Bunt, *Islam in the Digital Age*, p. 4.

106 Scott, *Conscripts of Modernity*, pp. 8–9.

107 Stanton, "Islamic Emoticons," p. 91.

108 Hofheinz, "Nextopia?," p. 35.

109 Campbell, *Exploring Religious Community Online*, pp. 60–61.

110 Phillips, "Cyberkurds and Cyberkinetics," p. 11.

111 Dawson, "Religion and the Quest for Virtual Community," p. 76.

112 Bunt, *Islam in the Digital Age*, p. 9.

113 Hackett, "Religion and the Internet," pp. 67–68.

114 O'Leary, "Cyberspace as Sacred Space," 51.

115 Ibid., p. 51.

116 MacWilliams, "Virtual Pilgrimages on the Internet," p. 317.

117 Hill-Smith, "Cyberpilgrimage," p. 239.

118 MacWilliams, "Virtual Pilgrimages on the Internet," p. 318.

119 Scheifinger, "The Jagannath Temple," p. 279.

120 Hackett, "Religion and the Internet," p. 68.

121 Campbell, Altenhofen, Bellar, and Cho, "There's a Religious App for That!," pp. 159–161.

122 Ibid., p. 162.

123 Bunt, "Surfing the App Souq."

124 Ibid.

125 Kalinock, "Going on Pilgrimage Online," pp. 13–15.

126 Echchaibi, "Mecca Cola and Burqinis," pp. 31–33.

127 Schlosser, "Digital Hajj," p. 38.

128 Ibid., pp. 39–40.

129 Osman and Shaout, "Hajj Guide Systems," p. 27.

130 Ibid., p. 28.

131 Rosiny, "The Twelver Shia Online," p. 252.

132 O'Connor, "Hong Kong Muslims on Hajj," p. 324.

133 Ibid., p. 324.

134 Ibid., p. 326.

135 Bunt, "'Rip. Burn. Pray,'" pp. 129–130.

136 Williams, "Surfing Therapeutic Landscapes," p. 82.

137 MacWilliams, "Virtual Pilgrimages on the Internet," p. 322.

138 Hill-Smith, "Cyberpilgrimage," p. 239.

139 Schlosser, "Digital Hajj," p. 41.

140 Kalinock, "Going on Pilgrimage Online," p. 14.

141   Bunt, "'Rip. Burn. Pray,'" p. 130.

142   Soja, *Thirdspace*, p. 1.

AFTERWORD: PRESUPPOSITIONS AND POSSIBILITIES IN THE STUDY OF ISLAMIC PILGRIMAGE

1   Ahmed, *What Is Islam?*, p. 542.

2   Schubel, "Karbala as Sacred Space," p. 189.

3   Murrani, "Baghdad's Thirdspace," p. 192.

4   Morikawa, "Pilgrimages to the Iraqi 'Atabat," p. 42.

5   Khosronejad, "Anthropology, Islam and Sainthood," p. 7.

6   Renard, *Seven Doors to Islam*, p. 70.

7   Wolfe, "The Pilgrim's Complaint," p. 252.

8   Ibid., p. 264.

9   Hazard, "The Material Turn", p. 59.

10   Hackett, "Religion and the Internet," p. 71.

11   Silverstein, "In the Name of Culture," p. 333.

12   Hazard, "The Material Turn", p. 58.

13   Schopen, "Archaeology," p. 11.

14   Ibid., p. 18.

15   Ibid., p. 20.

16   Said, *Orientalism*, p. 302.

17   Ernst and Martin, "Introduction," p. 14.

18   King, *Orientalism and Religion*, p. 25.

19   Vial, *Modern Religion, Modern Race*, p. 191.

20   Ibid., p. 249.

21   Smith, *Map Is Not Territory*, p. 295.

22   Meyer and Houtman, "Introduction," p. 16.

23   Orsi, *Between Heaven and Earth*, p. 195.

24   Smith, *Map Is Not Territory*, p. 291.

INDEX